D0492026

REC.

BETRAYED

THE ENGLISH CATHOLIC CHURCH AND THE SEX ABUSE CRISIS

RICHARD SCORER

Biteback Publishing

First published in Great Britain in 2014 by
Biteback Publishing Ltd
Westminster Tower
3 Albert Embankment
London SE1 7SP
Copyright © Richard Scorer 2014

Extracts from *Father and Me* reproduced by kind permission of Eamonn Flanagan.
Extracts from *The Tablet* reproduced with the permission of the publisher. www.thetablet.co.uk

ISBN 978-1-84954-682-9

10 9 8 7 6 5 4 3 2 1

A CIP catalogue record for this book is available from the British Library.

Set in Caslon and Typeka

Printed and bound in Great Britain by
CPI Group (UK) Ltd, Croydon CR0 4YY

CONTENTS

ACKNOWLEDGEMENTS

I have written this book in tribute to those many survivors of abuse brave enough to come forward and tell their stories and others who may yet do so. It is a matter of public interest that the tragic events of the last few decades are more fully understood, the better to prevent repetition in the future. Many people whose experiences have informed this work have shown courage in reliving distressing events. To them, and in particular Chris Carrie, Danny Mackle, Graham Wilmer and Eamonn Flanagan, go my profound thanks.

Many other people – survivor campaigners, journalists and fellow members of the legal profession – have assisted me with this book. I am grateful to all of them, but l in particular I should like to thank Dr Margaret Kennedy, who made available to me her archive from the early years of MACSAS/CSSA, read the book in manuscript and offered numerous comments and suggestions. Helpful comments on drafts were also provided by Dr Phillip Gilligan, Eamonn Flanagan, Graham Wilmer, Sue Cox, Jenny Fasal and Jonathan West, and of course my patient editors at Biteback, Sam Carter and Olivia Beattie. In addition, I am very grateful to the following who assisted with aspects of my research, offered critical comments and/or were willing to discuss their views and experiences: Alana Lawrence, Lucy Duckworth,

Alan Draper, Dr Elizabeth Mann, Mark Hollinghurst, David Greenwood, Justin Levinson, Donald Findlater, Elena Curti, John Wilkins, Peter Tatchell, Deirdre Healy, Molly Whittall, Victoria Beel and Jonathan Timbers.

In writing this book I would have wished to speak with senior safeguarding officials in the Catholic Church (NCSC). They declined to speak to me, I understand on legal advice. However, as explained in the text, a number of current and former diocesan safeguarding officials spoke to me strictly off the record, as did a number of Catholic priests including some in senior positions – all were very courteous and helpful in sharing views. Again, I am extremely grateful for their willingness to speak to me. I am also grateful to Ignatius Kusiak, owner of *The Tablet*, for permission to quote from that excellent publication, as I have done frequently throughout the book. Any errors, either of fact or interpretation, which remain are mine and mine alone. And thank you too to Helen, Rhiannon and Jamie for their love and forbearance.

CHAPTER 1

INTRODUCTION

'How much filth is there in the Church, even among those who, in the priesthood, should belong entirely to God.' Pope Benedict's lament at a Good Friday Mass in 2005 came twenty years after the first big Catholic abuse scandal erupted, in the United States. Two decades on, the crisis showed no signs of abating – in fact, it was soon to deepen with revelations from Germany implicating Pope Benedict himself. In 1983, Gilbert Gauthe, a priest in Lafayette, Louisiana, was exposed as a paedophile. The case set in motion events which have devastated the Catholic Church across the world. In 1985, Gauthe's defence attorney, Ray Mouton, and a Vatican official, Tom Doyle, wrote a 92-page report in which they pleaded with the US Church to confront the issue of sexual abuse. If left to fester, the report predicted, the scandal would involve up to 1,000 predatory priests and cost the US Church $1 billion in legal settlements.[1] It warned that child abusers presented a particular danger because 'recidivism is so high'. It urged the Church to deal with the media: 'Silence implies cover-up.' The problem had been brewing for decades; Mouton and Doyle begged the Church to face it head on.

The report went to senior Catholic leaders, including Cardinal Bernard Law of Boston. It was ignored, then buried. The scandal which has since unfolded in the USA and internationally has been much vaster, its impact on the Church and its congregations far more profound, than Mouton and Doyle predicted. Across the Catholic world, victims have been traumatised, parishes left broken and respect for the priesthood has been shattered. The scandal is still unfolding and is likely to continue for many years hence.

In accounts of this tragedy, events in England have received little attention. In the USA, damages awards have driven many Catholic dioceses to the brink of bankruptcy. In theocratic Ireland, the Church was so enmeshed with the state that the collapse of one has forever transformed the other. In England, the societal impact of the scandal has been less profound, leading some to play down its seriousness; in his anti-papal polemic *The Case of the Pope*, Geoffrey Robertson QC suggests that 'insofar as the church has had a success story in dealing with paedophile priests, this is in the UK'.[2] Robertson is no apologist for the Church, but his view reflects a common assumption, fostered by Catholic leaders, that there were relatively few cases in England and that such problems as existed have been eliminated by the Nolan reforms, a raft of changes to child protection in the Catholic Church in England and Wales which were introduced in 2001.

The statistics and historical records, however, indicate otherwise. Of course, the vast majority of Catholic priests are not involved in any form of sex offending; many do outstanding and selfless work, usually unheralded, for their congregations and wider communities. But the number who have been convicted of sexual crimes is not insignificant. In writing this book I have established that at least sixty-one Catholic priests have been convicted of sexual offences in the criminal courts in England and Wales since 1990. But that is a minimum number; there may be more. One of the many criticisms of Church safeguarding procedures is the lack of centralised and publicly available information about convicted priests. One would imagine that after the devastation caused by the abuse crisis, the Catholic Church in England and Wales would have compiled a single centralised record of known offenders, and would confirm publicly that those convicted of offences resulting in imprisonment of twelve months or more had been removed from the priesthood, or at the very least that a process to remove them had been initiated, as proposed by Nolan.[3] Not so. For those involved in child protection, the absence of this minimum level of centralised data recording remains surprising but perhaps very telling. It speaks to a reluctance to acknowledge, openly, the scale of the problem.

The priests and religious (i.e. members of monastic orders) convicted of sex offences in criminal trials in England and Wales, however, are likely to be the tip of an iceberg. Abusers often abuse multiple times. Out of every 100 reported cases of child sexual abuse, on average ninety-seven victims reporting abuse are deemed to be telling the truth but only four of the cases will result in the conviction of the offender. This leaves over ninety sex offenders per hundred without a criminal conviction. The true number of clerical sex offenders in England and Wales will likely number in the many hundreds or even thousands.

But absolute numbers are only one element of the story. Many institutions have had a problem of child abuse; the critical issue is how that problem is handled. And here, too, the Catholic Church in England and Wales has failed both victims and its wider congregation. Contrary to the claims of some Church leaders, the patterns of abuse, denial, institutional complicity and cover-up which have characterised the Catholic abuse scandal in other countries have also been present here: they are remarkably consistent throughout the Catholic Church in every part of the world. For the past twenty years the leaders of the Catholic Church in England and Wales have repeatedly stated that they are responding appropriately to reports of child sexual abuse, and that effective safeguarding protection procedures have been put in place. However, cases have repeatedly revealed that Church authorities covered up past reports of child abuse and allowed clergy and religious to remain in post despite allegations of – and in some cases, past convictions for – child sexual offences. In many instances further abuse then took place. In this book, which is intended to be both a history of the Catholic abuse scandal in England and Wales over the last thirty years and an analysis of Catholic safeguarding as it now operates, I examine the detail of some of these cases. Many, if not most, are 'historic'[4] but some, like the recent scandals at Benedictine schools, are contemporary and post-date the Nolan reforms. They illustrate that whilst Nolan has undoubtedly improved child protection in the English Church, that task is 'very far from accomplished'.[5]

• • •

I begin this book with an overview of the debates on clerical sex offending in the Catholic Church worldwide. The remainder of the book is devoted to the detail of events in England and Wales. That detail is necessarily selective: I cannot examine every one of the sixty-one cases in which priests have been convicted. My selection is designed to illustrate recurring themes. In Chapter 4

I look at cases involving complaints of abuse from the 1960s to the 1990s, an era characterised by institutional denial and suppression of allegations. Cases were routinely covered up, priests moved to different parishes and parents of victims actively discouraged from going to the police.

In England and Wales, it was only in the early 1990s that this culture of cover-up was publicly exposed, in a series of dramatic cases starting with Father Samuel Penney in Birmingham. The impact of the Penney case was devastating for the English Church: now it was plain that priests, even apparently very devoted and selfless ones like Penney, could be child rapists, a fact which many committed Catholics had struggled to accept. But the Penney case also laid bare the culture of denial which had been operating in the English Church for decades. In the mid-1990s the Church introduced a raft of new guidelines on child abuse, but these had no meaningful enforcement machinery and were more honoured in the breach than in the observance. Throughout the 1990s, exposés of denial and cover-up contin- ued, but Cardinal Hume, the leader of the English Catholic Church during this period, seemed to escape responsibility for the crisis: he died in 1999, and the heat was taken by his succes- sor, Archbishop (now Cardinal) Cormac Murphy-O'Connor. The conviction in 1998 of Father Michael Hill of the Diocese of Arundel and Brighton triggered investigations into earlier decisions by Murphy-O'Connor, who many felt had turned a blind eye to Hill's behaviour throughout the 1980s. Litigation in this case, combined with Murphy-O'Connor's appointment in 2000 as Archbishop of Westminster, created a media firestorm. After an initially defensive reaction, Murphy-O'Connor set up the Nolan Commission, which drove through a series of unprecedented changes to child protection in the Church, events examined in Chapters 8 and 9.

The effectiveness of the Nolan reforms over the past decade is a matter of fierce debate. A 2007 review concluded that grave problems remained and that the implementation of Nolan had been flawed. 'The task is far from accomplished,' the Cumberlege Report concluded. 'If the tensions that have come to the fore in this review are left unaddressed by those in the Church with the authority to deliver, we believe they risk a serious reversal of some of the important gains made to date.' This was strong language, although some survivor groups believed that even these stark conclusions had been watered down before publication. The tensions identified by Cumberlege included a continuing resistance to change amongst bishops, a lack of funding, and an overreliance on volunteers for child protection. And, critically, as I discuss in Chapter 9, canon law, with its cumbersome procedures for handling accusations against priests, was at odds with the secular model of child protection, which holds that the interests of the child must come first.

Baroness Cumberlege tried to address this issue, but she seems to have failed: as at the time of writing the Vatican has not yet granted formal recognition to those parts of Nolan which conflict with canon law. Controversially, and reversing a key Nolan reform, Cumberlege put the bishops back in charge of child protection, the very area in which they had failed so disastrously in the past. Cumberlege believed that this was the only way to fully engage bishops and congregational leaders in the challenge of child protection;[6] others have seen it as a recipe for further disaster. Meanwhile, as I show in Chapter 10, scandals at St Benedict's Ealing, Downside and other Catholic schools in the Benedictine Congregation have raised continuing questions about the effectiveness of child protection in Catholic institutions. Survivor groups, previously willing to engage with the Church, have largely abandoned dialogue, doubting the Church's good faith and its commitment to pastoral care of survivors, and have called for a public inquiry into the Church's handling of abuse allegations. The protection of vulnerable adults has been largely ignored, and in its handling of legal cases – resisting fair compensation at every turn – the Church has betrayed its duty to victims. I examine these issues in the final chapters of the book.

When launching the Nolan Report in 2001, Murphy-O'Connor had declared his ambition that the Catholic Church should become a 'beacon' for child protection. Over a decade on, progress has been slow and patchy, and many believe that the absence of real independent oversight means that the Church will always put its own, institutional, interests ahead of those of the victims in its handling of complaints of abuse. Whilst safeguarding in the English Catholic Church has improved since Nolan – and much of the credit for this must go to Cardinal Murphy-O'Connor, who pushed through the Nolan reforms in the face of intense (and occasionally unfair) criticism of his track record and integrity – there are serious continuing problems. As we shall see, the letter of the law has changed, but the spirit lags behind.

CHAPTER 2

'GOD WILL FORGIVE ME'

Why have so many Catholic priests been implicated in sex offending? Over the past thirty years, much academic study, particularly in the USA, has been devoted to the dynamics of clergy abuse. Explanations for the abuse crisis and the manner in which it has been handled, however, tend to reflect political and theological biases. Both conservative and progressive Catholics tend to accept that most blame rests with the bishops for mismanaging the problem. The facts of individual cases leave little room to suggest otherwise. Explanations then diverge.

Conservatives see the abuse crisis as a product of the more liberal climate in the Church brought about by the Second Vatican Council and societal changes in the 1960s. In this view, the crisis can be blamed on liberalism and moral relativism, a failure to enforce discipline within the Church, and a tolerance of homosexuality. Part of the conservative argument is that canon law fell into disuse from the 1960s and therefore within the Church penal measures were no longer deployed against suspected abusers, leaving them free to abuse again. This was a view repeatedly voiced by former Pope Benedict, who claimed that one of the causes of the abuse crisis was that from the 1960s onwards ecclesiastical penal law (i.e. canon law) ceased to be applied. As Benedict argued in 2010: 'The prevailing mentality was that the Church must not be a Church of laws but rather, a Church of love; she must not punish. Thus the awareness that punishment can be an act of love ceased to exist. This led to an odd darkening of the mind...'[7]

It is deeply ironic that it is former Pope Benedict himself who made this argument, since his track record in enforcing canonical discipline against high-profile sex abusers was chequered to say the least. As Prefect of the Congregation for the Doctrine of the Faith, whose duties included the investigation of priestly abuse, the then Cardinal Ratzinger wilfully failed to pursue serious allegations of sex abuse against Father Marcial Maciel. Maciel, founder of the extreme right-wing Legion of Christ, was a favourite of Pope John Paul II. He abused scores of Legion seminarians, fathered six children by three women and sexually molested several of his offspring. The Vatican knew of Maciel's behaviour from the mid- to late 1970s onwards but protected him for many years. As Matthew Fox observes, in the 1970s and 1980s Cardinal Ratzinger was 'too busy denouncing liberation theologians the world over to go after a darling of the Pope'.[8] At one point Cardinal Ratzinger told a Mexican bishop that it would not be 'prudent' to punish someone who had 'done so much good for the Church'.[9] So much for a 'Church of laws'. Former Pope Benedict, who has also faced serious questions about his actions in child abuse cases as Archbishop of Munich, is personally ill-equipped to sermonise about canonical and moral decline.

However, the conservative case cannot be dismissed out of hand simply because of the hypocrisy of its proponents. Superficially, the argument that canon law fell into disuse from the 1960s, leaving suspected abusers free from any ecclesiastical sanction, has a germ of truth. Geoffrey Robertson argues that canon law is a 'secret legal system designed to shield paedophile priests from criminal trial around the world'. But in fact, as far as we can tell, canon law seems to have been hardly deployed at all in Catholic abuse cases in England, at least in the cases we know about – and these almost entirely date from the 1960s onwards. It might well be argued that many of these cases would have been better handled from the victim's standpoint had ecclesiastical penal law been applied. Some sort of systematic investigative and punishment process, albeit a deeply flawed one, would have been set in train, whereas in fact allegations were simply buried and complainants sent packing. As the Irish journalist Tom Mooney says in his study of clerical abuse in the Diocese of Wexford: 'What is ironic about the Church's mishandling of abuse cases, from Bonn to Boston, is that a faithful adherence to canon law would have helped chastise offenders within its rank and file, while also igniting a light at the end of the tunnel for victims.'[10] Similarly, the Catholic commentator Austen Ivereigh argues:

> It was the bishops' failure to follow canon law in the 1970s and 1980s which in many ways lay behind the clerical sex-abuse crisis. Sexual abuse of minors is one of the most serious offences in the Code [of Canon Law], one of the *gravora delicta* for which penal sanctions, up to and including dismissal from the clerical state, are demanded. The purpose of those sanctions, as the Code puts it, is 'the reform of the offender, the reparation of scandal, and the restoration of justice'. In the 1970s and 1980s the failure to repair scandal and restore justice through penal sanctions left the victims, and the wider Church, indignant and angry.[11]

This argument, however, is true only in a very limited sense: in a Church which suppressed allegations with no form of investigation or redress at all, the handling of complaints by reference to some sort of canonical due process and punishment might have been better than what actually occurred. But not much better. As I emphasise throughout this book, canon law, with its emphasis on secrecy, its unrealistic time limits and its insistence on 'moral certainty' in the proof of allegations, was, and is, an obstacle to the proper handling of sex abuse cases, which in my view should be reported to secular authorities under a mandatory reporting law and dealt with outside the institution. No safe system for dealing with sex abuse allegations has the institution under scrutiny as judge and jury in its own cause: as Robertson says, canon law 'fails the first test of proper legal process, namely that it does not provide an independent and impartial court. The sodality of the priesthood is intimate and self-supporting, and prosecuting and defendant counsel will have a close empathy with their colleague, the defendant.'[12] And canon law cannot impose the necessary penalties: as Mooney says, it can 'chastise' the abuser, but 'chastise' is what you do to errant children; sex offenders need to be sent to jail. Canon law is inherently unsuitable for sex abuse cases, as became even more apparent after 2001 when Nolan tried to introduce secular procedures for child protection which proved to be in conflict with it.[13]

In any case, the conservative argument that canon law only fell into disuse because of the liberal climate created by Vatican II is not supported by evidence: canon law does not seem to have been much used in abuse cases before Vatican II either. In cases we know about from the 1950s, canon law is as notable by its absence as it is in later decades. The point is difficult to resolve definitively because the cases from the 1950s that we can analyse now are relatively few in number and available documentation about them is sparse. For technical legal reasons relating to the Limitation Acts, it is virtually impossible to bring a legal claim in England in respect of abuse which occurred before 1954, so for this reason and due to the age of victims the legal claims which might otherwise cast a light on Church practices at that time are rarely brought. But from what we know, canon law was rarely employed. This conclusion tends to be supported by evidence from other countries. The Murphy Report in Ireland found that canon law appeared to have fallen into disrespect and disuse from the mid-twentieth century onwards. Or – to be more accurate – what fell into disuse was that part of canon law which involved the application of penal sanctions against clerical sex offenders; as the Murphy Report acidly observed, most officials in the Dublin archdiocese continued to be 'greatly exercised by the provisions of canon law which deal with secrecy'.[14] But at any rate, the decline in the use of canonical sanctions against abusers preceded Vatican II.[15]

Sometimes the conservative argument is put more generally: from Vatican II onwards there was a pervasive decline in moral standards so that the traditional Catholic certitudes of yesteryear were discarded in favour of what Pope Benedict called the 'dictatorship of relativism'.[16] The actor and Catholic traditionalist Mel Gibson encapsulated this view in his claim that 'Vatican II corrupted the institution of the church. Look at the main fruits: dwindling numbers and paedophilia.'[17] Presumably, moral decline permeated the Church so that traditional abhorrence of child abuse was compromised by relativistic notions about sex, morality and punishment. Again, this argument has a superficial attraction. The moral environment in society and the Church undoubtedly changed in the 1960s, and it is not impossible that some of these changes blunted the moral faculties of decision-makers in the Church. In Chapter 4, I examine the case of Father Michael Ingram, an English Dominican priest who for many years openly advocated sexual relations between adults and children. Ingram, who was associated with the Paedophile Information Exchange (PIE) in the 1970s, was convicted of buggery of boys in 2000 but committed suicide before sentencing. His revolting views on adult–child sex were entirely at odds with Catholic teaching. Yet Ingram was never really condemned by his order: on one occasion he was ordered not to speak at a PIE meeting, for fear of adverse publicity, but there is no evidence that his views on child sex were otherwise censored. It seems that the Church at that time might itself have been infected by the liberal attitudes to paedophilia advocated by some of the '68 generation', such as the student leader Daniel Cohn-Bendit – ideas which, in the 1970s, also gained some traction in left-wing organisations such as the National Council for Civil Liberties and the Howard League for Penal Reform.

Would a more conservative Church have censored Ingram, indeed expelled him from the priesthood as soon as his views became known, thus preventing him from abusing some of his victims? Possibly, but this is supposition and Ingram, although high-profile in his day, was only one priest. It is, of course, difficult to know how a more conservative moral climate might have influenced human behaviour in particular situations. But when – for example – the parents of boy M complained to Father Michael McTernan in 1972 that Father Christopher Clonan was abusing their son (see Chapter 5), Father McTernan's failure to act on that complaint is hardly explained by the liberal climate of the day. Father McTernan simply wanted to cover for a fellow priest and protect the institution. The conservative argument that post-Vatican II moral laxity is the cause of the abuse crisis seems unconvincing when set against the detail of actual cases, where repeatedly we see the Church hierarchy covering up sex abuse to protect its own interests and power: a consistent theme throughout the history of the Catholic Church, as Karen Liebreich shows in her study of abuse cover-ups in the Piarist Order in the seventeenth century.[18]

Rose-tinted spectacles are the blurriest of lenses: as we now know, child abuse was widespread in Catholic institutions before the 1960s. In the Republic of Ireland, state commissions of inquiry have identified hundreds if not thousands of cases from the 1950s, 1940s and earlier. In that era, the Republic of Ireland was everything a conservative Catholic might yearn for and, according to the Archbishop of Dublin, ecclesiastical penal law was widely used, yet child abuse was widespread. Conservative Catholic values and institutions did not protect children from abuse in 1930s and 1940s Ireland; indeed, those very institutions were riddled with abuse. The deep conservatism and religiosity of Irish society deterred terrified victims from disclosing. As Pope Benedict himself admitted, Ireland was a 'self-enclosed Catholic society', so to speak, which remained true to its faith despite centuries of oppression, but in which, then, evidently certain attitudes were also able to develop'.[19] Abuse cases seem to have increased after Vatican II, but this has little to do with moral decline. It is not that there was more abuse from the 1960s, rather that victims were starting to talk about it more openly. Increased societal awareness and recognition of child abuse led to more disclosures. Also, within the Church, Vatican II may have helped to create an atmosphere in which it was more acceptable to challenge clerical authority, giving victims greater confidence to come forward.

Another conservative claim is that the abuse problem is a consequence of modern tolerance of homosexuality in the Church. In making this argument, conservatives point to the pattern of victim selection. The secular media talks about 'paedophile priests' and an 'epidemic of baby rape' in the Church, so the public impression may be that the victims are predominantly young children. However, as many commentators have pointed out, victims in Catholic child abuse cases tend, predominantly, to be pubescent and post-pubescent teenage boys. The John Jay study concluded that 'the majority of alleged victims were post-pubescent, with only a small percentage of priests receiving allegations of abusing young children.'[20] It also concluded that of all victims whose gender was reported, 81 per cent were male and 19 per cent were female.[21] This pattern appears to be confirmed by the cases resulting in the criminal convictions of Catholic priests in England and Wales. Of the sixty-one priests convicted of sexual offences since 1990, four were convicted of offences involving the making of indecent images of children and the gender of their victims is not readily identifiable from publicly available information. However, of the remaining fifty-seven, forty-seven (82 per cent) were convicted of offences against males only; three (5 per cent) were convicted of offences against females only; and seven (13 per cent) were convicted of offences against both males and females: figures similar to the John Jay study. Similarly, of the male victims, the overwhelming majority were in the nine-to-sixteen age range.

Of course, data on this topic is likely to be inherently biased. Younger children may be less likely to disclose sexual abuse. In criminal proceedings in particular, allegations made by younger children may be viewed as less likely to lead to a conviction, given the greater probative and prosecutorial difficulties posed by their evidence. Amongst the English priests who have been convicted for child abuse, for example, there are at least two cases where allegations relating to very young children were dropped from the indictment because the age of the victims meant that the criminal standard of proof was unlikely to be satisfied. Similarly, at the other end of the age spectrum, the abuse of vulnerable adults has also been neglected because of legal issues around consent; indeed, the very definition of 'vulnerable adult' is contested.[22] As Margaret Kennedy has shown, the sexual exploitation of adult women by priests is hugely underreported.[23] Therefore, the data should be treated with caution. And in acknowledging a bias in victim selection towards teenage boys, there is also a risk of ignoring or downplaying female experiences, and of disregarding allegations which do not fit the most common template, so that the pattern of victim selection becomes self-reinforcing. Nevertheless, the pattern of criminal cases in England and Wales is undoubtedly similar to the John Jay research. In cases involving the abuse of minors (as opposed to adults) the victims, typically but by no means exclusively, tend to be boys aged between nine and sixteen. For this reason, some commentators, particularly Church apologists, have claimed that 'paedophilia', which in its DSM-III-R definition specifically refers to 'sexual activity with a prepubescent child', may not be an accurate characterisation of the Catholic abuse problem, and have suggested that 'ephebophilia', the sexual preference for pubescent boys, is a more appropriate term.[24]

Conservatives have then argued that this preponderance of teenage male victims indicates that the problem is primarily a homosexual problem which can be solved by excluding gays from the priesthood. For some, this argument is reinforced by the undoubted fact that a significant proportion of Catholic priests *are* in fact gay. Estimating numbers of gay priests is fraught with difficulty but evidence from several studies indicates that there are higher than average numbers of homosexual men (active and non-active) in the Catholic priesthood: Donald Cozzens suggests anything between a quarter and a half of priests are gay.[25] Similarly, studies by Sipe and Wolf from the early 1990s suggest that the percentage of priests in the Catholic Church who admitted to being gay or were in homosexual relationships was well above the national average for the USA.[26] A John Jay study suggested that homosexual men entered the seminaries in noticeable numbers from the late 1970s through the 1980s.[27] Many think this led to a 'gay subculture' dominating the seminaries. The reasons for a gay priesthood have been much debated but may not be hard to identify. The gay rights campaigner Peter Tatchell sees it thus:

> In the era of criminalisation and extreme homophobia, some gay men saw the Catholic Church as a safe haven. It was an all-male community, full of high camp ritual, which was well known to contain a high proportion of gay or bisexual men. Within the confines of the Church, discreet homosexuality was mostly not a problem.[28]

Deploying – and distorting – these statistics, Vatican officials have repeatedly attempted to draw a link between homosexuality and child sex abuse. Speaking at a press conference in April 2010, the Vatican Secretary of State, Cardinal Tarcisio Bertone, explicitly blamed homosexuality for the abuse crisis: 'Many psychologists and psychiatrists have demonstrated that there is no relation between celibacy and paedophilia ... They do believe, however, that there is a relation between homosexuality and paedophilia ... That is true ... that is the problem.'[29] In the storm of protest which followed, Father Lombardi of the Vatican press office 'clarified' Bertone's remarks by suggesting that the comments 'obviously referred to the problem of abuse by priests and not the population in general'.[30] Bertone's comments were supported by a Dr Richard Fitzgibbons, a prominent Catholic psychiatrist who serves as a consultant to the Congregation of the Clergy at the Holy See and who regards homosexuality as an illness: 'Cardinal Bertone's comments are completely supported by the John Jay study report and by clinical experience. In fact, every priest whom I treated who was involved with children sexually had previously been involved in adult homosexual relationships.'[31]

In his 2002 'Letter to Catholic Bishops', Fitzgibbons attributed the sex abuse scandal to a combination of same-sex attraction (SSA) and lack of religiosity. Priests 'suffering' from SSA – and thus, in Fitzgibbons's view, prone to commit sexual abuse – have, according to Fitzgibbons, experienced 'profound emotional pain' during childhood due to loneliness, problems in their relationships with their fathers, rejection by their peers, lack of male confidence, and poor self-image. These experiences lead priests 'to direct their sadness and anger towards the Church, her teachings on sexual morality, and the magisterium'.[32] Such priests 'consistently refuse to examine their consciences, to accept the Church's teachings on moral issues as a guide to their personal

actions, or regularly avail themselves of the sacrament of reconciliation'. Priests who 'suffer' from SSA and who are therefore
prone to abuse need to become

> more knowledgeable about the emotional origins and healing of
> same-sex attractions, as well as the serious medical and psychiatric
> illnesses associated with homosexuality ... We have observed many
> priests grow in holiness and happiness in their ministry as a result
> of the healing of their childhood and adolescent male insecurity,
> loneliness and anger and, subsequently, their same-sex attractions.

Fitzgibbons's views are probably representative of a substantial
body of opinion in the Vatican and the institutional Catholic
Church. Even some on the progressive wing of the Church,
whilst not necessarily seeing homosexuality as intrinsically
disordered, express unease about the gay subculture of seminaries and wonder privately whether it has been a factor in the abuse
crisis. One prominent lay Catholic progressive expressed to me
his fears that 'the gays are driving out the straights' from the
seminaries, and felt that progressives are reluctant to debate the
implications for fear of seeming homophobic. However, views
on homosexuality and its relationship to the abuse crisis are
not consistent across the Catholic hierarchy. In relative terms,
the leadership of the English Church has for many years been
notably less homophobic than the Vatican. In 1992, when the
then Cardinal Ratzinger, with the approval of Pope John Paul II,
issued a declaration justifying discrimination against homosexuals, Cardinal Hume was privately appalled by the language and
tone of the document. In discreet discussions with gay rights
campaigners such as Peter Tatchell he made it clear that he saw it

as fuelling prejudice.'As a result of the dialogue I had with Hume, he issued a clarification which went as far as it was possible to go in distancing himself from Ratzinger's document.'[33] Similarly, Cardinal Bertone's comments in 2010 linking homosexuality and child abuse were directly contradicted by the secretary-general of the Catholic Bishops' Conference of England and Wales, Father Marcus Stock: 'There is no empirical data which concludes that sexual orientation is connected to child sexual abuse ... The consensus among researchers is that the sexual abuse of children is not a question of sexual "orientation", whether heterosexual or homosexual, but of a disordered attraction or fixation.'[34]

Nevertheless, the Bertone/Fitzgibbons view is embodied in official Vatican policy. In 2005 the Vatican issued an 'Instruction Concerning the Criteria for the Discernment of Vocations with regard to Persons with Homosexual Tendencies in view of their Admission to the Seminary and to Holy Orders'. As the title of the document confirms, it is concerned exclusively with candidates for the priesthood who have homosexual leanings. Under the policy, men with 'transitory' homosexual tendencies may be ordained deacons following three years of prayer and chastity, but men with 'deeply rooted homosexual tendencies' may never be ordained. Technically the document upholds the traditional Catholic distinction between homosexual orientation and homosexual acts: it is the acts rather than the orientation which are grave sins. Therefore, as Archbishop Dolan of New York pointed out, technically the Vatican directive was 'not tout court a no-gays policy'.[35] However, the document is clearly aimed at barring almost all homosexuals from seminaries on the premise that homosexuality amongst some Catholic priests is a significant cause of the abuse crisis.

In reality, however, Father Stock is right: there is no empirical evidence to substantiate the argument that sexual abuse of boys is a product of homosexual orientation. The claim by Fitzgibbons that every clerical child abuser he had treated had previously been involved in adult homosexual relationships seems highly questionable. I am aware of no such instance in the many Catholic abuse cases I have dealt with, all of which have involved priests who seemed obviously incapable of forming intimate adult relationships and fixated on teenage minors precisely because of an inability to relate properly to adults. As Cozzens argues, the age of the victim indicates a level of psychosexual immaturity on the part of the perpetrator.[36] Fitzgibbons's claim that Cardinal Bertone's comments are 'completely supported' by the John Jay study is simply untrue; the study did not assert any such conclusion. Indeed, another John Jay study suggested that 'the abuse decreased as more gay priests began serving in the church'.[37] A study by Tallon and Terry examined the data gathered on clergy abusers in the USA and concluded that where priests had multiple victims, fewer than half of them had repeatedly abused victims of the same age and gender.[38] In general, academic literature does not provide evidence to support the alleged link between clerical homosexuality and clerical child abuse. Dr Fred Berlin, of the National Institute for the Study, Prevention and Treatment of Sexual Trauma in the USA, says that 'there is no evidence that an adult gay male is any more likely to seek out a boy for sexual activities than an adult heterosexual man would be to seek out a little girl for sexual activities'.[39] Indeed, if there is a 'gay subculture' within the Church, homosexual priests will presumably find willing partners amongst their fellow priests. Thus it is illogical to argue, as the Vatican has sought to do, that the gay subculture is the cause of the abuse crisis.[40] On the contrary, for those priests of homosexual orientation the gay environment of the priesthood provides them with an outlet for adult homosexual activity which, absent a flourishing homosexual subculture in the Church, they might not find so readily. Sexual attraction to children is different and distinct from sexual orientation. Some paedophiles or ephebophiles are attracted to people of the same sex whilst others are attracted to the opposite sex. The attraction is not based on their sexual orientation, but on a fixation towards young people.

For gay rights campaigners, the Vatican's anti-gay arguments are simply a way for Catholic traditionalists to kill two birds with one stone: gays can be blamed for the abuse crisis, and that blame can be used to reinforce Catholic condemnation of homosexual behaviour. As Tatchell says: 'scapegoating gay people within the Church is both a way for the Vatican to wash its hands of responsibility for the sexual abuse that has taken place and also a way to further demonise gay people and justify the church's anti-gay policies'.[41] Tatchell is in no doubt as to the dynamic underlying the attempts to conflate homosexuality and child abuse: 'Many gay clergy have entrenched the homophobia of the Vatican. They espouse it with great enthusiasm, seeking to atone for their own homosexuality by being ever more homophobic.'

There are two other ways in which data about victim preponderance is deployed by Church apologists. Some claim that sexual abuse visited upon adolescents is less harmful than abuse involving younger children. A Canadian bishop vocalised this view following the Mount Cashel scandal: 'We are not dealing with classic paedophilia. I do not want to argue that homosexual activity between a priest and an adolescent is therefore moral.

Rather, it does not have the horrific character of paedophilia.'[42] Based upon experience of acting for many hundreds of victims in legal cases, I strongly disagree. Indeed, the psychic devastation caused by abuse can be especially profound and long-lasting in teenage boys, who are struggling with insecurities about their developing masculinity. In fact, this is a reality the Catholic Church would understand far better if it engaged properly with survivors, rather than trying to outsource pastoral support to external organisations.[43]

A second claim is that the distinction between paedophilia and ephebophilia excuses or at least explains the Church's decisions to return abusing priests to active ministry. Philip Jenkins argues that 'in the prevailing psychiatric opinion of the 1970s and early 1980s it would have been quite appropriate to return to a parish setting a man who had been successfully treated for ephebophilia but not for paedophilia'.[44]

Jenkins was writing about the USA, but the same has been said in an English context. The argument is flawed, for reasons illustrated by two cases from that period detailed in this book where psychiatric input was sought at an early stage: Crowley (Chapter 4) and Hill (Chapter 7). Both men abused pubescent and post-pubescent boys, but there is no evidence in either case that the distinction between ephebophilia and paedophilia formed any part of the Church's decision-making process. Because of a failure to investigate allegations properly, Crowley was wrongly treated as a voyeur of adolescent sexual activity, not as the participant he actually was. These investigative failings are likely to have been a recurring theme at that time: as the Murphy Report observed about Dublin, a notable feature of the Irish Church's handling of abuse allegations was 'the refusal to acknowledge or recognise an allegation of child sexual abuse unless it was made in strong or explicit terms ... A number of bishops heard suspicions and concerns but they did not take the obvious step of asking what was involved.'[45] In Crowley's case, the Church turned a blind eye to evidence of more serious crimes, and so Crowley was treated far more leniently than his offences demanded. This leniency had nothing to do with the age of victims; it was a result of failing to investigate what had really happened. In the Hill case, the precise age of his victims was never suggested to be relevant and the medical evidence specifically highlighted his 'risk of recidivism'. In some medical reports Hill was referred to as 'homosexual' rather than 'paedophile', but none of the medical practitioners who treated him from 1982 onwards seem to have been in any doubt that he posed a continuing risk to children. The problem in the Hill case was that those warnings were not heeded.

• • •

The progressive critique of the abuse scandal – advanced by progressives and liberals within the Church and endorsed by many outside it – sees the root causes of the scandal as residing in a toxic mix of authoritarianism, clericalism, celibacy and sexual immaturity which characterises the Catholic Church and some of its priests.

In authoritarian cultures, leaders are not challenged: the Catholic Church's undemocratic, unaccountable structure and culture, it is argued, facilitates abuse of power. The Pope, the Byzantine papal bureaucracy (the Curia), the bishops – all operate in an authoritarian atmosphere of deceit, denial, secrecy, silence and cover-up. Power corrupts; absolute power corrupts absolutely; and, as Lord Acton also said – and he was speaking of the papacy – there is no worse heresy than that the office sanctifies the holder of it. The papacy is underwritten by the doctrine of papal infallibility; the Pope is accountable only to God, and his word is law. The bishops are accountable only to the Pope. When this authority is challenged, the Church hierarchy reacts by denying and suppressing the information and trying to protect the organisation at any cost; there is no countervailing power within Church structures to question the actions and decisions of its leaders. Rather than reporting allegations to secular authorities, the bishops simply buried them and, if there was a risk of public exposure, moved the priest elsewhere. Bishops – operating in an atmosphere of untrammelled papal and episcopal authority – could not conceive of acting transparently and in accordance with secular norms and laws. And as Margaret Kennedy has observed, they also

> feared what is happening now, the faithful leaving in droves. They knew that ordinary Catholics would vote with their feet when they discovered that their priests were not as 'holy' as they made out. Catholicism is based on the mystery of the priest and what he does on the altar ... they knew they would lose power if the faithful found out.[46]

Anyone who has followed the development of the abuse scandal in the English Catholic Church over the last thirty years will recognise this picture. As the cases examined in this book will show, at least until the 1990s, and in many instances much later, allegations of abuse were suppressed in ways which could never have happened if the leadership of the Church had believed itself to be accountable to its congregations, to the law and to wider society. That accountability has now developed to some extent, not because of any change in the structure of the Church, which remains intrinsically authoritarian, but because victims started to voice their stories openly, gaining courage and collective power through campaigning organisations, and using the legal system and the media. These pressures have operated in different ways in different parts of the world. In the United States, multi-million-dollar awards to victims of abuse have driven many dioceses to the brink of bankruptcy. The financial imperative for the Catholic Church in the US to stamp out child abuse within its ranks has become irresistible. To a degree the same has happened in Ireland, where the Catholic Church, to which the state effectively subcontracted the education and welfare of its children for many decades, has had to contribute millions of euros to state redress and compensation schemes for victims of abuse.

In England, the position has been different. Damages awards to victims of abuse – quantified by judges, not juries – have been more modest. Six-figure awards have been relatively rare; I explain why in Chapter 13. No diocese has been threatened with bankruptcy. The financial pressure on the Church in England has been nowhere near as acute as in Ireland and the USA. Here, the media has been the single most important factor in forcing the Church to change. The Penney case in Birmingham was subject to a devastating exposé by the BBC, *Breach of Faith*. The Archbishop of Birmingham, Maurice Couve de Murville, came across as slippery and dishonest. At that time, however, the media was quiescent with Cardinal Hume; his saintly reputation protected him from difficult questions. The Church's failings in the Michael Hill case only came to light because of detective work by a BBC reporter, Angus Stickler, and survivor groups, and the following few years, during which Archbishop Murphy-O'Connor was subjected to a sustained assault on his record, can be seen as a transitional period in which the Catholic hierarchy faced, for the first time, the challenge, questioning and accountability which is the norm in a modern democracy. Subsequently, Murphy-O'Connor did much to redeem himself by pressing forward with the Nolan process and his successor, Vincent Nichols, has welcomed the accountability which the media brings to the Church's activities. For all that, the Church remains an authoritarian institution. That authoritarianism is rightly seen as helping to create the conditions for the abuse crisis. The way in which the allegations were dealt with, with priests protected and victims pressured not to report, hugely accentuated the problem and an authoritarian, unaccountable culture explains this response.

Also central to the abuse crisis, in the progressive analysis, is clericalism, described by some as the 'cancer at the heart of the Church'. Clericalism positions the Catholic clergy as superior to the laity and in a state of power over them. Clericalism is a cast of mind, a mentality that is strictly hierarchical and in which the priest sees himself as belonging to an exclusive club and sees the role of the laity as being to 'pay, pray and obey'. Members of the clerical caste believe themselves to have a monopoly of wisdom and of access to the Holy Spirit. Clerical power in the Catholic Church is bestowed by ordination, and in Catholic theology ordination changes the man's very essence. The taking of holy orders bestows upon the priest the power to turn bread and wine into the body and blood of Christ and to forgive sins. As explained by one Catholic bishop:

A man once ordained is ontologically changed. He is a priest. Something mysterious happens. It is an action of grace, and something quite real ... The priesthood is not just the deputing of an individual to take on a particular role. It is more than a function; it is a radical reorientating of the whole reality of the person. He is changed at the level of his being ... it is such a transformation of the person that a distinctly priestly character can be identified in him.[47]

Ordination places the priest on a higher plane: hence, a priest who is subsequently laicised is 'reduced' to the lay state.

Clericalism acts to preserve the interests of the club: to protect its own, even at the cost of truth and justice. The reputation of the institution is given primacy over the needs of victims, whose voices are suppressed. As Austen Ivereigh observes, the abuse crisis is a 'consequence of a culture of clericalism which still prevails, an attitude that places concern for a priest's reputation above the welfare of a child, and a mindset that leads to dissident theologians being prosecuted more swiftly than abusers of children'.[48] In that sense, clericalism elides with the authoritarianism just discussed; it is the other face of that coin. But the culture of clericalism is also a means by which abusers gain power over their victims. Priests, 'acting *in Persona Christi*, not as a mere instrument of Christ's work but rather as Christ's real image and representative', may believe that they are set apart from and above the laity, more superior and more holy; that they can do no wrong.[49] Where priests are minded to commit abuse, that sense of superiority may shelter them from the reality of their behaviour and may instil fear, deference and submission in their victims.

Clerical sex offenders interviewed by Donald Findlater and his team at the Lucy Faithfull Foundation described how they used religion, and specifically the authority and charisma of the priesthood, to achieve power over their victims. The priesthood, one said, is an 'extraordinary, trusting, revered position ... I had the respect and used it as a cover.'

Another explained:

I used it to gain their trust, I used the power of God. I knew my power, my status, would be a stumbling block for them. As a member of the church, I represented God. My victims would be prevented from disclosing. My victims were very vulnerable. I knew that beforehand. My beliefs, my status – what I was doing must be right (to my victim) because Father X was doing it.

Or, as another said: 'It's about the power of being a priest, standing in the community, standing in the family. Manipulating the family. Being there as the adviser. This guy has all the answers.' Or:

I used [religion] to get the trust of the child. Because I was a priest I had access. I had access to the child. I had access to the family. I had respect in the community, nobody would suspect me. The power you felt, the power to be trusted. The power and control that I had. As a priest I had an automatic key to people's trust. As a school chaplain I had easy access to children. I was automatically seen as a person to be trusted, by teachers, parents, children ... Nobody would dare question me.

Another said:

As an actual part of my ministry I had access to schools and families. My victims and their family saw in me a particular light. The person who was bringing them to God and God to them. My integral part of all of their lives and the good that flowed from that. All of that was a massive cover hiding the abuse and the child would have found it impossible to separate the abuse from that. They felt that they would not have been believed.

These priests saw that to many parishioners, a priest could only ever do good:

A person who spoke and acted in the way I did, who enabled them, couldn't possibly be other than a good person. If somebody comes to me with their problems, disputes, breakdowns, a whole range of stuff – if there was someone making sense of all this – how can this person be anything other than good?

Priests find it easy to inveigle themselves into families in the parish: 'I had the name of being a good priest, a counsellor for young people, and a Holy man, a good man. Parents directed their sons to me. I would listen, invite the person to come back: you need help and I'm here to listen.'

Priests in the Findlater study were open, too, about the grooming process, which would involve progressively increasing intimacy using the power and assumed right of the priest to probe their victim's inner thoughts: 'I was grooming. I knew that my agenda was to get the person to talk about their fantasies. They believed that because I said it, this must be a catharsis. I got them to become progressively more intimate.'

How can a priest, a man of God, reconcile sexual abuse of a

child with faith? The Findlater study shows that religion and clerical status can themselves provide shelter from reality and evasion of responsibility. As one priest said:

> God chose me, he knew what he was getting, he alone knew all of me, the good and the bad, but he still chose that person, and the bad was allowed to remain with the good. It doesn't seem to matter to God; he knows me, warts and all. God knows both parts of me and allows one for the sake of the other. The more I felt the need to abuse, the more I plunged myself in the pastoral ministry, the more I helped the poor, the sick, choosing areas very taxing and demanding, it drained me more and I went back to the solace of abuse. That circle of giving and being drained, the vacuum inside me – filled up through the solace of abuse – but this created a different void – a void of guilt – a terrible mess – people would say you were drained out, you do too much for us, this fed in, often those would be the families I was abusing – the child was swept along – the abuse was doing their bit for Father. I got angry with God, yes – how did I get in this? … But mixed with the shrug of shoulders – you chose me, it's your fault.

Another priest explained it this way:

> When I was offending, I couldn't convince myself that God didn't know. I brought it into prayer, treated it as a problem. I handed the problem over to God. It doesn't fit with how I am, but this is the way you made me. It's up to you to sort it out. I treated it as God's problem rather than mine. It didn't outweigh the good I was doing. I hoped God would intervene.

And once abuse is committed, Christian concepts of forgiveness are misused to permit reoffending. Forgiveness, of course,
is supposed to follow true penitence. But the facile injunction to
forgive still dominates Catholic thinking about the abuse crisis:
an article about child protection in the *Pastoral Review* from
2006, needless to say not written by a survivor, emphasises that
'the yoke of Christ that is laid upon us is forgiveness and the love
of those who do evil to us. The final reality that alone can heal all,
victim and perpetrator alike, is forgiveness.'[50] But as one priest
said in the Findlater study:

> The thing that is very specific to being a Christian is the whole
> area of sin and forgiveness. It is very possible for distortions to
> creep in there. In my own case it was a very obvious distortion. I
> take sin seriously in the first place. Part of the whole business of
> sin and forgiveness is that I am fully aware of my sin, the implica-
> tions of what I've done, part of that is accepting the consequences
> that may follow from my actions, but I think that a lot of these
> things tended to short-circuit and distort – I said to myself: 'I
> believe in a God who forgives, who forgives unconditionally',
> which is true, but it was using these things in an illegitimate way,
> permissive way, to permit myself to offend because I said 'No
> matter what I've done God will forgive me'. And that is true, but I
> was leaving out the consequences, what it meant for other people,
> I was glossing over that. It was damaging to me as a person in so
> many different ways.

Clericalism, authoritarianism and distorted theology may have
underpinned and compounded the clerical abuse scandal but they
do not fully explain why Catholic priests sexually abuse children

in the first place. In searching for explanations, researchers have focused on sexual immaturity in the priesthood and the interplay with celibacy and the emotional loneliness which accompanies it. Donald Findlater points out that the formation of a priest, particularly a Catholic priest, is not informed by an understanding of sex: 'Priests have to pretend that they are asexual but they are put in intimate situations with parishioners and they have no tools to manage these issues. Supposedly celibate, they are told that sexual thoughts should not cross their mind. It is entirely unrealistic.'[51]

The problem is compounded by the sexual immaturity of many priests who have entered seminary at a young age before their sexual maturation is complete. Their sexual behaviour is frozen in their teenage years, which may partly explain the clerical abuser's fixation with adolescents. The point is expressed perfectly by one of the priests interviewed in Findlater's study:

When I was fourteen I realised that I was more interested in boys than girls; I said to myself, this is not for me, I want to be a priest. It went from there. I never faced up to my sexuality. It froze at fourteen. I began to abuse at the age of twenty-eight. I realised my sexuality came alive at the age I shut it away, at the age of fourteen. The Church prohibits sex, thoughts of sex, but I needed to be touched by people, to be intimate. I was scared of adults so I chose children.

Many clergy also lead lives of emotional isolation: 'I was in a permanent state of isolation and loneliness. I chose boys who I thought were like me – vulnerable, boys whose fathers showed them no affection. I offered it.'

Another explained:

My fantasies weren't specifically sexual, all my fantasies were about friendship, cuddling; when I got aroused I just made a joke out of it. I told myself it wasn't sexual, it was about friendship, but I felt guilty, I went to confession and told priests, then I stopped, then I'd get lonely again. The loneliness would get deeper. My own loneliness, my own need, I wasn't thinking of the child.

That emotional isolation can be a function, of course, of mandatory celibacy. Of all the possible causes of the abuse crisis, celibacy is the one most cited by the media, and indeed by many Catholics. Dissident Catholic theologians such as Hans Küng have long suggested a link between celibacy and clerical sex offending, but senior figures in the Catholic hierarchy have occasionally voiced the same thought. In 2010 the Archbishop of Vienna, Christoph Schönborn, acknowledged that celibacy could be a cause of the scandal and called for an 'unflinching examination' of the issue, which required 'a great deal of honesty, both on the part of the church and of society as a whole'. Archbishop Schönborn, in the usual manner of senior Catholic clerics engaged in kite flying, later 'clarified' his remarks by insisting that he was 'in no way' seeking to question the celibacy rule or call for its abolition.[52] The issue is unlikely to go away, however, and celibacy is undeniably a factor in the causative mix, although the arguments linking it with the abuse crisis can sometimes be oversimplistic.

In its crudest form, the argument that celibacy is a cause of the crisis posits that priests, being sexual beings like everyone else, cannot in practice adhere to their vows of celibacy and thus need a sexual outlet, which is supplied by children, because they happen to be available; because of the tradition of gender segregation in Catholic settings, only boys will generally be available to male priests.[53] But this reductionist argument is too crude, given that in society generally a substantial proportion of child sex offences are committed by married men. It also ignores the reality that a substantial minority of priests, and possibly even a majority, are sexually active in any event, most of them with other adults; Sipe suggests that at best only 50 per cent of the priesthood are truly celibate in relation to avoiding sexual activity altogether, a figure which falls to 2 per cent if masturbatory abstinence is expected as a definition of proper chastity.[54] Mandatory celibacy does not quite reflect the reality of many priests' lives. That said, it is clear that the involuntary nature of the vow of celibacy poses problems, particularly for clergy who enter the priesthood with little or no sexual experience: a vow which can seem straightforward to an immature teenager entering seminary may provoke much inner anguish a decade or two later. As one report concluded, priests often 'bring, to adult church leadership, a serious sexual and relationship immaturity. Sexual desire is not eliminated by commitment to ministry.' Clergy are 'caught in a trap' because they 'experience sexual desire as part of their humanity but also experience shame and distress at the presence of such desire'. This can lead to a whole range of problems including a 'distinctive pattern of sexual abuse that is rooted in sexual addiction'.[55]

Celibacy may also have contributed to the abuse crisis in more indirect ways. For individuals who are sexually fixated on children, celibacy provides a respectable cover: celibacy 'signals purity, not danger' and so becomes a camouflage for nefarious action.[56] There will always be individuals of this type who are drawn to the Catholic priesthood. At the same time, the requirement of mandatory celibacy has had a disastrous impact on clerical recruitment. Falling numbers of ordinands meant that standards of vetting and assessment of new recruits were effectively lowered, increasing the risk of men of unsuitable psychological makeup entering the priestly life, and raising the risk of sex offending.

Finally, in enumerating the causes of the abuse crisis, we cannot ignore a fundamental fact: the power structure responsible for this scandal is entirely male. Feminist analysis of the abuse scandal emphasises the role of patriarchal power, seeing child sexual abuse (and the abuse of adult women in the Church) as intrinsically linked to male supremacy; the Catholic Church, even more than most institutions, is seen as a belief system and organisation founded upon oppression of the powerless. Whether one agrees with that view, there is surely force in the arguments of some female theologians that a greater presence of women in Church power structures would have prevented or at least reduced clerical abuse. As one pointed out, correctly: 'It is clear that statistically, women abuse much less than men. And, in terms of reporting, are much more likely to report abuse.'[57] It is difficult, of course, to prove empirically that a greater involvement by women in religious power structures would reduce abuse, because even the Protestant churches which have introduced women bishops have done so only recently: there is simply not enough history from which to generalise. The experience of one female Anglican bishop in New Zealand, Penny Jamieson, is illuminating: as a bishop, she found that handling incidents of clergy sexual abuse was 'like firing an open torpedo shot at the underlying and still very well-functioning patriarchal structure of the church'. Jamieson recalled:

All the other bishops that I have known who have been called upon to deal with incidents of clergy sexual misconduct – all of them male – have found it incredibly hard to break the bond of brotherhood with their male colleagues and ensure a just outcome by taking steps to terminate the priests' license for ministry. I have watched them make every excuse in the book. Some have overcome their conditioning, some have not.[58]

That 'bond of brotherhood', which Jamieson found so potent in the Anglican Church, is even more impregnable in the all-male Catholic priesthood. It is, undeniably, a factor in the crisis, but as Jamieson herself found, the maleness of the priesthood is only part of the problem. When, as a bishop, Jamieson was herself required to challenge clerical misconduct, she acknowledges that 'I also found taking such action very hard. I realised that is because I see much of the security of my ministry as a bishop in making and retaining good relationships of trust and respect with all my clergy.' That sodality of an 'intimate and self-supporting' priesthood – male or not – is itself a central factor in the abuse crisis, and even more so in its cover-up.

CHAPTER 3

A COVER-UP?

Why has the Catholic Church acquired a reputation for deliberate, orchestrated cover-up? Any organisation facing challenge will instinctively seek to defend itself; in that respect, the Catholic Church is hardly unique. With the revelations about the BBC and Jimmy Savile it would be absurd to suggest that the Catholic Church is the only institution to have attempted to suppress complaints of abuse in order to protect its reputation. Nevertheless, and with good reason, the phrase 'cover-up' has become commonplace in coverage of the Catholic abuse scandal.

In England and Wales, our knowledge of how the Catholic Church has handled abuse cases over the past few decades is necessarily limited. We are trying to shine a torch on some very dark corners and much of what truly happened will remain hidden. Whilst criminal trials can occasionally shed light on the handling of complaints about a particular priest, the purpose of a criminal prosecution is simply to convict the offender, not to examine institutional knowledge and culpability. Institutional failings generally never see the light of day if the offender pleads guilty. Occasionally, in preparing criminal cases the police will stumble on past complaints of abuse from other victims and thereby piece together a pattern of knowledge, and sometimes that information seeps into the public domain, particularly where such evidence is given in open court.

However, our knowledge of how the Church has handled complaints of abuse comes largely from two sources: media investigations and civil (compensation) cases. Both depend on the courage of victims, and victims may have become more emboldened to speak out as child abuse becomes more openly discussed; but in other respects the media and legal cases are now depleting assets. High-quality investigative journalism is in retreat, undermined by the shift from newspaper and TV to the internet. With a few exceptions like Exaro, the internet has failed to make up for the decline in the traditional investigative journalism of the *Sunday Times* Insight team or the old-style *Panorama* – a trend which should concern everyone who cares about the accountability of powerful institutions. Meanwhile, legal cases have helped to expose institutional culpability, but as a vehicle for holding the Church to account, they are limited. Court rules mean that much of what may surface in legal cases cannot be reported.

Of course, even where documents are forced out of the Church, they may not reveal much: very few personnel files of convicted priests contain incriminating information, at least not at the point at which they are disclosed to claimant lawyers. The *Catholic Directory* can sometimes disclose telltale signs that a priest has been in trouble: if a priest's entry is tracked through successive years of the *Directory*, it is sometimes found that his name mysteriously disappears in particular years, or that his address changes from a particular parish church to 'c/o Bishop's House'. This may be an editing error, but it can also indicate that a priest has been taken 'out of circulation' until the embarrassment of an allegation has faded. But the history has to be pieced together through inference.

In theory (and in canon law), internal Church documents regarding paedophile priests should be found in the rather Dan Brown-sounding 'secret archive'. The Code of Canon Law provides that

> there is also to be a secret archive, or at least in the ordinary archive there is to be a safe or cabinet, which is securely closed and bolted and which cannot be removed. In this archive documents which are to be kept under secrecy are to be most carefully guarded.[59]

Canon law forbids the removal of any documents from the secret archive; only the bishop is permitted to have the key. The documents to be kept in the secret archive include:

> documents from historic criminal cases [i.e. within canon law] concerning matters of a moral nature; documentary proof of canonical warnings or corrections when someone has been about to commit an offence, or is suspected of having committed one, or has been guilty of scandalous behaviour; documents relating to preliminary investigation for a penal process that was closed without a formal trial; documents relating to any other documents the bishop considers secret.

So the secret archive ought to be a fruitful source of material about past allegations, and claimant lawyers have learned to force disclosure, on affidavit, of the contents of the archive, sometimes with striking results. But the reality is that in the past many allegations were dealt with informally, with no relevant documentation being created: see the Dunn case in Chapter 4. Diocesan child protection coordinators who have attempted, post-Nolan, to unearth evidence of past allegations have more often than not been disappointed to find that the secret archive yields little or nothing of relevance.

In any event, cases which are truly embarrassing for the Church are invariably settled out of court, and often with confidentiality provisions (technically, 'gag orders' cannot be imposed on claimants, but the risks of litigation sometimes leave them with little choice). Also, as discussed in Chapter 13, changes in the legal framework governing abuse claims mean that institutional culpability is now largely irrelevant to victim compensation. Previously, in order to secure compensation, it was necessary for lawyers to prove that the institution had been negligent in the handling of abuse cases: i.e., that it knew or ought to have known that abuse was being committed and failed to intervene appropriately to protect actual and potential victims. Therefore, it was necessary for claimant lawyers to hunt down and forensically examine evidence of institutional knowledge and cover-up. Compensation cases became a vehicle for exposing the Church's historic failings. However, a series of interlocking court decisions over the past few years, culminating in the *JGE* case in 2012, have determined that the Catholic Church is vicariously liable for the actions of its priests where these are sufficiently closely connected with the performance of priestly duties. Thus, compensation will generally flow as of right if the abuse can be proved, if any time-limit hurdle can be overcome and if the abuse occurred within the course of the priest's pastoral duties, which are analysed broadly.[60] This is better for victims seeking compensation: securing a damages pay-out is now simpler and quicker. Yet paradoxically, many examples of institutional culpability that might previously have been exposed will now remain hidden. Getting to the truth of what really happened in many cases, and, most importantly, who knew what and when, is exceptionally difficult; we probably see only the tip of an iceberg. In the future, it may be even more difficult to probe beneath the surface, a point which reinforces the need for proper external oversight of the Church's handling of allegations.

In many of the cases described in this book there is compelling evidence that allegations of abuse were ignored and suppressed; that priests were moved to new parishes to quell public scandal; and that victims and their parents were actively discouraged from going to the police. In this sense, 'cover-up' is a reasonable description of what occurred. But the term is an emotive one: some campaigners against Church abuse intend it to refer to some wider organised conspiracy, perhaps orchestrated from Rome. Meanwhile the use of the term is challenged by Church apologists, who argue that it ignores historical context.

Proponents of a wider conspiracy focus in particular on the Church's non-cooperation with civil authorities in abuse cases and the secrecy apparently mandated by Vatican documents and canon law. Of course, an unwillingness to bend to secular authority has been one of the defining features of Catholicism over hundreds of years: the traditional papal stance is encapsulated in an 1864 Encyclical Letter, *Quanta Cura* ('On Current Errors'), which condemned the 'wicked and so often condemned inventions of innovators [who] dare with signal impudence to subject to the will of the civil authority the supreme authority of the Church and of this Apostolic See given to her by Christ

Himself, and to deny all those rights of the same Church and See which concern matters of the external order'.[61] Something of that same age-old Vatican mentality can be seen in the now notorious confidential letter dated 31 January 1997, addressed to the Irish Catholic hierarchy and signed by Archbishop Luciano Storero, Pope John Paul II's envoy to Ireland. The letter was a response to new child protection policies put in place by a commission of Irish bishops. The policies included a mandatory obligation to report allegations to the police. The letter stated that in following this new policy the bishops would be breaching canon law. Not only that, but the letter warned that implementing punishments that were outside of the law would likely end with the Vatican overturning the decision.[62] However, although this letter acquired particular notoriety it can be seen as just one of a long line of Vatican edicts designed to 'shield paedophile priests from criminal trial around the world'.[63]

When canon law was codified in 1917 the abuse of children under sixteen was specifically outlawed as a sin: the modern version is Canon 1395.2 of the 1983 Code, which provides that 'a cleric who in another way has committed an offence against the sixth commandment of the Decalogue[64] … with a minor below the age of sixteen years, is to be punished with just penalties, not excluding dismissal from the clerical state if the case so warrants'. But under the 1917 Code this and certain other canonical crimes were reserved for handling by the Sacred Congregation of the Sacred Office, which in 1965 became the Sacred Congregation for Doctrine of the Faith (now just plain CDF).[65] Proponents of the conspiracy theory point to the Vatican directive *Crimen Sollicitationis*, originally issued by the Sacred Congregation of the Sacred Office in 1922 and updated in 1962, which set out detailed instructions on the procedures to be adopted in dealing with the canonical crime of solicitation, and which is notable for an obsessive emphasis on secrecy.

The existence of *Crimen Sollicitationis* came to world attention in 2003 amidst much controversy: a lawyer for victims unearthed it in the Vatican archives. In 2006, a BBC documentary, *Sex Crimes and the Vatican*, presented *Crimen* as a 'smoking gun', proof of a Vatican-ordered conspiracy to protect paedophile priests. Tom Doyle, a well-known canon lawyer and campaigner against clerical sex abuse, argued in the programme that *Crimen*, which imposed an oath of secrecy in relation to the victim, the offender and any witness in an abuse case, was 'indicative of a worldwide policy of absolute secrecy and control of all cases of sexual abuse by clergy'.[66] The American Catholic journalist John Allen contested that view, arguing that *Crimen* was 'exceedingly obscure' and that most bishops had never heard of it prior to the controversy in 2003, 'so to suggest it played a crucial role in shaping the church's response to the crisis is an exaggeration'. Further, Allen claimed, the document went out of force in 1983, and only concerned secrecy in ecclesiastical procedures:

> There was nothing in it, nor anywhere else in Church law, that would have prevented a bishop (or anyone else) from reporting a crime of sexual abuse to the local police or a prosecuting attorney. That the bishops failed to do so is indicative of a widespread pattern of damage control ... This was a matter of cultural and institutional psychology rather than formal law.[67]

Shortly afterwards Doyle offered a more nuanced view than his original comment implied:

Although I was a consultant to the producers of the documentary, I am afraid that some of the distinctions I have made about
the 1962 document have been lost. I do not believe now nor have
I ever believed it to be proof of an explicit conspiracy, in the
conventional sense, engineered by top Vatican officials to cover
up clergy abuse. I do not believe that the Vatican or any group of
bishops needed a conspiracy.[68]

Indeed, Doyle has always maintained that the Codes of Canon
Law – 1917 and 1983 – contained the legal means to deal with
clerical sexual offending; those means were provided by Canon
1395, together with Canons 1717–19, which set out procedures
for investigating sexual wrongdoings. The failure to use them
correctly was the fault of the bishops charged with implementing the law, not the law itself: it was an issue of an organisational
culture grounded in 'secrecy, clericalism and institutional
self-preservation'.[69]

Since *Crimen* came to light in 2003, the Vatican has always
denied that the oath of secrecy in it (and indeed the overriding obsession with secrecy throughout the whole document)
mandates non-cooperation with law enforcement authorities, but
Geoffrey Robertson argues persuasively that this is incompatible with paragraph 23 of *Crimen*, which requires the accuser to
commence by making a formal denunciation under oath: after he
signs it, 'he is to be administered the oath to maintain confidentiality, of necessity under pain of excommunication'.[70] From this,
Robertson infers that a victim who took his story to the police
would risk excommunication, and the Murphy Commission
in Ireland certainly saw it as constituting 'an inhibition on the
reporting of child sex abuse to the civil authorities or others'.[71]

Allen is almost certainly wrong in claiming that *Crimen* lapsed in 1983: a successor document published by the CDF in 2001 explicitly confirmed that *Crimen* had been 'in force until now'.[72] However, Allen is probably right that many bishops in recent years had never heard of *Crimen*. Although it seems likely to have been sent to most diocesan bishops in 1962, with an accompanying instruction from Pope John XXIII that it must be 'observed in every detail',[73] it was never published alongside other official legal documents of the Holy See, and Doyle concedes that 'it is quite possible that most of the bishops who have served during the past thirty years were not aware of the 1962 document'.[74] Some commentators have questioned whether *Crimen* even extended to child sex abuse taking place outside the confessional (technically the crime of solicitation relates to the abuse of the sacrament of penance by a priest who solicits the penitent to sin against the Sixth Commandment), although Doyle argues convincingly that it clearly applied to other sexual crimes perpetrated by clerics.[75] But as Doyle concludes: 'The cover-up happened whether or not bishops were aware of the 1962 document.'[76] That cover-up was a product of institutional culture; to the extent that it was known about, *Crimen* merely gave legal force to a longstanding culture of secrecy. The evidence from actual cases, at least in England and Wales, is that bishops generally handled allegations informally, pressurising victims into silence and, if necessary, dispatching priests elsewhere with barely anything in the way of a written record. For this reason, the argument over *Crimen* may be a red herring. Secrecy and cover-up did not need to be formally mandated because they were what the Church – especially its bishops, who are chosen for their loyalty to Rome, not for their independence of mind – did instinctively.

Crimen Sollicitationis was revised in a declaration promulgated by the then Cardinal Ratzinger (at that time head of the CDF) in 2001 (*Sacramentorum Sanctitatis Tutela*) and further revised in 2010. S*acramentorum Sanctitatis Tutela* made it clear that the CDF would ultimately deal with all cases of sex abuse by Catholic clergy: it was in response to the many thousands of cases which then landed on Cardinal Ratzinger's desk that he made the statement about 'filth' in the Church quoted at the start of this book. The objective, it was claimed, was to promote a unified approach to such cases. But both documents continued to emphasise secrecy and neither mentioned duties to report to the statutory authorities, a surprising and perhaps telling omission, especially as the question of whether the Vatican did or did not support reporting to the civil authorities has been a major source of controversy.[77] Whether or not the idea of a Vatican-orchestrated conspiracy to cover up sex crimes by clergy was a myth, the then Pope did little in these documents to dispel it.

On the issue of cooperation with civil authorities, however, Vatican apologists now point to the 'Circular Letter on Sexual Abuse' issued in May 2011 by the then head of the CDF, Cardinal William Levada. The 'fifth consideration' in this letter stated:

Sexual abuse of minors is not just a canonical delict but also a crime prosecuted by civil law. Although relations with civil authority will differ in various countries, nevertheless it is important to cooperate with such authorities within their responsibilities. Specifically, without prejudice to the sacramental internal forum,[78] the prescriptions of civil law regarding the reporting of such crimes to the civil authority must always be followed.

However, this is hardly a clear and unambiguous instruction to report allegations of abuse to the police; it simply says 'obey the law of the land'. Since most countries do not have a mandatory reporting law, this still permits considerable 'wriggle room' in terms of what the Church is, or is not, obliged to report. It did not represent any fundamental change to the culture of keeping allegations 'in house'. Although some senior Catholic clerics such as Charles Scicluna, formerly Promoter of Justice at the CDF, seem to have tried to modernise the Church's position, resistance to mandatory reporting to civil authorities is still deeply entrenched in the Vatican.[79]

On the other side of the argument, Church apologists strongly reject the notion of 'cover-up', arguing that the Church cannot be criticised for failing to act more forcefully in abuse cases before the 1990s because the true nature of paedophilia was not properly understood at that time. What is now seen as a 'cover-up', they argue, may have been a perfectly reasonable, or at least excusable, decision in the light of medical knowledge as it then stood. The argument is expressed in varying ways but usually takes the form of saying that the risk of recidivism was not properly appreciated and the Catholic Church cannot be blamed in hindsight for not knowing as much about this feature of paedophilia as is known now. The decision to move a priest to a new parish was taken in understandable ignorance of the risk of reoffending and the damage his abuse had already caused.

Again, the argument can appear persuasive in the abstract but is revealed as disingenuous when applied to real cases. It is undoubtedly the case that knowledge and understanding of child abuse has improved over the last forty years and so, as a general proposition, the argument that the Catholic Church could not have been expected to understand as much in earlier decades is self-evidently true. However, as the Murphy Report in Ireland repeatedly emphasised, we should not lose sight of the bigger picture: child abuse has always been a criminal offence; the state of medical knowledge cannot be, and never has been, a reason for failing to report a serious crime to the authorities. Priests and bishops have always claimed to be moral arbiters in society; they purport to be touched by God and invested with spiritual authority; by definition they are supposed to know the difference between right and wrong. Child sexual abuse is and always has been immoral and shocking to any normal person. It is and always was a crime against the laws of the land; to say that this was not properly appreciated before the 1990s is untrue, intellectually dishonest and frankly absurd, particularly coming from a Catholic hierarchy who, as the Murphy Report observed, 'were all very well educated people'.[80] Diarmuid Martin, current Archbishop of Dublin and one of the bravest voices against sex abuse from within the Catholic hierarchy, put the point simply in 2009: 'The sexual abuse of a child is and always was a crime in civil law; it is and always was a crime in canon law.' Martin went on: 'There is no room for revisionism regarding the norms and procedures that were in place.'[81] Doyle would agree, indeed would rightly see the very existence of provisions such as Canon 1395 or indeed *Crimen Sollicitationis* as proof of the Church's longstand-ing knowledge of sex abuse: an awareness that stretches back two thousand years. In relation to recidivism, the claim that the Catholic Church did not understand the true nature of paedo-philia before the 1990s is unconvincing. The Murphy Report in Ireland found that in 1981, the then Archbishop of Dublin had 'a clear understanding of both the recidivist nature of child sexual abusers and the effects of such abuse on children'.[82] The Murphy Report rejected the notion that bishops in the Archdiocese of Dublin were on a learning curve about child abusers, as the Archbishop of Dublin took out insurance in 1987 to cover the cost of any liability that might arise from child sexual abuse by clergy. The bishops in Dublin also knew about a significant number of cases, hence the Murphy Report's rejection of the claim that the bishops were 'lacking in any appreciation of the phenomenon of child sexual abuse'.

In England, it was claimed in the Hill case that Bishop Murphy-O'Connor was unaware of the risk of recidivism due to the state of medical knowledge in the early 1980s. But the medical evidence on Hill specifically referred to 'the reputation this condition has for recidivism'. That was in 1983. Some of the medical evidence was, arguably, ambiguous in other respects, a point discussed in Chapter 7. But on the risk of recidivism it was unequivocal. In fact, although the Hill case garnered endless headlines, Murphy-O'Connor was possibly less blameworthy (in relative terms) than some of his colleagues: he attempted early on in the saga to seek medical input (see the Penney case by way of contrast). In many other cases, decisions to move a known abuser to a new posting were made without obtaining medical evidence. The Church cannot really rely upon 'the state of medical knowledge' at any given time to excuse its failings when it did not, in many cases, seek medical advice.

Although emotive, the term 'cover-up' is a justifiable shorthand for what has occurred in the Catholic Church over past decades. The Murphy Report concluded of the Archdiocese of Dublin that its 'preoccupations in dealing with cases of child sexual abuse ... were the maintenance of secrecy, the avoidance of scandal, the protection of the reputation of the Church, and the preservation of its assets. All other considerations, including the welfare of children and justice for victims, were subordinated to these priorities.'[83] As we shall see, that conclusion applies with equal validity to the English Church.

CHAPTER 4

EASILY SILENCED:
1960s-1990s

'I was totally in awe of priests. I believed that if I said anything I would burn in hell for evermore.'[84] From today's vantage point, when child abuse dominates public discourse and the Catholic Church has been 'holed below the waterline',[85] it is easy to forget how much fear could be felt by ordinary Catholics. From the 1960s to the 1990s, complaints of abuse were systematically suppressed by dioceses and religious orders. The cases I explore in this chapter are just a selection of the many allegations we now know about from that period, but they illustrate common themes. Most victims were devout, and were easily silenced. Allegations were kept well hidden; if victims thought of involving the police, they were rapidly disabused. It was only years later, realising they were not alone, that victims started to summon up the courage to talk about their experiences, and it became possible to see what had really occurred.

• • •

Graham Wilmer's first day at the Salesian College is ingrained in his memory: 'Our housemaster – a dowdy old priest who smelt of BO and tobacco – showed us to our desk. The shoulders of his faded black cassock had a heavy dusting of dandruff on them. It made him look a little like a cake decoration.' But the old priest moved 'with the stealth of a lion' when he saw Graham talking: 'He struck me across the face with his open hand. I had not even seen him coming.'

It was 1963; starting school in Chertsey, Surrey, Graham was one of thousands of pupils of the Salesians of Don Bosco, the second largest Catholic order in the world. The order, according to its website, enables 'poor and suffering children to live better lives and build brighter futures. We operate 5,000 schools and technical training centres, 23 colleges, 216 clinics and hospitals, 225 orphanages and shelters and a wide variety of social and economic development activities' worldwide. The order has 'an active presence in more than 130 countries spanning five continents'. All in all, there are nearly 34,000 priests, brothers and sisters who serve the Salesians of Don Bosco, supported by many volunteers. The order has also featured heavily in the abuse scandal.

Graham quickly adjusted to the Salesian teaching method ('do what we tell you or you get beaten') and his first three years at the college were, by and large, a happy time. He enjoyed school, made good friends and did well academically.

In 1966, a new teacher, 'tall, young and energetic', joined the staff, and befriended Graham. Hubert Madley was less than ten years older than Graham; he insisted that Graham call him 'Hugh'. 'Why he chose me is something I don't fully understand but, whatever his reasons were, I was the one.' He offered to take Graham home on his motorbike. Graham realised afterwards that these rides, which became more and more frequent, 'served more than one purpose'. It gave Madley the opportunity to groom him, whilst separating him from his friends. After a little while, Madley persuaded Graham's parents to allow him to give Graham extra maths lessons at the family home.

A bit later, the arrangements changed. Madley was suddenly taking Graham home by car. The first assault occurred towards the end of the car journey to Graham's house. 'Madley put his hand onto my right leg. I tried to remove it, but he resisted and moved it up. I was frozen with fear. I simply did not know what to do.' Graham wanted to get out of the car, but Madley prevented him and told him that it was 'only a bit of fun'.

In Graham's bedroom, Madley repeated the assault. At the end, he told Graham in a threatening tone not to tell anyone about it. Madley left. He had already charmed Graham's mother. In the summer of 1967, Madley persuaded Graham's parents to let him take Graham on a camping holiday in Wales. Graham felt trapped. He contemplated running away, and even thought about trying to kill Madley. But by then, Madley had achieved 'total control'. They landed up in a derelict cottage.

> Madley told me to take off my trousers and lie face down. He removed all of his clothes, seemingly oblivious to the cold. He had a mad look in his eyes and seemed very agitated. He lay down on top of me and I felt him fumbling around with my bottom. After a few moments, he began to push his penis into my anus. I told him that he was hurting me, but he paused only briefly to spit on my anus. Then he began again, penetrating me for the first time...

The sexual assaults continued for around eighteen months. Graham's school work deteriorated sharply. He became desperately sad and reclusive; he lost weight and spent hours alone in his room. His school reports, which Graham has kept, showed very clearly that something was wrong. His parents were worried too, and spoke to the school. Their response was dismissive: Graham was 'a typical moody teenager'.

Brought up as a devout Catholic, Graham had stopped taking communion at Mass. He believed he was in a state of mortal sin. He could not go to confession and tell the priest what he had done. But

the rules were the rules – you do not mess with the Church, and you certainly do not mess with the Almighty. These sins were just so terrible that I knew that I would never be able to confess them and get away with it. I was doomed; I knew it and I believed God knew it.

But the death of Graham's best friend in February 1968 forced the issue. Graham was asked to serve as an altar boy at the requiem Mass. This meant one thing above all – he would have to go to confession. Agonising, he decided that he would have tell the priest that he had committed 'terrible homosexual acts'. A couple of days before the funeral, Graham went to confession and steeled himself to face the consequences. In his eyes, it was his fault that he had committed terrible sins, so he deserved whatever punishment was due. In confession with a Father Madden, he told the priest what had happened and identified Madley as the other participant.

Father Madden initially seemed sympathetic. He gave Graham total absolution, but told him that he needed to repeat these things to him outside confession; as it was, the sanctity of the confessional would prevent him taking matters any further.

Immediately after confession, he confronted Madley. Madley's response was dismissive: 'They will not believe you. I will just deny it.' But in the meantime, Father Madden had told the headmaster, Father O'Shea. Father O'Shea informed the rector, Father Gaffney, and the provincial superior, Father George Williams.

A few days later Graham was summoned to see O'Shea and Gaffney, together with another priest whom Graham had never seen. This man was the provincial rector of the Salesian Order in the UK. This priest, he was informed, was a 'specialist' in these sorts of matters, who would 'talk to him alone about what had happened'. Graham was interrogated on every aspect. He told them everything; at the end, they told him not under any circumstances to talk to anyone about it, including his parents.

As far as Graham knew, that was the end of the investigation. In the meantime his education had been wrecked and he went into a downward spiral. Struggling to settle and incapable of forming lasting relationships, he 'stumbled on through life, but the legacy of guilt, confusion and anger was never far from the surface'. So began

> my years in the wilderness. I worked as a window cleaner's assistant, a hospital porter, a van driver's assistant, a shop assistant, a cinema cleaner, a gardener's assistant and numerous other manual jobs. It was not difficult to get work, but I found it difficult to stay long in any job. I was easy prey for paedophiles. Such is the nature of child abuse. The more often you are damaged, the more vulnerable you become.

Eventually, in 1997, Graham had a breakdown. Overwhelmed by images of the abuse, he went to the edge of self-destruction.

In 1999, following counselling, he made a full statement to Surrey Police. They launched an investigation. In April 2000, Madley was arrested, but denied that anything had happened. Father O'Shea also denied knowing anything about it and, based on their denials, the CPS decided not to prosecute. The CPS did not even interview Father Williams.

Graham was unwilling to give up. In October 2000, he threatened to initiate a civil case against the Salesians. They responded by offering to mediate. Mediation, they suggested, would be 'far less painful and much quicker than going through the courts'. Following mediation, Graham accepted a damages payment of £20,000. This was in February 2001. The money was paid on condition of confidentiality. The settlement also provided that 'in consideration' of the damages payment, not only would Graham not pursue civil proceedings – a normal provision of any settlement of a claim – but also, and more controversially, he would not 'actively pursue any complaint to the police'.[86]

Graham wondered what he had really achieved. 'Did I get the justice I wanted so desperately? Did I bring my abuser to book?' Graham debated what he should do. The turning point was the murder of two schoolgirls in Soham, Cambridgeshire, in 2002. In 2003, after Ian Huntley had been convicted, it became clear that there had been previous allegations against him which the authorities had ignored. If the police had listened more carefully to previous complaints, Holly Wells and Jessica Chapman might still have been alive. As a result of the Huntley case, police practice on recording of allegations was changed. Graham decided to make a fresh allegation against Madley, knowing that this would be recorded on the police national computer. 'At least I could ensure that Madley would never be able to work with children again in a school.'

Graham was nervous, however, about his agreement with the Salesians; he was supposed to say nothing. As far as they were concerned, the matter was 'dead and buried'. He wrote to the Salesians, explaining his concern that Madley could offend again. Perhaps treading more delicately in the post-Nolan period, the order replied in an apparently sympathetic vein, saying that they would not seek to enforce confidentiality if Graham were to initiate 'a private criminal prosecution against Madley'. They emphasised that they had no information on Madley 'other than that which you have supplied'. This throwaway line was to haunt the order later.

Graham tried to lay the ground for a criminal prosecution by writing at length to Madley: 'I told him in unemotional language that I had now embarked on a course that would only end when the truth was finally out … I would never stop until I had brought him to justice.' In response, Graham expected a threatening letter from Madley's solicitors; he was stunned when Madley replied directly, suggesting a meeting. More letters were exchanged; Graham and a friend also telephoned Madley, and taped the conversations. Madley admitted everything, and begged for forgiveness. But what transpired from those conversations was devastating for Graham: it turned out that when he had made his disclosures in 1968, the provincial rector had interviewed Madley straight away. Even then, Madley had disclosed everything that had happened, and was asked to promise that he would never abuse another child. On the strength of that promise, the school organised for Madley to be given a job in another school, in Battersea. Graham had spent over thirty years assuming that he had not been believed, and assuming that Madley had branded him a liar. And Madley had gone on to teach elsewhere, putting other children at risk.

Six weeks later, Madley was charged under the 1963 Sexual Offences Act with three specimen charges, two of indecency with a minor, and one of buggery with a minor. Graham assumed that it was 'all over bar the shouting'. The trial began in August 2005. Unfortunately, by now, and presumably on legal advice, Madley had decided to plead not guilty. Interviewed by the police under caution, Madley had made a number of admissions, and these formed the basis of the prosecution case. Madley was by now growing old, but the police had believed that he was able to answer questions without the presence of an appropriate adult. But in the court's view, this was mistaken: Madley was depressed and vulnerable. 'It is my view', said His Honour Judge Inman, 'that the custody officers erred in not providing an appropriate adult for the two interviews.' The evidence was excluded, and the trial collapsed; Graham was back at square one.

Graham was left 'appealing to the court of public opinion'. He decided to publish an account of his involvement with Madley and his struggle for justice. In 2006, he found a publisher. The Salesian Order's lawyers tried to prevent publication, apparently under the impression that Madley had maintained his silence, and thus that anything Graham said would be a breach of the confidentiality agreement.

In 2007, however, in an extraordinary interview with his local paper, Madley, by then sixty-three, confessed to indecently assaulting Graham:

Madley, who is unmarried and suffers severe depression, went on to admit that he had indecently assaulted Mr Wilmer but said that he did not believe that he had had sex with him. 'I wish I could get it clear in my own mind, I must have done it. Why would he say it if it was not true? I think I did it. I cannot imagine that he would carry on pursuing the matter if it did not happen. I wish I could replay it in my mind' ... The former teacher, who at times spoke in disjointed sentences and occasionally broke down during the interview, says he wants to meet with Mr Wilmer to help remember what had happened and to help Mr Wilmer ... Mr Madley denied sexually abusing other children and insisted he posed no risk. Detective Constable John Hobbs, who led the 2004 investigation, agreed Mr Madley was unlikely to carry out further offences, but only because of his age and failing mental health.[87]

No police action followed this bizarre interview, but Graham has not abandoned his battle for justice: over the past few years, through meetings with the Salesians and the police, he has continued to lobby for the investigation to be reopened. Late in 2013 came a breakthrough: the police announced a comprehensive inquiry into abuse in Salesian schools – not just what happened to Graham, but in many other Salesian institutions. The new police inquiry, Operation Torva, appears to be wide-ranging, and is ongoing at the time of writing. But what is clear, although it only became known to Graham many years later, is that the Salesian Order always knew he was telling the truth; Madley admitted his crimes straight away and was simply transferred to another school. Two former pupils at that later school,

Salesian College, Battersea, have now made allegations against
Madley. The police investigation continues.

• • •

Father Michael Dunn arrived at the Church of Christ the King
in Thornaby, near Stockton-on-Tees in 1973. He was in his twen-
ties and joined as an assistant priest, supporting the much older
Monsignor Carroll. Carroll was 'a typical old-fashioned priest,
stern and austere'.[88] The overwhelmingly working-class congregation was respectful of Carroll but glad to see new blood. Dunn,
a 'trendy young curate with shoulder-length hair', was a powerful
personality. He quickly made an impact, especially on younger
congregants.

In 1975, one of his parishioners was a thirteen-year-old
schoolboy. John (not his real name) and his family were devout
worshippers at Christ the King. To John and his siblings,
Dunn was charismatic and exciting. John's sister remembers:
'He was magnetic. I developed a kind of teenage crush on him. He
was that sort of person. We all looked up to him.'

Dunn singled the family out for special attention, taking John
and a sibling on a trip to Ireland. John's mother found it odd
that Dunn seemed reluctant to tell Monsignor Carroll about the
trip, but thought little of it. The holiday was a great honour for
working-class Catholics, and she was keen for John to become
more involved in the Church. She trusted Dunn completely:
'The Church was my life. I went to Mass every day. I had absolute respect for priests. You trusted them totally.'

The holiday passed off innocently, and cemented John's
friendship with Dunn. Not long afterwards, Dunn started a

youth group at the church. It was poorly attended, but John was growing closer to Dunn and started spending evenings with him. There was no evening housekeeper at the presbytery, and Dunn often asked John to come over after school to answer the phone: 'I'd go to the church straight from school on an evening and hang out with him until 6 or 7 p.m.' They sat and chatted. Dunn had 'a sort of new-age charisma'. He was interested in music, playing the guitar and singing.

John began to spend more and more time with Dunn, and Dunn started to tell John that he loved him. 'Love' was a religious word, so at first John understood it in that way: 'This was being said by my priest, so I didn't find it odd or off-putting. It was strange how it was said. But I felt I could justify him saying this to me as he was a priest. Priests talk about love all the time.'

The family became uneasy about the relationship. John's mother felt that Dunn was displaying undue favouritism towards John. 'I treated all my kids the same. I didn't understand why Dunn would favour one over another.' She remembers 'feeling troubled. Something just didn't seem right, but I couldn't put my finger on it.' There was a disconcerting incident. John was a big fan of the rock group Queen. Dunn bought some Queen tapes for him. In his bedroom, John had a poster of the Queen song 'Somebody to Love'. Dunn added some words so that it read 'I've got somebody to love'. The family thought it was creepy and told John to take it down. John refused. He revelled in the attention from Dunn and looked up to him.

Dunn had occasionally hugged John, in an apparently innocent way. On one occasion in late 1975, they were talking in the presbytery. Dunn turned off the lights and started hugging him. Then he kissed him on the mouth, a full, passionate kiss. John felt desperately confused. 'Being so young and trusting, I didn't know if this was normal behaviour or not. I felt powerless to do anything. I felt very uncomfortable. A priest is a representative of higher authority and I trusted him.' Then Dunn undid his trousers and masturbated him, and made John do the same. 'I don't remember what, if anything, was said during this. At the time I was very confused about the rightness or wrongness of it. Afterwards Dunn gave me a lift home.'

John was 'utterly confused and bewildered'. The incident was the first of scores of sexual assaults over many months. Dunn coerced John into staying overnight at the presbytery, where they shared a bed. He became obsessive. As well as being curate, he was a member of the board of governors at the local Catholic school, giving him the use of an office in the school. He started to come into the school much more often, calling John into the office, where he was also assaulted. He took John on an overnight visit to his parents in Hull, and further afield, to Walsingham in Norfolk, where they stayed at a Church hostel.

John's mother was unaware that her son was being sexually abused, but she started to worry about the intensity of the relationship. It felt very uncomfortable, John spending so much time with Dunn. But John was completely under Dunn's control.

The abuse was so awful, and I felt powerless to stop it. I developed a habit of putting the three main aspects of my life into separate mental boxes in order to preserve my sanity. I felt that I had to put the shame and revulsion to the back of my mind, a sort of self-defence mechanism. I was denying any wrongdoing to my mother, and tried to convince her that it was an innocent friendship. I probably tried to convince myself too. It had become routine. My school friends started to notice how many times I would make excuses not to hang around with them after school. They soon started to realise that I was visiting the church almost every evening.

Snide comments followed John around the school. Being called out of class a lot led to some friction with John's teachers. Dunn's priestly authority, however, meant that he always got his way. John began to feel increasingly like an outsider, shunned by most of his friends.

In March 1976, John's mother was cleaning his room. In the sock drawer she found a letter. It was on salmon-pink writing paper and written in bluish-purple ink. It was from Father Dunn to John. Two full pages long, it was a love letter. John's mother could recall it years later: 'It was disgusting, saying things like "I feel you in my water" and other statements in this vein. I feel sick thinking about it.' She was totally distraught: 'A priest is supposed to speak of the love of God, but this priest was saying words of sexual love to my son.' She ran to see a friend, who was horrified. The friend advised her to see Monsignor Carroll right away.

John's mother met Monsignor Carroll at the church: 'It was just me and him. I took the letter. As usual he was very austere. He read the letter and just said, "Oh dear." I said that there was something very wrong and I wanted Father Dunn moved away. He told me to leave it with him.' She didn't trust Carroll:

He asked me to leave the letter with him. I refused. I knew he'd destroy it. I didn't feel he was taking it seriously. He said I didn't have to worry because nothing physical happened. I didn't

understand what he meant by 'physical'. I felt that he was trying
to make light of it. As I left he said: 'Do you think I will sweep
it under the carpet?' I replied: 'Yes, I do.' It took a lot of courage for me to say this. I had never contradicted a priest. He
didn't respond.

John's mother waited for Father Dunn to be moved. Desperately
upset but very devout, she carried on with church activities. One
evening, as she was cleaning in the church, she bumped into
Dunn and confronted him. Dunn was angry, and shouted at her:
'How could you do this to me?' John's mother was stunned. She
had expected Dunn to apologise: 'I was shaking.'

By June 1976 Father Dunn was still at the parish. John's family
could not believe that he still had not been moved. He continued
to see John. Bishop McClean[89] was visiting the parish in June
and John's mother demanded to see him. The bishop came to
the family home. They talked for about two hours. 'At the end he
said "leave it with me – I will see to it" or words to that effect.'
She remembers feeling elated when he had left, as if something
was going to happen.

But nothing happened. Dunn's obsessive, almost cult-like hold
over John continued, and John's mother felt powerless to stop it.
By this time she 'was more and more despairing. I started to feel
as if I was cracking up. I stopped going to church. It was very
hard because the church was such a big part of my life.'

By October 1976 John's mother felt she had to go and see the
bishop again. 'I went with my daughter. We didn't really have
much of a discussion. He didn't seem to take it seriously. He was
dismissive and insulting. Eventually my daughter stood up and
shouted at the bishop. She said something about going to the

papers.' Then they stormed out. Bishop McClean evidently took the threat seriously. Immediately after the meeting Dunn was moved to a church in Hull, becoming an assistant priest at Our Lady of Lourdes.

In 1981 Dunn moved on again, to York, and later back to Middlesbrough, where he was a parish priest at St Joseph's until 1994. The effects of the abuse stayed with John throughout his life. 'Over the years I have tried to put these events behind me. I needed to forget about what had happened. But I suffered depression. It had a devastating effect on my life.' He described to me wanting to be invisible at work, avoiding promotions so that he could stay in the background. But for many years he felt powerless to act.

By 2005, the Nolan reforms, which were supposed to include a comprehensive trawl of historic allegations, had been in place for four years. Bishop McClean had died on the job in 1978; Monsignor Carroll had also passed away. Whatever institutional memory remained of events in 1976, Dunn was still practising as a priest – since 1994 he had been at St Francis's in Hull. John now summoned up the will to confront him. After reading a book called *Altar Boy*, about a boy who was abused by a priest in Ireland, John decided to contact Cleveland Police.

The police investigation was a model of thoroughness; numerous witnesses were interviewed, including former school teachers dating back to 1975. They were able to piece together how Dunn groomed his victim. As the police observed, there were no threats; Dunn cleverly abused his position of trust. DC Norman Ross, who led the investigation, described how Dunn 'attacked this young boy's very beliefs and used them against him'. John's family were not well off; the offer of money to spend on clothes, toys or holidays for their children was too good to refuse. In 2005 Dunn was convicted and jailed at Teesside Crown Court. He pleaded guilty to two specimen charges of gross indecency and one of indecent assault on the child between 1975 and 1976. Sentenced to eighteen months on each charge, Dunn was exposed not by the Nolan reforms but by the courage of his victim and by careful detective work.

• • •

Father Michael Ingram was an English Dominican priest who died in 2000 shortly after being convicted of child sex offences. By 2000 Ingram had left the Dominican Order, but his offences – or at least the ones we know about – had been committed in the 1970s,[90] when he was a parish priest at Holy Cross Priory Church in Leicester. Over many years, Ingram used the priesthood to gain access to vulnerable children. He acquired a reputation for youth work and purported to undertake 'child counselling'. He organised camping trips for troubled and disadvantaged children: the offences for which he stood trial in 2000 were committed in part during a camping holiday on the Isle of Wight.

Ingram left the Dominican Order in 1989. For a while he evaded justice. The trial in 2000 was the third attempt to prosecute him. In 1991, whilst working as a 'freelance drugs counsellor' in Cambridge, he was investigated for child sexual offences in the late 1980s, but the complainant withdrew the allegation. In 1994 Ingram was investigated by the Metropolitan Police, this time for sex offences in the late 1960s, but the prosecution was discontinued. In 1998, however, a much larger investigation,

Operation Minute, was initiated following complaints from two men who, as children in the early 1970s, had attended the camping holiday near Carisbrooke Castle. The holiday was an ad-hoc event organised by Ingram, their local parish priest, under the guise of Holy Cross Boys' Club. During the holiday Ingram assaulted and buggered several boys. Witnesses on the camp recalled that Ingram was prone to violence.

Ingram died from injuries sustained in a car crash whilst awaiting sentencing. The inquest found that he had driven his car into a wall; he was found at the wheel of the car wearing only underwear, his sordid death following a sordid life. A verdict of suicide was recorded.

The judge at Ingram's criminal trial described him as 'a devious, guileful and intelligent man'.[91] But in truth Ingram should have aroused much more suspicion during his years in the priesthood. Over several decades, in addition to his work as a priest, Ingram was an open advocate of sex between adults and children: his repulsive views on child sex were aired in a stream of publications, so were hardly hidden. Some of his ideas made it into respectable academic journals, but much of the time his main outlet was articles and events explicitly associated with paedophile campaign groups such as PIE (Paedophile Information Exchange). His views were so totally at odds with Catholic doctrine that it seems extraordinary that Ingram could have survived in the priesthood – but he did.

Throughout his career Ingram claimed to be an expert on child development and child sexuality, but his precise qualifications were never entirely clear and aspects of his CV may have been fabricated or embellished. He seems to have joined the Dominicans in 1958, at the age of twenty-six, although on his CV later he claimed to have been a Dominican since 1952. Once established in the order, he showed an interest in child psychology and child development, attending a part-time course in educational psychology at Oxford University's Institute of Education in the mid-1960s. In later years he claimed to have attended courses at the Tavistock Clinic and at the Maudsley Hospital, leading centres of expertise on child development, and claimed to be a qualified 'child counsellor' or 'child psychologist'. However, it is unlikely that he had formal qualifications to justify either title. Certainly he did not have a psychology degree, and the assumption amongst those who knew him that he was professionally qualified seems to have taken root simply because he repeated it so often and encouraged others to so describe him. According to his CV, exhibited at his trial, he claimed to have worked as a 'child counsellor' at St Thomas' Hospital in London from 1968 to 1970. Between 1970 and 1973 he worked as a 'child counsellor' in Leicester, combining this role with priestly duties. The CV stated that from 1973 he was a 'consultant' with the International Catholic Child Bureau in Geneva, 'including two years as chaplain to the English-speaking community in Geneva, and two as secretary-general of an international commission in Geneva, with active participation in international conferences in different parts of Europe and in Vancouver'. The latter seems to have been a reference to Ingram's involvement in a subcommittee of the Conference of International Catholic Organisations, set up to examine the world population problem. The *Catholic Directory* records Ingram as being based at Holy Cross Priory throughout the whole of the 1970s, but he seems to have taken sabbaticals and at times was uncertain as to whether he wished to remain in the priesthood. On his CV he also claimed to be 'author of minor sundry articles on religious and moral education, one major one on child abuse, and one major one for the Pathfinder Fund Boston, USA, on the ethics of triage'. He had, he claimed, 'lectured extensively on child psychology and child abuse, especially in adult institutes of education. Also in Harvard and other universities in the eastern USA.' Following his departure from the Dominican Order in 1989, he claimed to be a 'freelance youth counsellor in Cambridge, specialising in drugs problems'.

Some of the job titles sound nebulous and there is little doubt that Ingram was a fraud as well as a child abuser. But he was also able to publish in prestigious journals and his views gained currency in radical circles. Ingram tried to build an academic reputation on research which purported to show that sex between children and adults was not necessarily harmful per se and in fact could be beneficial to the child, who might not otherwise experience love and affection. Moreover, Ingram claimed, in so far as harm is caused by abuse, it is not caused by the sexual acts themselves but by society's reaction to them. The processes of investigation and interrogation, Ingram argued, were more damaging than the sexual contact itself. In his lengthy article 'The Participating Victim', published in the *British Journal of Sexual Medicine* in 1979, Ingram explained the development of his thesis:

> My first encounter with cases of boys being 'indecently assaulted' puzzled me as a student of child counselling. I was asked to counsel traumatised children who had evidently a totally different reaction from that of their parents, or the moral welfare committee. They regarded the experience with a certain robustness, if not relish, that started me thinking about the problem in a new light.[92]

The *BJSM* article purported to be a scientific analysis of 'ninety-two cases of sexual contact between adult and child'. The children involved in the 'study' were all pre-pubescent ('without pubic hair or, in the absence of information about this, under fourteen and did not have a "broken" voice'). The children, Ingram claimed, had all been referred to him for counselling, either because of actual sexual assault or because of behavioural disorders or family problems. Ingram claimed that he had then contacted and interviewed the men involved sexually with these ninety-two children. They were 'mostly men who loved children, and in most cases they were doing a great deal of valuable work in the community'. Many of the men complained that 'the children were so provocative and seductive, and they had found abstinence impossible'. Ingram claims that in sixty-six of the ninety-two cases, the boys involved actively sought affection from the men. Conceding that this may not have been a specifically sexual invitation, he concluded:

> If I doubt the extent of the claims for child seductivity, there is no doubt that it is there, and that children do encourage sexual activity with a man, and participate in it willingly. I do not think there is any evidence from my study that any of the children were worse off for the activity, and many, no doubt, may be better off for a relationship with a loving adult outside the family.

Of course, the detailed methodology of this so-called study of ninety-two boys – and the men who abused them – was not disclosed; Ingram did not explain how he validated his conclusion that 'many' of the children involved were 'better off' for the experience. But the whole article is an apologia for paedophilia, falsely paraded as scientific research based on empirical case studies so as to give the impression of academic rigour and objectivity.

By the late 1970s, Ingram's views were being widely cited as expert support by advocates of paedophilia, and he was regularly invited to write for pro-paedophile journals and speak at meetings. In early 1977, for example, he published 'FILTHY: Reaction to Paedophilic Acts' in the *Journal of Libertarian Education*, in which he argued that children are 'quite capable of indulging in sex games with willing adults, and even of provoking or initiating them'. Ingram claimed that he had made a 'study' of fifty-seven boys who were 'indecently assaulted' (Ingram's quotation marks). 'Eight of them resisted the assault which was discontinued for that reason. The rest appear to have been willing for it to take place. Thirty-eight of the boys returned to the same man for more...' Ingram concluded that 'society should not cut off from children the contribution that can be made to their welfare by those whose only fault is that their love leads to acts that society fears without reasonable cause, and whose importance diminishes in comparison with what their love can do'.[93]

The high point of public controversy over the activities of the Paedophile Information Exchange occurred in 1977, and Ingram was drawn in. One event was a conference at Swansea University on the theme 'Love and Attraction'. The conference was organised by the British Psychological Society but seems to have been hijacked by Tom O'Carroll, a notorious paedophile campaigner, who invited Ingram to the conference. In his book *Paedophilia: The Radical Case*, O'Carroll describes Ingram's involvement:

I had known Father Michael for some time. I had received his hospitality at the Holy Cross Priory, Leicester, where he lived, and I had read his study of ninety-two man–boy paedophilic relationships – a study which had come out of his work as a child psychologist … he knew that a lot of relationships were loving ones, in which more good was done than harm. What's more, I knew that his study, giving substance to these views, had not been published, and I felt that it deserved to be – which is why I arranged for him to attend the Swansea conference … I contacted the conference organisers on his behalf, and they accepted his paper without demur … I hoped attention would be drawn to the Ingram paper.[94]

In fact, the Swansea conference turned into a PR disaster for O'Carroll: porters, kitchen staff and auxiliary workers at the conference threatened to go on strike if he was allowed to attend, and the university banned him.

In September 1977, PIE held a meeting at Conway Hall in London. Ingram was due to attend as a mystery guest speaker, but withdrew on the instructions of his Dominican superior, who evidently feared adverse publicity. However, his speech was read out and he continued to advocate his view openly in public forums. In 1986 Ingram was one of several contributors to the *Betrayal of Youth* ('BOY'), a pro-paedophile book edited by PIE campaigner Warren Middleton. 'Many paedophiles', claimed Ingram in his chapter, 'are genuine child lovers. They are affectionate and caring and have a lot to offer children.'[95] Citing his own 'research', Ingram claimed that sexual contacts between adults and children seem to be of two kinds: 'Firstly, there are those which result from an intense affectionate relationship, and this is usually found where the child comes from a deprived background, or is him/herself emotionally deprived. The other involves the rather boisterous, adventurous game of mutual masturbation, or just simply grabbing one another's genitals.'

He went on: 'We are always hearing about the possible bad effects of adult/child sex, but what about the possible benefits?'[96]

Other than preventing his appearance at Conway Hall, at no point did the Dominican Order attempt to censor Ingram's views on paedophilia, which he published and advocated freely over two decades whilst working as a Dominican priest. In fact, Ingram did find himself censored by the Vatican, but not in relation to child sex. He was one of several 'international Catholic experts' who co-wrote *The Problem of Population: A Challenge to Mankind Today* in 1976, with Ingram contributing £1,000 from his own money to the cost of publication. The book dissented from Catholic orthodoxy in advocating artificial contraception, and suggested that the problem of world overpopulation meant that traditional Catholic moral principles might need to be re-examined. The Vatican demanded that the book be removed from sale, and Ingram's sense of injustice about this censorship of his views on the population question seems to have prompted him to consider leaving the priesthood. But he remained in the Dominican Order for another thirteen years.

Why did Ingram's Dominican superiors allow him to propagate these views? The context of the time cannot be ignored: during the 1970s, views similar to Ingram's were not unusual in radical left-wing circles. In his 1975 book *The Great Bazaar*, the 'soixante-huitard' student radical Daniel Cohn-Bendit celebrated erotic encounters with five-year-olds at his anti-authoritarian kindergarten.[97] In 1977, the French newspaper *Le Monde* published an open letter signed by sixty-nine French intellectuals protesting the imprisonment of three men

convicted of sex with minors. Signatories included Jack Lang, a
future minister of culture, and Bernard Kouchner, later French
foreign minister under President Sarkozy.[98] In 1976 the National
Council for Civil Liberties (NCCL) filed a submission with
the Criminal Law Revision Committee arguing that 'childhood
sexual experiences, willingly engaged in, with an adult result
in no identifiable damage ... The real need is a change in the
attitude which assumes that all cases of paedophilia result in
lasting damage.'[99] The NCCL's general secretary at that time
was Patricia Hewitt, later a Labour Cabinet minister.[100] In 1977,
the NCCL was asked by the *Evening Standard* for its views on PIE.
'NCCL has no policy on PIE's aims, other than the evidence
that children are harmed if, after a mutual relationship with an
adult, they are exposed to the attentions of the police, press and
court,' said an NCCL spokesman.[101] In April 1978, the NCCL
published a briefing paper on the Protection of Children Bill
that was before Parliament. The author, Harriet Harman, now
deputy leader of the Labour Party, was worried that the draft
Bill placed the onus on adults caught with film or photographs
of nude children to show that they were possessed with a view
to 'scientific or learned study'. 'Our amendment places the onus
of proof on the prosecution to show that the child was actually
harmed,' she wrote.[102] And in 1982, Patricia Hewitt, still at the
helm at the NCCL, published *The Police and Civil Liberties*, in
which she considered O'Carroll's imprisonment for conspiracy
to corrupt public morals. 'Conspiring to corrupt public morals is
an offence incapable of definition or precise proof,' complained
Hewitt. O'Carroll's involvement in child porn 'overshadowed the deplorable nature of the conspiracy charge used by
the prosecution'.[103]

However, the NCCL focused on the legal/civil liberties aspect, not advocacy of paedophilia as such. Clearly, some of those who held these views went on to prominent positions in public life. But such views were in no sense mainstream in the 1970s. They were views held by a small minority of vocal activists on the radical left of politics who, to apply Edmund Burke's famous phrase, were really no more than 'half a dozen grasshoppers making the fields ring with their importunate chink'. Some of those people later entered mainstream politics, and would – doubtless – abhor these views now. Whilst a minority in left/liberal society flirted with legalising paedophilia, the NCCL excluded members of PIE after the DPP started arresting them: O'Carroll was jailed in 1981 and, although Hewitt attacked the prosecution, PIE's affiliation with the NCCL was formally ended in 1983.[104] This confirms that for most people, even far-left activists, paedophilia itself remained transgressive. The most accurate reflection of mainstream opinion was the kitchen workers' strike at Swansea University, in protest at O'Carroll.

Nevertheless, radical attitudes to paedophilia appear to have infiltrated the Church. As Pope Benedict later suggested:

A theory was even finally developed at that time that paedophilia should be viewed as something positive ... In such a context, where everything is relative and nothing intrinsically evil exists, but only relative good and relative evil, people who have an inclination to such behaviour are left with no solid footing. Of course, paedophilia is first rather a sickness of individuals, but the fact that it could become so active and so widespread was linked also to an intellectual climate through which the foundations of moral theology, good and evil, became open to question in the

Church. Good and evil became interchangeable; they were no longer absolutely clear opposites.[105]

The Catholic journalist Mary Kenny, reviewing the writings of moral theologians in Irish publications in the 1970s and 1980s, argues that during this period Catholic essayists were increasingly influenced by non-Catholic and radical notions about sexuality:

> Freud, D. H. Lawrence, Carol Rogers, Erikson and Adorno were among the authorities frequently cited. Some priests were publishing influential material in journals calling for a new progressiveness towards sexuality. By the early 1980s they were writing that we should not identify morality in terms of sex, that there should be fewer prohibitions and more uncensored dialogue about sexuality.[106]

Kenny noted that Professor Patricia Casey, psychiatrist at the Mater Hospital in Dublin, found that some therapists during this period were quite influenced by the views of Alfred Kinsey, who had suggested back in the 1950s that sexual relations between adults and children were 'not necessarily harmful'; it was 'only society's attitude that caused the harm' – very close to Ingram's view, of course. Kenny concluded that 'if we had stuck to the Church's original view of Freud and Freudianism – that it tended to "excuse" sins, instead of repenting and atoning for wrongdoing – some of these grisly situations would not have been perpetuated'.

What are we to conclude from the Ingram saga? Clearly, during the 1970s and 1980s the open advocacy of paedophilia – or at least of the view that adult–child sex was harmless – was tolerated in some parts of the English Church: it was not seen as necessarily beyond the pale. That view was completely at odds with Catholic doctrine and with most of public opinion at the time, so in allowing itself to be infiltrated by these views, the Church was not reflecting wider social norms. In Ingram's case, the failure to censor and expel him allowed him to use his status as a priest to abuse children. But the fact that Ingram was tolerated suggests that his ideas had wider traction in the Church. If you believe that sex between adults and children is harmless, you will turn a blind eye to it: which is precisely what the Church did, frequently, during this period.

• • •

Father David Crowley, a priest of the Leeds diocese, was jailed in 1998 for fifteen counts of sexual abuse of teenage boys. His offences spanned the years 1981–92 and included acts of gross depravity. Crowley's personality encapsulates the features associated with clerical sexual offenders in so many studies: emotional and sexual immaturity and fixation on adolescents against the background of alcohol abuse. His case is also a long saga of missed opportunities to protect children. Concerns about Crowley surfaced regularly during the two decades between his admission to the priesthood and his conviction for sexual offences, but on each occasion he was given another chance; the Church's policy of dealing with complaints 'in house' prevented his crimes from being exposed until it was too late.

Born in 1954, Crowley seems to have been attracted to the priesthood at a young age, but his unsuitability became apparent early on. At Ushaw seminary, fears about his immaturity delayed his ordination, although this eventually went ahead. In 1980, concerns were voiced about Crowley's sexuality. Following a suggestion of homosexual solicitation he was sent to Our Lady of Victory in Stroud for treatment.[107] Within a few months his faculties (i.e. permission to preach) were restored: his erratic and sexually immature behaviour seems to have been attributed to a rough-and-ready working-class background.

In the early 1980s Crowley was posted to a parish in Huddersfield. In 1987 there was a 'grave scandal': several parents in the parish complained that Crowley had encouraged their teenage sons to get drunk and engage in sexual activity with one another. At this point Crowley admitted to hosting strip poker sessions and watching a nine-year-old boy performing an act of gross indecency on a thirteen-year-old, but claimed that he was a mere bystander. He also admitted to sharing a bed with a boy, but denied sexual activity.

Even on the known facts it was obvious that criminal offences had probably been committed, but the police were not informed. The parents of at least some of the boys wanted to go to the police, but seem to have been dissuaded from doing so on the promise that the Church would take Crowley out of circulation. The Diocese of Leeds determined that no police involvement was necessary, although that decision was made without any systematic investigation of the parents' complaints. To meet the parents' concerns, Bishop David Konstant suspended Crowley from the priesthood and told him that the 'grave scandal' meant that 'it will not be possible for you to work again as a priest in this diocese'.[108] It is clear, however, that in making this statement Bishop Konstant did not turn his mind to barring Crowley permanently from the priesthood, merely from the Diocese of

Leeds, because the case had been such an embarrassment locally and the diocese wanted him well out of the way. Crowley was sent back to Stroud for further treatment, and was told that he would remain suspended from the priesthood for a period of at least five years, to be followed by laicisation unless his behaviour radically improved.

Medical assessments concluded that Crowley was suffering from arrested development but was not a paedophile as such. Due to emotional immaturity, the psychologists reasoned, Crowley was drawn to teenage boys, and under the influence of alcohol and out of a desire to impress and befriend the boys he had behaved irresponsibly. One assessment concluded:

> He did not fit into the usual psychological profile of a true paedophile. [His] behaviour would not be too alarming in an early adolescent boy. In an adult [age thirty-three] who has sacred trust and is a member of the clergy it is of course enormously serious and utterly inappropriate and a bar to his practising the priesthood. He has already been told that there is no possibility of his ever functioning as a priest in the diocese of Leeds.[109]

A subsequent report concluded that although Crowley had behaved 'in a grossly unsuitable way, he was not a paedophile'. It concluded his behaviour was caused by 'misuse of alcohol and emotional immaturity'.[110]

These comments highlight the limitations of psychological assessment, which is only as reliable as the factual premise underlying it. The conclusion that Crowley was essentially suffering from arrested development and was not a 'true paedophile' was based on the false premise that Crowley was a mere bystander in sexual activity involving teenage boys, rather than an active participant. This was not the case and had a police investigation been initiated in 1987 it is likely that the full facts would have been uncovered and he would have been jailed there and then. The Church, however, proceeded on the basis that Crowley was suffering from immaturity and alcohol problems and that both of these could be cured. Despite being told that he would suffer a long suspension, in fact Crowley returned to the priesthood within a few months. In late 1987, Bishop Konstant asked Christopher Budd, Bishop of Plymouth, to take Crowley into his diocese. A psychologist suggested that Crowley should be subject to a 'contract', which was duly was drawn up. Crowley undertook to abstain from alcohol, attend meetings at Alcoholics Anonymous, attend Our Lady of Victory for aftercare visits, have no ministry with youth and not socialise with young people. How this contract was to be enforced was unclear, but Bishop Konstant passed that problem over to Bishop Budd.

In September 1987 Crowley was posted to Torquay as assistant priest. In 1989 he was appointed to a similar role in Barnstaple. But in September 1990, Father Cornish, the parish priest in Barnstaple, made a sudden announcement: 'David Crowley will not be returning to this parish.' Crowley's departure was rapid, and the reasons for it remain unclear, but seem to have involved fears on the part of Father Cornish that Crowley was developing relationships with teenage boys locally. It was evident, in other words, that Crowley could well be violating his contract. Yet again, rather than being removed permanently from ministry and laicised, Crowley was sent for assessment and therapeutic treatment, on the premise that his latest misdemeanours were just another manifestation of his arrested development.

The treatment having been completed, Crowley seems to have been shunted back to the Leeds diocese, where Bishop Konstant had said that he would never work again. In 1998, a spokesman for the Leeds diocese was reported in the press as admitting that there had been concerns in 1990 that Crowley had failed to honour the 1987 contract. But the 1990 'assessment, as the previous one, did not indicate the danger he was to young people. The Church authorities and professional advisers were deceived.'[111]

This is disingenuous: the 'deception' was entirely self-inflicted, because the 1987 scandal had never been properly investigated and if it had been the whole premise on which Crowley was subsequently assessed would have been different. But by 1990, even on the known facts, Crowley had been assessed as unsuitable for the priesthood on no fewer than four separate occasions in his career, had broken the contract in Barnstaple, and had a history of orchestrating sexual activity between children. No sensible person would have allowed him to continue in the priesthood. However, in breach of the earlier commitment that Crowley would never again work in the Leeds diocese, in August 1991 he was installed as a temporary priest at a parish in North Yorkshire: part of the Diocese of Leeds.

Crowley seems to have remained there for about a year. Before arriving, he signed a further 'contract'. But no policing measures were put in place. Crowley ingratiated himself with parishioners and, when asked about his past, drew sympathy by claiming to be a reformed alcoholic. Deviously, he told parishioners that he had been the victim of 'false allegations' of sexual abuse, as a consequence of which he was 'going to be extra careful about protecting himself from the risk of false allegations in the future'.[112] These statements fostered the impression that Crowley was honest about his past and transparent in his dealings with parishioners of all ages. To protect himself, he claimed, he always made sure that he was never alone with just one altar boy; he would see them in groups. Crowley then inveigled himself with a group of altar boys, encouraging them to smoke, drink alcohol and watch pornographic films with him. He offered boys 'massages' and got them to reciprocate, and then sexually assaulted them. Whatever supervision of Crowley was supposed to be in place was totally ineffective, and Crowley was able to have boys staying the night with him at the presbytery, as well as taking the altar boys for a regular outing after Sunday Mass. The sexual abuse of boys committed by Crowley during this time involved 'a wholly exceptional degree of depravity'.[113] In August 1992 Crowley was moved back to Leeds and held various temporary positions until August 1993, when he was appointed as a full-time hospital chaplain at St Luke's Hospital and Bradford Royal Infirmary. In 1996, one of Crowley's earlier victims was undergoing counselling and the counsellor contacted the police. Crowley was arrested and in June 1998 pleaded guilty to twelve indecent assaults on boys under sixteen and three charges of indecency with a child. The offences covered West Yorkshire, northern England and Devon between June 1981 and August 1992. Prosecuting counsel Peter Benson told the court:

> The abuse was systematically contrived and the Crown say the accused cleverly exploited his position of trust and authority as a Catholic priest to seduce impressionable young boys. He would set about winning their trust by allowing them to smoke and plying them with alcohol as a prelude to seducing them. He would often target the emotionally vulnerable young

men who he came into contact with as suitable candidates for his attentions.[114]

After the trial, the Diocese of Leeds claimed publicly that 'the first report to the authorities as to the activities of David Crowley was made by the Church'. The basis of this statement is unclear since Crowley was working as a hospital chaplain at the time of his arrest and the investigation was instigated by a victim, not by the Church. Cardinal Hume ducked any discussion of the wider lessons of the case: he was 'distressed and horrified by the affair but had no authority over Crowley or the Bishop of Plymouth'.[115]

In the light of the Crowley case it is little wonder that victim campaigners are deeply sceptical of commitments made by the Catholic Church on child protection. Throughout this saga, the church's overriding concern was not any crimes which may have been committed against children but minimising public scandal and, also, Crowley's own welfare. In 1991, the Diocese of Leeds, in breach of its earlier commitment that Crowley would never again serve there as a priest, placed him in a parish role in North Yorkshire, where he committed sexual abuse of the most extreme kind. Despite signing a further 'contract', the supervision of Crowley during this assignment was minimal to non-existent and he was able to have unrestricted access to altar boys extending to sleepovers at the presbytery. Then, just as the English Catholic Church was finalising new national child protection guidelines,[116] Crowley – whose past was known personally both to the author of the guidelines, Bishop Budd, and to Bishop Konstant, and who was self-evidently someone who needed to be removed immediately from active ministry – was appointed to a hospital chaplaincy, putting him amongst vulnerable people;

he remained in that role until his arrest in 1996. As one of
Crowley's victims told me: 'You look at everything that happened
and you learn to never, ever believe anything the Church says.'[117]

CHAPTER 5

'SMOOTH DE COUVE'

'A difficult man to know, read or even like.'[118] From 1982 to 1999 the Archbishop of Birmingham, Maurice Couve de Murville, was one of the most senior figures in the English Catholic hierarchy. But in popular esteem he was consistently overshadowed by the much-loved Cardinal Hume at Westminster and the more forthright Archbishop Worlock in Liverpool. In public he seemed arrogant. Those who knew him privately also found him cold and aloof. Upper class, French-born and unexpectedly plucked from academic obscurity to manage a sprawling diocese with many social problems, Couve de Murville disliked challenge, and ran the archdiocese as an autocracy. Working-class, ethnic Irish congregations did not embrace him, and he was a poor administrator. His nickname in Catholic circles, 'Smooth de Couve', alluded not to any public ease, which he entirely lacked, but to his skill, as a fellow ultra-traditionalist, in inveigling himself with Pope John Paul II's Vatican. His first major engagement as archbishop was to welcome Pope John Paul II to Coventry in 1982. At that time, basking in the limelight, he started to be mentioned as a successor to Hume. His moment in the sun did not last long, and in Birmingham his limitations quickly became evident. Catholic bishops normally tender their resignation at age seventy-five, but

Couve de Murville left in June 1999, just before his seventieth
birthday. Above all else, Couve de Murville was overwhelmed
and eventually broken by the abuse scandal, which dominated
the Birmingham archdiocese throughout the 1990s.

Throughout that period, the archdiocese featured so regularly in
news reports that journalists speculated luridly about 'paedophile
rings' amongst Catholic priests in the area. In fact, the primary
explanation for Birmingham's prominence may be more prosaic.
Birmingham is one of the largest dioceses in the country.[119]
Many Irish immigrants settled in the area in the mid-twentieth
century, particularly in Birmingham and Coventry, creating a
large pool of loyal congregants and, inevitably, potential victims.
These factors help to explain the archdiocese's prominence in
the scandal. But only in part; the leadership of the archdiocese
undoubtedly worsened the situation by its wilful mismanagement of cases, and Couve de Murville frequently distinguished
himself by his incompetence and lack of empathy. The poverty of
his leadership was a significant reason why the scandal spiralled
out of control.

• • •

'Extraordinarily charismatic and popular': almost everybody
who encountered Father Samuel Penney during his years as a
parish priest testified to his magnetic personality. Penney was
jailed in 1993 for seven years after admitting charges of sexual
assault against ten children. Penney was charged with specimen offences, and many other victims did not come forward.
His offences spanned a 25-year period. His case was the most
devastating of all those which came to light in the Birmingham

archdiocese, laying bare the culture of denial and cover-up which pervaded the archdiocese in the decades leading up to his conviction, and which many say persisted for some years afterwards.

Penney was an Irishman from Cork, but he had close family in England and both his parents were buried in the cemetery attached to St Joseph's Church in his final parish, Nechells, in inner-city Birmingham. After attending seminary in England, Penney was posted to St Peter's Church in Leamington Spa. The dynamic 28-year-old curate rapidly gained a reputation for his devotion to youth and community work. He was intimately involved with many families. One mother of a disabled child, speaking nearly twenty years later in a BBC documentary on the case, thought he'd 'fallen from heaven'.[120] Her child had a hole in the heart; before Penney arrived, mother and child had to take buses to hospital. Now Penney was on hand to give those lifts: 'somebody God had sent'.

One of the families Penney befriended was a devout Catholic family with five children aged between seven and sixteen. Penney sexually abused all the children, both the boys and the girls. He swore each of them to secrecy, telling them no one would believe them. Each was terrified and assumed they were the only one. It was twenty years before they broke their silence and it was their case which triggered Penney's eventual arrest in 1993.

In January 1975, Penney was appointed as curate in Burton on Trent, assisting the then parish priest, Father Riley. He began a close relationship with the Flanagans, a 'regular Irish Catholic family'. Eamonn Flanagan, who was twelve when Penney arrived, became one of his victims and later wrote a powerful account of their relationship, *Father and Me*. Flanagan remembers Penney's first day in Burton: the new curate immediately announced at

Mass that he would be visiting all the families in the parish over the coming months in an attempt to get to know them. This was unusual. Over his time in Burton, and foreshadowing later events in Nechells, Penney went out of his way to cultivate a loyal following amongst parishioners. Throughout his many years of abusing children, Penney's powerful personality and passion for helping the poor and needy shielded him from greater scrutiny. He was very successful in building up a following in Burton: 'Lapsed Catholics returned, non-Catholics converted, all because of Sam.' Even when his abuse was ultimately revealed, his bishop maintained that he was a good priest.[121]

Flanagan, like several of Penney's other victims, became an altar server. After a long period of grooming, Penney sexually abused him for a decade: the abuse started when Flanagan was a 'naive, sexually unsure' twelve-year-old and lasted until he was twenty-two, with the most intense period between twelve and sixteen, when abuse took place virtually on a daily basis. The mental torture of the abuse became all-consuming. Flanagan lived for years with the constant terror of Penney coming to his house, Penney waiting for him outside school, Penney infiltrating and dominating every aspect of his life. But how could he speak out against a priest? Penney's reputation and the esteem in which he was held within the community made it impossible for Eamonn to challenge him:

Father Penney was the greatest priest ever born. The messages came at me from the man himself, family, friends, and parishioners. Yet abuse was taking place daily in my home or in the presbytery. On trips away it was even easier for him. I had no control, I had no strength. I was terrified and yet still had to be around him. I was unable to break free. He gave sermons from the altar, handed out the sacred host to the congregation and within twenty minutes he would be using that mouth, those hands to kiss and masturbate me ... it seemed as though being a priest meant everything but abusing me meant nothing.[122]

Flanagan knew he was being manipulated but found the power of priesthood overwhelming.

Demonstrating his extraordinary manipulativeness, Penney himself acknowledged to Flanagan that what was going on was wrong and that he was trying to deal with it: 'I am continually trying, Eamonn. I have been up at six each morning praying in front of the Blessed Sacrament.' Penney put the abuse down to Flanagan's satisfaction of his emotional needs:

In life you have a few quality friends and you are one of mine ... you know how we get on, we do so much together and we talk so well. I have never had a friend like you ... I will be moved in a few months, just hold on until I'm gone.[123]

Flanagan was one of many victims: Penney later admitted to offences spanning the years 1967–92. Although his relationship with Flanagan persisted for ten years, his other involvements were generally shorter. Until his seven-year stint in Nechells, Penney moved parishes with notable regularity. This inevitably increased the number of his victims and in later years it also raised questions about the Church's knowledge of his behaviour – did the frequent moves have a sinister explanation? In 1978, Penney left Burton to do a liturgy course in Ireland. He was away for a year. After brief hiatus at the end of his course, he was given a temporary parish in Stourbridge in the West Midlands. After that, he went to Upton-on-Severn and then in 1979 to Blackmore Park in the Malvern Hills. Blackmore was Penney's first proper post as a parish priest. The posting made little sense. On the face of it, Penney was a dynamic priest with a deep mission to help the poor. He was an obvious candidate for an inner-city parish with a large Catholic congregation.

Penney's behaviour with children was bound to come to light eventually. The scandal is how long the archdiocese allowed him to continue in his ministry whilst knowing of the serious allegations against him. Penney could use violence when children resisted. Whilst attending a camp, he tried to force himself on a thirteen-year-old boy who was sleeping next to him. The boy fought back, and Penney punched him violently around the back of the head, rendering him virtually unconscious. The incident became known to a Father Tom Farrell, who arranged for the boys to be brought back from the campsite. The boy's father seems to have physically attacked Penney in revenge. But nothing was done.

One night in in 1984 Penney had a group of boys staying over with him. He propositioned one of them, inviting the boy into his room and then demanding that he join him in bed. The boy refused. Penney locked both of them in the room, and they argued all night. Penney had selected the wrong victim: the boy told his mother. After confronting Penney in person, the mother took her complaint straight to Archbishop Couve de Murville. A senior archdiocesan official, Monsignor Dan Leonard, was deputed to meet her. The mother recalls telling Monsignor Leonard everything that had happened: 'No details were left out.'[124] The mother asked Leonard if this had happened before;

'Yes,' he replied. Within two days, Penney had left his post. The Archbishop later admitted that Penney was moved because of a complaint of 'too close an association' with a boy, but tried to suggest that the mother had not actually alleged anything sexual, just that Penney was slightly too familiar. That was not how the mother remembered it: 'We were dealing with a paedophile; we trusted they would deal with it as in any other institution.' The speed with which Penney was moved suggests that the incident came as little surprise to the archdiocese. The decision to move him was undoubtedly made on the hoof in reaction to the mother's complaint. Penney had a three-month break before being assigned to his new post in Nechells. When she heard that Penney had been given a new parish the boy's mother was stunned: 'In reporting the incident, after all, we assumed that he would be permanently removed from parish-type duties which allowed so many chances for paedophilia. We were staggered when we heard that not long afterwards he was back in parish life.'[125]

Nechells is in the centre of Birmingham and at the time had a sizeable congregation of around eight hundred. On the face of it, it was a perfect fit for a priest of Penney's background and social activism. Nechells is a mixed multicultural area scarred by widespread poverty. St Joseph's Church was close to Spaghetti Junction, on a hill surrounded by rundown factories. The streets were littered with broken glass, and steel mesh guarded the windows of the presbytery. Although many residents of the parish are Afro-Caribbean, their presence was stronger in the Church schools than in the congregation, which was dominated by first- and second-generation Irish immigrants. With his Irish background, Penney was immediately able to identify with his flock. His predecessor was seen as an overly traditional priest: conscientious in visiting his parishioners, just as Penney was to be, but conservative in doctrine and distant from their lives and values. Penney, by contrast, instinctively understood the pastoral needs of an inner-city parish suffering from chronic deprivation.

But given Penney's special skill in preying on vulnerable children, poverty-scarred Nechells was possibly the worst choice of parish. Arriving in the parish, Penney was immediately seen as a breath of fresh air, a powerful, dynamic personality who galvanised the community. Always ready to visit the sick and dying, Penney came across as caring, unstuffy and interested in the daily struggles of his parishioners. He seemed sensitive to the realities of their lives in areas like sex and divorce, taking a liberal, non-judgemental view to the point that several of his parishioners recalled him talking as if there was no such thing as sin.

Penney's house at the church became an 'open house', particularly for young people, for whom he became something of an icon. Persuading local businesses to sponsor his community initiatives, he set up local youth clubs and helped to run them. He encouraged young people to join in the activities of the church, in the choir or as altar servers, and became known for handing out presents to youngsters: trainers, even bicycles. In a parish stricken by poverty, these gestures had a powerful influence on parents and children. It became common for youngsters to stay at Penney's house: sometimes ten or more children might be sleeping over at the weekend.

Some older and more conservative parishioners found Penney too 'new-agey'. His desire to be called 'Sam' rather than 'Father' and his reluctance to wear clerical dress occasionally grated against traditional Irish sensibilities. A few parishioners drifted away to worship at neighbouring churches. But they were vastly outnumbered by the many new converts or lapsed Catholics inspired by Penney to return to the congregation. Penney's following grew rapidly. He created a sense of total trust and loyalty. It was, to coin a later phrase, a mass grooming.[126]

In 1986, Penney was arrested and charged with abusing a Vietnamese boy. The boy didn't speak good English, and the charges were dropped after Penney counterclaimed that the boy had been stealing from the presbytery. We know that at this point Archbishop Couve de Murville interviewed Penney again. This was, at the very least, the second incident involving Penney which had come to the attention of archdiocesan officials. But the archbishop allowed Penney to continue with his ministry, and said nothing to police about the 1984 complaint. The archbishop's explanation when questioned by the BBC several years later was that Penney was 'a master of deceit. He deceived many parents and he deceived the Church.'[127] But the Church knew more than parents knew, and had no excuse.

In 1990, under pressure from family members, Flanagan disclosed the abuse he had suffered from Penney. Flanagan – now twenty-seven – wrote to Penney in Nechells: 'Last weekend I told my family about your abuse of me from age 12–22. I want no further contact. Eamonn.' And then, in June 1990, Flanagan's parents met with their local parish priest. They told him about Penney's behaviour. The priest immediately told Bishop Pargeter, the auxiliary Bishop of Birmingham. But absolutely nothing seemed to happen. Penney remained a parish priest. Then, almost a year later, Flanagan was told that he needed to go and see the bishop and tell him directly, otherwise no action could be taken. In the interim, Penney had been abusing other children.

In July 1991, Flanagan, with his local priest, met with Bishop Pargeter. He was informed that Penney had denied the allegations; this was after a nun had been deputed to investigate, and had found 'nothing suspicious'. At this point, Flanagan asked whether the archdiocese was aware of any previous complaints against Penney. He was told that Dan Leonard, now the Vicar-General, had been trying to stop Penney from going on camps 'for four years, but we just can't stop him'.[128] It was apparent that the archdiocese knew quite a lot.

Flanagan laid out his story, and asked that Penney be removed from all further contact with children and all parish work. Not just temporarily, but forever. His demand was rejected. A priest, he was informed, could not simply be moved in that way. Despite Flanagan threatening to go to the press, the archdiocese seemed unwilling to act.

Two weeks later, Flanagan was informed that the archbishop would be 'dealing with the matter shortly'. He discovered, a few days later, that Penney had been moved away from Nechells. But his parishioners had no idea why. Penney had previously spent brief periods away from the parish for medical treatment. Parishioners were allowed to assume that Penney was leaving for rest and recuperation after years of hard work. In fact, the arch-diocese had decided to send Penney for therapy – initially on a 'prayer course', and then to Heronbrook House, for psychiatric treatment. But nobody was told the full story. Penney continued to visit Nechells, attending Masses and fundraising activities. Parishioners continued to visit him with their children, and some of those children were abused.

A year later, in July 1992, Penney was arrested and charged with the sexual abuse of the five siblings in Leamington. At Sunday

Mass in Burton, Flanagan's parish priest asked his congregation to pray for Penney and all the victims. As he awaited trial, two other families came forward from Nechells. Penney's abuse of children had lasted for a quarter of a century. He was sentenced to seven-and-a-half years in prison.

In May 1993, Archbishop Couve de Murville was interviewed for the BBC television *Everyman* programme 'Breach of Faith'. He maintained that the first knowledge on the part of the Church of Penney's possible sexual abuse of children had come in July 1991, with a complaint from Eamonn Flanagan. This statement was patently untrue: Flanagan's complaint had been made a year earlier, but in any event the Church had moved Penney to Nechells in 1984, and was also well aware of the 1986 allegations. The archbishop, whose career had been spent preaching Christian morality, had no compunction about telling a barefaced lie. Shifting uneasily in his chair, and failing to meet the interviewer's eye, he dismissed the mother's account that she had complained about sexual advances to her son in 1984: 'That is not the truth as we see it.'[129]

The archbishop's response, many felt, was coloured by snobbery. More comfortable at an Oxbridge high table, or burying himself in medieval French liturgy, the archbishop seemed to regard working-class complainants with regal disdain. When Couve de Murville came to Nechells in November 1992, he stood in the church and woodenly read out a prepared statement apologising for the pain caused by Penney's behaviour. During the service the archbishop was challenged directly by one of the victims, who shouted at him during the ceremony. Couve de Murville, she said, had known that Penney was an abuser and did nothing. After the service, the archbishop asked to see the victim and her family. In a breathtaking display of arrogance he proceeded to 'forgive them' for their outburst in the church. They reminded him forcefully that he had no authority to forgive and told him that the parish priest had done little to help the victims in any case.

The Penney scandal was devastating for Nechells and for the wider Catholic community in Birmingham. The impact of Penney's arrest and conviction extended well beyond the immediate victims. It reverberated throughout the parish and the archdiocese for many years. Alan Draper, who studied the impact on the parish of the Penney scandal as part of his theological studies at the Maryvale Institute, recalls that 'there was a strong feeling that the parish had been abandoned by the diocese during the crisis'.[130]

For John Wilkins, editor of the Catholic magazine *The Tablet* between 1981 and 2003, the Penney case was a turning point. Wilkins first heard about the case through the 1993 BBC documentary. He obtained a transcript and had no doubt whatsoever that Eamonn Flanagan was telling the truth. The impact was overwhelming:

> Priests were thought to be rather like God. Ontologically, a priest changes into another Christ. The image of the priest with the child, the safety of the child with the priest, that was iconic. Now it was shattered. It was a huge shock. Parish priests were loved. Now they had feet of clay.[131]

Wilkins wrote a powerful editorial in *The Tablet* calling for openness. The impulse of the Church authorities, he complained, is to hush things up, to look to the safety of the institution, to isolate and forsake the victim or victims ... and to move the perpetrator elsewhere (where he does the same thing again). That leaves not only a person or persons wounded to the heart, with a festering sense of wrong that may break out in dramatic ways years afterwards, but families and parish communities wounded as well. Moreover, the wound is now double, for to the sexual abuse is added the grievous hurt of the pattern of disbelief and denial on the part of the authorities experienced by those who have approached them in the cause of justice...[132]

The Tablet is not an official organ of the Catholic Church but it is a significant voice within the Catholic community and the editorial was a powerful rebuke to the hierarchy. Brendan Flanagan, Eamonn's brother, told *The Tablet* the following week:

On Friday it was my privilege to be in the same room as Eamonn when he received a telephone call. The caller told him about *The Tablet*'s editorial. Its words could have been our words. Eamonn said: 'This is the greatest day of my life!' You will never fully appreciate the blessed release we all felt. At last Eamonn had support from within the Church, from people we and the clergy respect. It is twenty years since he was first abused. It is a long time to wait for support from your own.[133]

• • •

'With hindsight perhaps he should have been stopped sooner.'[134] Archbishop Vincent Nichols was talking about Father John

Tolkien, another priest of the Birmingham archdiocese. Tolkien was the son of the author J. R. R. Tolkien (*The Lord of the Rings* and *The Hobbit*). The allegations against him were never proved in a court of law but several compensation claims relating to abuse by Tolkien have been settled by the Archdiocese of Birmingham. They included a claim by Christopher Carrie, who campaigned over many years to expose Tolkien's behaviour.

The Tolkien family were Catholic converts; J. R. R. Tolkien's mother converted to Catholicism as a teenager, much to her family's disgust, and following her early death, the orphaned J. R. R. Tolkien was partly brought up under the guardianship of a local Catholic priest. J. R. R.'s son, John Francis Reuel Tolkien, was born in 1917 during his father's period of invalidity from war service. John Tolkien grew up in Oxford, where his father was appointed Professor of Anglo-Saxon in 1925. John was educated at a Catholic boarding school in Berkshire before reading English at Oxford, and after graduation he started training for the Catholic priesthood in Rome. The English College in Rome was exiled to Stonyhurst College in Lancashire during the war and John Tolkien spent the war years there. He was ordained in north Oxford in 1946 and began his career as a priest in Coventry. In 1947 he moved to the English Martyrs Church in Sparkhill, in inner-city Birmingham, the city which had inspired his father's fantasy novels. Whilst at Sparkhill he also became a scout leader of the local English Martyrs Scout Troop.

From 1957 to 1987 Tolkien lived in Stoke-on-Trent, until 1966 working as a priest at Knutton Roman Catholic Church in Staffordshire and then as priest in charge at the Church of Our Lady of the Angels and St Peter in Chains, Hartshill, a Stoke suburb. Tolkien occupied numerous positions of responsibility in the community, as chair of a board of school governors and chaplain to several student organisations. His final career posting as a priest was to St Peter's in Eynsham, Oxfordshire, where he remained until his retirement in 1994. A wealthy man by dint of his family background, he made considerable personal donations to the cost of church building. 'Owlish and bespectacled', he led what appeared to be a selfless life, ministering to the needs of thousands of families.[135] But in all probability, Tolkien molested many boys.

Christopher Carrie, a working-class boy from a devout Catholic family in Sparkhill, never forgot his first encounter with Tolkien. In November 1956, Carrie was eleven years old. The encounter followed his appearance at the local juvenile court for petty crime. Deemed to need firmer guidance, Carrie became a member of the English Martyrs' 159th Boy Scouts; Tolkien was the group scoutmaster.

Carrie was called in to see Tolkien at the English Martyrs presbytery. Carrie was nervous, but Tolkien seemed even more so. 'Now, Christopher, you are of an age when you should be told, that is you should learn, what should I say, err, the birds and the bees, that is, err, the facts of life ... Your mother has asked me to have a chat with you.' Tolkien then made a long, perverted speech, asking Carrie about his private parts and describing the act of sexual intercourse. Towards the end of the conversation he told Carrie that he needed to physically examine him 'in order to write a report on your well-being'.[136] Carrie was ordered to strip naked and perform various physical exercises including press-ups.

Tolkien then sexually assaulted him in what the priest claimed was a 'special blessing', which involved pouring 'holy water' onto his penis and massaging it. Carrie was ordered by Tolkien to return the following week, when a second assault took place, again in what Tolkien claimed was a religious ceremony: this time the act of 'prayer' involved Tolkien massaging Carrie's penis between his praying hands. As Carrie was leaving, Tolkien cautioned him not to speak to anybody about his 'blessing' lest he 'offended Jesus and suffered the loss of my very soul'. 'I was very, very frightened,' Carrie said later.

Carrie did nothing about the two incidents until much later in his adult life when he suffered a breakdown and 'seriously began to question my personality'. As a result of his breakdown he lost his marriage, felt disgusted and devastated by what had occurred, and decided that he wanted to challenge Tolkien. He described the years in between:

A quarter of a century has passed since Father Tolkien formed the secret pact between Jesus, himself and me. The threat of eternal damnation, should I reveal the secret, no longer holds any dread for me. I now know he was a wicked person abusing his position as a priest to sexually molest children. I often thought of meeting him again, and facing him with the harm his corrupted influence had caused. How to achieve such a meeting seemed a daunting task given the passage of time. I had no way of knowing where he was, or even if he was still alive. The first step, on what was to prove a very long journey, was initiated by one of Tolkien's own brethren.

Through a relative who was a Catholic priest, Carrie discovered that Tolkien was still alive. Even at this point Carrie struggled with approaching Tolkien:

The teaching of Catholicism buries itself deep in the soul. It is a mortal sin to speak ill of God or his disciples – priests. That is what I had been taught from the age of five. Regardless of truth, if what you said harmed Mother Church it was deemed sinful.

Carrie eventually tracked Tolkien down to Oxford, spurred on by the death of a school friend from the English Martyrs who may also have been abused by Tolkien. In the late summer of 1993, having established that Tolkien was still working as a parish priest in Oxfordshire, Carrie went from church to church looking for him.

He then contacted and met with Archbishop Couve de Murville. Carrie provided the archbishop with a detailed account of the abuse and a résumé of what he knew of Tolkien's recent activities. The archbishop promised to investigate and wrote to Carrie on 10 October 1993, explaining what action he intended to take:

> Passage of more than thirty-five years makes it difficult to establish precisely what happened and when, but I have carefully investigated your complaints as far as possible. I have also interviewed Father Tolkien. He is more than seventy-six years old and not in good health. It may be helpful for you to know that he is now going to retire and cease the active practice of his ministry as a priest.

Nowhere in the letter did the archbishop attempt to deny or rebut the allegations.

But the archbishop's promise that Tolkien would 'cease his

active ministry' was not honoured. In June 1994, Carrie found Tolkien presiding at Mass at the Church of St Gregory and St Augustine in Oxford. Standing at the back of the congregation, Carrie heard Tolkien intoning the words 'when you come before the great prosecutor on final judgement day, be sure to have your case well prepared'. It felt like some of the parishioners were attending a celebrity Mass conducted by J. R. R. Tolkien's son. At the end of the Mass, Carrie confronted him, and Tolkien agreed to a meeting at his home. The failure to remove Tolkien from active ministry was a grave breach of a promise with potentially serious consequences: Tolkien had placed a notice in the vestry of an Oxfordshire church, inviting parents to send their children to him for 'one-to-one' liturgy instruction.

Carrie saw Tolkien two weeks later. Covertly recording the meeting, he put it to Tolkien that he had sexually abused him in the 1950s. The taped record confirms that Tolkien accepted that he had committed at least some of the alleged abuse. Asked whether he remembered stripping Carrie naked and putting holy water on his penis and massaging it, Tolkien, crying, replied: 'No, I don't deny that part of it. No. But I deny that I masturbated anybody.' Carrie asked him if he himself had been sexually abused as a child. Slipping into reminiscence, Tolkien described the environment in which he had grown up:

You know, I believe every boy experiences some of what you described ... for instance, when I was a boy I was constantly surrounded by my father and colleagues of my father. Almost without exception his colleagues were academics of one sort or another and, you know, some of them were pretty strange fellows. Well, I say strange, what I mean is that they were highly intelligent, no question of that. Often people would stay over for the night at our house. Most times there would be so many of them we would just have to make do. Sleep-where-you-could sort of thing. I often awoke the next morning to find someone sharing my bed. More often than not it would be ... well, I don't intend to name names, just to say this one particular person who I loved dearly, not in a sexual way, you understand. This person would be fast asleep, huddled up next to me when I woke in the morning. Well, let's say things had gone on in the night. I knew this. Well, if you wake up with your pyjamas off and they were on when you went to sleep you would wonder, wouldn't you?

Asked who the person was, Tolkien refused to say:

I won't say. The person was a very close friend of my father, a highly respected man of letters. No. It would be a total betrayal on my part. I can't see that it did me any great harm. I'm not like you, tittle-tattling to all and sundry about things that happened years ago.

In September 1994 Carrie made a formal complaint about Tolkien to West Midlands Police. Interviewed at Bradford Street police station, he waited to hear what the authorities intended to do. He carried on waiting but heard nothing. Hearing that the Church had new child protection rules – the 1994 Pastoral and Procedural Guidelines[137] – Carrie approached Bishop Terence Brain, who had responsibility for them. In October 1995 Bishop Brain assured Carrie that he would personally go to Oxford, speak to Father Tolkien and find out his response to Carrie's allegations, and then contact Carrie again.

But he never heard back from Bishop Brain. Despairing at this lack of action, Carrie decided to publish his story: the result was his book *Klone'it*, an anagram of Tolkien, which described his encounters with the priest as a boy and his campaign to expose him for who he really was. Carrie had to get his book published privately, and it brought forth a volley of legal threats.

In 2000, Carrie put his book on a website; this brought further coverage, and Carrie was encouraged to contact the police again. He duly did so. This time, they took his complaint seriously. A new police investigation was initiated in January 2001. Tolkien was arrested and interviewed, and it looked like Carrie's tape of his meeting with Tolkien back in 1994 would see the case into court. But the police investigation came too late. In February 2002, the Crown Prosecution Service (CPS) decided not to prosecute. The case was evidentially strong, but by now the ageing Father Tolkien's medical condition apparently precluded a trial. The CPS statement confirmed that 'the case passed what is termed the evidential test; it was felt that there was sufficient evidence for a realistic prospect of conviction'. However,

the CPS has advised the police not to bring charges against Father John Tolkien following allegations of historic sexual abuse. After careful consideration of all the circumstances of the case, the CPS decided that it would not be in the public interest to proceed. This decision was made following the submission of expert medical opinion regarding Father Tolkien's state of health.

All that Carrie had left by way of legal redress was a compensation claim, which he duly initiated in 2002 in the hope that he could somehow force Tolkien into a courtroom. During the case I secured statements from five other individuals who alleged that they had been sexually abused by Tolkien at one time or another: three in Stoke and two in Birmingham. The archdiocese argued, initially, that the case should be thrown out on time-limit grounds. This argument was self-evidently weak: the archdiocese had known about the allegations almost a decade before, but had taken no action at that time. Shortly before the time-limit point was due to be decided by the court, the archdiocese settled. It was agreed that the settlement amount would remain confidential, but Carrie refused to agree confidentiality in respect of the entire case.

I represented Carrie in his civil case and I have no doubt he is telling the truth. His account has been entirely consistent throughout many years of retelling and it is clear that his actions were never motivated by financial gain. Indeed, he took almost ten years from his confrontation with Tolkien in 1993 to instigate a damages claim, doing so only on my advice that this was the only way left to secure some measure of accountability from the Church. He was intensely frustrated when settlement of the case (for full value) deprived him of his day in court. Other complainants against Tolkien independently made similar accusations. But with Tolkien's death in 2003 the allegations remain just that: accusations which can never be properly adjudicated by a court of law. The Tolkien family are left with unresolved allegations; Carrie and other victims will never have their chance to put their accounts to a jury.

Following Tolkien's death, the Birmingham *Sunday Mercury*, which had tried to expose him, carried a powerful editorial:

Father John Tolkien is dead but the harm that he did in his lifetime will not die with him. The victims of his career of sex abuse are still suffering. This newspaper was threatened with legal action to stop us telling the truth. In the past the Catholic Church itself has also preferred silence, rather than facing up to the scandal of paedophile priests. In the case of Father Tolkien, one victim claims that he was assured – by an archbishop no less – that the elderly Tolkien would be retired. He took that to mean a dangerous man would be kept away from children. Yet, nine months later, Tolkien was still working as a priest and even offering one-to-one services to teach youngsters. How could this happen?

Whether out of sheer naivety or a desire to cover up uncomfortable facts, the Roman Catholic Church is not good at answering such difficult questions. Denial will achieve nothing. Nor will protecting pervert priests at the expense of their victims. There is no room for prevarication when it comes to protecting children. Only by bringing this story out into the open can we hope to make sure there are no more John Tolkiens.[138]

• • •

Like Samuel Penney, Christopher Clonan was an Irishman who came to England to follow his vocation. Born in County Meath, in the early 1970s Clonan arrived at Christ the King Catholic Church in Coundon, Coventry, as an assistant priest. The priest in charge – Clonan's line manager – was Father Michael McTernan. Coundon was one of the leafier suburbs of Coventry: a Warwickshire village which had been amalgamated into the city in the 1930s as population growth and house building expanded the city limits.

Clonan shared some of Penney's Irish earthiness. A construction worker before becoming a priest, he was known as 'Father Fix It' for his skills in church building projects. Vivacious and amiable, with a strong Irish accent and a liking for Scotch, he 'swore like a trooper, loved a drink and puffed countless cigars'.[139] He liked snooker and pool, and built a snooker club in the presbytery for use by the church community. This was one of the places where he molested boys over a twenty-year period.

An allegation about Clonan surfaced early, but was buried just as quickly. In 1974 a boy, referred to as M in later court proceedings, told his father that Clonan had touched him inappropriately. The father left a note for Father McTernan, saying he wanted to talk with him. About two days later, McTernan came to their house, where the boy's parents saw him and told him what had happened. As the parents remembered it, McTernan said very little except to suggest that they might speak to Clonan. The boy's father said there was not much point in doing that. After a time McTernan left, and the family heard no more. As the father explained: 'The matter certainly didn't die in our household but it appeared to me to have died with Father McTernan.' The boy's mother's statement described how McTernan initially made no comment about Clonan's behaviour but 'just sat looking into the fire'.[140]

Questioned by the police in 1992, Father McTernan claimed to have no recollection of the meeting: 'I cannot remember ever visiting their house and discussing with them any problem in relation to their son … and matters concerning Father Clonan.' Mr Justice Jack, ruling on this evidence in the *Maga* case in 2009[141] was unimpressed by McTernan's response: 'A very strong case can be made that the parents of M would not have invented their complaint to Father McTernan.'[142] But in any event Father McTernan seemed to concede he may have known something, telling the police in 1992: 'I had no reason to suspect that there had been anything untoward between M and Father Clonan. However, I must confess I feared the worst.'[143]

Father McTernan's failure to act on the 1974 complaint left Clonan free to abuse boys for a further eighteen years. In July 1992, the parents of another boy told Clonan that their son had said that he had abused him. Clonan telephoned Father (by now Monsignor) McTernan to tell him of this, and that he was leaving the country. In an echo of the Laurence Soper case in Ealing,[144] Clonan disappeared, fleeing Coventry for Ireland, where, it seems, he spent a few months lying low in a Dublin psychiatric hospital. In late 1992, he flew to Australia, joining some of his ten siblings and his mother in Melbourne. Thereafter, his whereabouts became a mystery, one which fed much press speculation just as the Birmingham archdiocese and its loyal congregations were reeling from the Penney scandal.

Father McTernan died in 1996. The true extent of his knowledge of Clonan's behaviour with boys, and Clonan's subsequent whereabouts after fleeing the country, can only be guessed at. As Mr Justice Jack later observed in *Maga*, when Father Clonan telephoned Father McTernan in 1992 to tell him that there was an allegation against him, Father McTernan did not even ask him what it was about. At some point, Father McTernan reported on his conversation with Clonan to archdiocesan colleagues, but the important question of precisely when he did so, bearing in mind that Clonan had signalled an intention to flee the country, has never been answered: no note of the conversation exists in archdiocesan files. As the scandal unfolded, the archdiocese seemed incurious about exactly what Clonan had done and where he had gone. The explanation offered by the archdiocese in later court proceedings was that the police were conducting a criminal investigation and they thought it appropriate to leave matters to the police.

The archdiocese apparently could not assist regarding Clonan's whereabouts. Nonetheless, in 1992, not long after Clonan had disappeared, some belongings were collected from the presbytery by a friend of Clonan's and taken to Ireland. On 24 September 1992, Monsignor Dan Leonard, the senior archdiocesan official then handling the matter, wrote to a Reverend W. Baker in Melbourne, Australia, saying that the Church had been unable to trace Father Clonan's whereabouts since he left hospital in Dublin despite exhaustive enquiries. A local newspaper cutting dated 14 January 1994 states that it was understood that Father Clonan had applied for a visa for Australia and had instructed his Coventry solicitors to sell his house in Coundon and another owned by members of his family.

The article was sent to Archbishop Couve de Murville by Father McTernan's successor at the Church of Christ the King in Coundon, Father Eamon Clarke. Father Clarke complained to his superiors that that he was not being kept informed: 'On the occasion of my appointment you assured me that the problem was over as there was no case to answer. With respect I think you were mistaken since not a week goes by without some rumour or allegation being made.'[145] Meanwhile Clonan's whereabouts in Australia continued to remain a mystery. In June 2000 a Monsignor Moran of the Birmingham archdiocese wrote to a Monsignor Hynes in Rockhampton, Queensland, saying that the police had information that in 1993 Father Clonan had applied to work in the Rockhampton diocese, and asking for help as to his whereabouts. He explained: 'Archbishop Vincent Nichols wants to be seen to be cooperating with the police in relation to the protection of children and therefore, we feel obliged to help the police to find him if at all possible.' An answer was received saying that the bishop had a vague recollection of an enquiry from Father Clonan, but it had not proceeded. In his later judgment in the *Maga* case, Mr Justice Jack extended the time limit for the claimant to bring his claim: in investigating Clonan and the allegations against him, and indeed in trying to find him, 'the Church did not make enquiries and take steps which, given its position, it should reasonably have taken'.

A few years after his disappearance, reports started circulating that Clonan had faked his own death to avoid arrest and criminal charges. In 2004 British police flew to Australia to investigate the claims. It transpired that in Australia, from 1992 onwards, Christopher Oliver Clonan had reinvented himself as Christie Oliver, a property developer and retired former casino operator. 'Christie' had taken up residence in the town of Bendigo, ninety miles north of Melbourne, where his brother Andrew lived. Living quietly on the high street in the Bendigo suburb of Kangaroo Flat, he managed a boarding house for students, sold timber at local markets and played pool in the pub. His disguise was very effective. Residents of Kangaroo Flat were later stunned to discover that Clonan was a child-molesting priest on the run from the law; when told, one of them fainted.

Clonan's brother Andrew told the British police that Clonan had died suddenly of a brain haemorrhage in 1998. The night before his death, said Andrew, they had enjoyed a bottle of Scotch together.[146] But Andrew's story was inconsistent:

previously, during Clonan's lifetime, he had told the *Coventry Evening Telegraph* that he had last seen his brother in December 1993 as he put him aboard a Qantas flight to Manila. In Andrew's earlier account, Christopher Clonan's application for Australian residency had been rejected due to the concerns about his character: 'They kicked him out of Australia. I took him to the airport myself.' Later, however, Andrew conceded that his brother had sneaked back into the country and established himself in Kangaroo Flat, before dying in 1998. 'We try to protect the living, not the dead,' was Andrew Clonan's reported explanation for his previous story. Subsequently Andrew produced a death certificate, stating that Christopher Clonan had died on 22 October 1998, aged fifty-six, and was cremated in Bendigo Crematorium. Andrew Clonan said that his wife had identified the body in the presence of police, and that his brother was cremated. Cremation, of course, was very unusual for a Catholic priest, but it was claimed that the family was short of money.

Suspicions that Clonan faked his death have persisted. A source quoted in the Birmingham *Sunday Mercury* newspaper claimed that several priests had spotted Father Clonan in Birmingham on a number of occasions since his disappearance. The source claimed he had lost a lot of weight, but was otherwise similar, and that he was using an Irish passport which claimed that his profession was a teacher. However, the death certificate and DNA taken before cremation appear to support Andrew Clonan's statement that his brother died alone in 1998 in Kangaroo Flat. Coventry police, who collected this evidence whilst in Australia, say they are satisfied that Clonan is dead.

In terms of compensation paid, the Clonan case has been one of the most expensive by far for the English Church. Simon Grey, one of Clonan's victims who waived his anonymity, received an out-of-court settlement of £330,000 – at that time one of the highest ever awards in a UK child sex abuse case. Mr Grey argued that six years of abuse at the hands of the priest turned him into a violent alcoholic who had spent time in jail and tried to set fire to himself. Another Clonan victim was awarded £635,000, the highest reported award of damages in a civil claim against the Catholic Church in England. The courts were unimpressed by the archdiocese's conduct in the Clonan case over the previous thirty years.

• • •

Another prolific sex abuser in the archdiocese, Father James Robinson, also disappeared overseas. Robinson fled to California in the mid-1980s, but the saga ended with his extradition back to the UK in August 2009 and his trial and conviction at Birmingham Crown Court in 2010. Robinson, by then aged seventy-three, was convicted of twenty-one charges of sexual assault, all against boys under sixteen. The charges related to the period 1959–83. Robinson had abused at churches in Staffordshire, Birmingham and Coventry. He was sentenced to twenty-one years' imprisonment. Judge Patrick Thomas QC described his crimes as 'unimaginably wicked'. Robinson, he said, was a 'devious and manipulative' priest who caused 'immense and long-lasting damage' to his victims. He criticised Robinson for refusing to return to the UK to face trial, saying he clearly imagined he was beyond the reach of the law.

Robinson, said the prosecution barrister, had 'something of a knack for spotting the quiet child of the family'. His status as a priest gave him unfettered access to children, whom he groomed by giving them gifts and taking them on trips in his sports car. He would become a trusted family friend, able to mix freely with family members, before engaging his victims in sexual activity. All his victims had been left profoundly emotionally damaged.

Robinson had been traced to California by a BBC journalist, Paul Kenyon, in 2003. At that time California law did not permit extradition to the UK and Kenyon found Robinson to be 'pretty cocky': Robinson evidently believed that he would not be forced to return to the UK to stand trial. But a few years later the law in California changed, and Robinson was extradited back.

The archdiocese said after the trial that it 'sincerely regretted Robinson's betrayal of the trust placed in him'. But the question of what the archdiocese knew about Robinson, and when, was only hinted at during the trial.

Robinson was paid £800 per month by the archdiocese until December 2001. By that time, the archdiocese had long been aware of the allegations against him, probably for over two decades. Robinson had claimed that he was unable to afford to return to Britain for trial, even though the archdiocese had sent him a cheque for £8,400. Judge Thomas sidestepped the issue of the archdiocese's role, but observed that 'others may take the view that a full investigation and a full disclosure of the results of that investigation are due to members of the Church and Robinson's victims'.

And so it was: priests of the archdiocese and, it was later alleged, the then Archbishop of Birmingham, George Dwyer, had known about Robinson for nearly thirty years and allowed him to continue to abuse. The nature of the archdiocese's knowledge was the subject of civil litigation before Robinson's criminal trial. Father Robinson's immediate superior in the period 1972–74 was Father Matthew Corrigan, the parish priest of the Holy Family Church in Small Heath, Birmingham. Corrigan's assistant priest was Father Sheehy. It was alleged that a boy complained to Corrigan and Sheehy around that time that Father Robinson was showing him undue attention. The boy, who was twelve at the time, said that he didn't like Father Robinson; he didn't like Robinson staying overnight at his house, and he didn't like the way Robinson organised the altar boy rota so as to ensure that he had to serve whenever Robinson (at that time a junior priest of the church) was celebrating Mass. When questioned, Father Robinson's explanation for spending an unnatural amount of time with the boy was that he was 'explaining the facts of life' to him: an explanation which might reasonably have aroused suspicion amongst the other priests but seemingly did not. Meanwhile, in or around 1972–73, the same boy complained to a Father Lynch at the Birmingham Oratory that Robinson was sexually assaulting him. This complaint was made during confession. The boy recalled making the same complaint, also during confession, to a Father Winterton at the Birmingham Oratory and similarly to a Father McTernan at St Teresa's Church in Perry Barr a few months later.

This boy, however, was not the only complainant. In 1972, another complainant – later referred to as E in court proceedings – became aware that a friend of his, P, had been sexually assaulted by Robinson on many occasions from the age of eleven onwards. E complained to several prominent individuals within the arch-diocese about Robinson's sexual assaults on P and his unsuitability for the priesthood: an administrator at St Chad's Cathedral in Birmingham, an administrator at Father Hudson's Home, a house mother and the superintendent at St Vincent's House. No action was taken, and in late 1976, E took his complaint to Archbishop Dwyer, only to be ignored again. Later, in 1985, a letter was sent on behalf of Archbishop Couve de Murville to the Chancellor of the Archdiocese of Los Angeles. At this point, Robinson had just moved to the USA. After describing Father Robinson's work as a priest as 'highly regarded', the letter explained that

> the immediate reason for his being in the United States just now is that a few months ago he met a man with whom he had an unwholesome relationship about thirteen years ago. We have no reason to believe that there has been any recurrence of this problem, but Father Robinson says that he would feel safer a long distance away and untraceable by this man.[147]

The nature of that 'unwholesome relationship', which the archdiocese knew about in 1985, has never been explained. The civil courts never adjudicated on the other complaints about Robinson as the damages claim was settled out of court. The archdiocese maintained that the obligation of confidentiality owed by Fathers Lynch, Winterton and McTernan in respect of the confessional meant that those priests could do nothing about Father Robinson: the sanctity of the confessional is inviolable.[148] Whether the rules of the confessional – part of canon law, not the law of the land – can displace obligations arising under civil law in respect of child protection has never been decided by an English court. But of course, the information about Robinson available to the archdiocese in this case was not only gleaned in the confessional: it came from several different sources, and acting upon it could have prevented many years of suffering.

• • •

'Your victims were not only young but they were helpless. You were the nearest thing they had to a father figure. You are a disgrace to the cloth and to the Church you proclaim.'[149] So stated the trial judge as he sentenced Father Eric Taylor to seven years' imprisonment. Taylor was jailed in 1998 after being convicted of indecent assault and buggery of children. His crimes were committed from 1957 to 1965 at Father Hudson's Home in Coleshill, Warwickshire. Aged seventy-eight at the time of his conviction, Taylor denied all the charges, claiming that he had been left impotent after serving in a prisoner of war camp during World War II.

Father Hudson's Society was the social care agency of the Birmingham archdiocese, and in Taylor's day ran a number of residential care homes for children. At the end of the trial, the society issued a joint letter with the Birmingham archdiocese expressing their 'profound sadness and sorrow for the actions of Father Taylor'.[150] The statement appeared to offer counselling and support, but the subsequent compensation claims by victims were, for a long time, vigorously defended. Settlements were eventually conceded only after several years of litigation and media pressure.

At the end of the trial it was disclosed that Taylor had previous convictions for indecent assault. Taylor, who had converted to Catholicism during his time as a prisoner of war in Austria, became an assistant administrator at Coleshill in 1957 and remained there until 1965. In 1975, whilst working in Warwickshire, he was fined £250 by Worcestershire magistrates after admitting five indecent assaults on boys in the Warndon area. In 1988 all Father Hudson's Homes were closed as residential units for children. Taylor had left Father Hudson's many years earlier, but continued to work as a supply priest for the archdiocese until 1996, when he moved abroad. All the while, the archdiocese knew of his 1975 conviction but allowed him to remain in ministry. Taylor was arrested during a visit home in 1997 and convicted in 1998. He died in prison in 2001.

Formed in Coleshill in 1902 to help poor children, Father Hudson's had an unhappy history. The society was heavily implicated in the forced emigration of children to Australia, which started in the late 1930s. Some ninety-two children were sent to Australia from Coleshill.[151] The migrant children scandal was itself seen by some former residents as cover for paedophilia: abuse a child then ship him to Australia where he cannot complain. Hudson's Home – remembered by many of its inmates as a bleak, austere environment with sadistic nuns and child-molesting priests – became a byword for nastiness. One inmate, Danny Mackle, recalled a dehumanising regime. Forced to rise early every morning and pray for an hour, he also had to kneel for lengthy evening services. In between he was forced to undertake countless physically demanding tasks such as scrubbing the kitchen floors. He did this for six years; the kitchen floors were 100 feet long and the task took over an hour every day. Kneeling was also a punishment: 'If I got into trouble I'd have to kneel on the cold marble floor, arms outstretched.' Relentless physical brutality during his adolescence left him with lifelong knee problems: when I represented him in his legal case nearly forty years later, he was still having knee surgery. During his time in Coleshill he was also experiencing regular sexual assaults from Taylor, and another priest who died before he could be put on trial. The nuns were known too for their emotional cruelty: 'They told us that as children in care we were the sons and daughters of Satan.'

After years of nightmares – 'I tried to put the past to bed, but I was breaking down every day'– Mackle eventually took Hudson's to court, but the fear that Taylor inspired in children silenced many of them. During the criminal trial one former inmate of the home stood by Taylor.[152] Patrick Mullins, an orphan, spent his childhood at Hudson's: he was Danny Mackle's roommate. In the early 1970s, becoming active in the Young Conservatives, he was feted by Prime Minister Ted Heath and became Birmingham's first Youth Mayor. In the 1970s, he moved to Western Australia. When the Taylor trial took place, he hit out at the men who were giving evidence against Taylor, suggesting they were doing it for compensation. But in 2012 Mullins disclosed that he too had been abused by Taylor:

That man didn't believe in God, he only believed in little boys. That is all he believed in. The judge called him a disgrace to the cloth. That is an understatement. The nuns definitely knew of his sexual attachment to the boys and turned a blind eye to it, he being a priest. He was regarded almost as a God … I worked in the presbytery where he lived. He was a psychopath … He had no empathy for his victims; he felt no guilt. He was a predator in the strictest sense of the word. I used to see him hiding behind walls waiting for boys. He had his hunting ground.

Mullins apologised to other victims for not disclosing earlier, and for castigating complainants during the 1998 trial. To date, only Taylor has been convicted of sexually abusing children at the home. Taylor was not the only priest at Father Hudson's who has been named as a child molester, but the home closed in 1988 so the likelihood of further prosecutions must be modest. But the Hudson's story seems to run and run; the brutality of the home makes it difficult to forget. In 2008, the *Sunday Mercury* suggested that a teenager at the home had been 'disappeared' after it was discovered that he was having an affair with a nun. The allegation has never been substantiated. In 2009 the *Sunday Mercury* revealed further allegations from eleven people who reported sexual and physical abuse by priests and nuns.

The horror of life at Hudson's, supposedly a charitable foundation aiming to give vulnerable children a better life, has haunted many of them ever after. Danny Mackle, desperate to confront the man who had ruined his childhood, decided to visit Taylor in prison:

I heard he was in Blakenhurst [Prison]. I decided to just turn up. You had to fill in a form – family or friend? I wrote down 'friend', just to get in. I was led inside. Door after door slammed behind me, keys jangling on the warders' hips. It was just like Hudson's. I was having flashbacks to my childhood. My heart was racing. Then I was taken in to see him. And there he was, in his orange vest.

Everything I wanted to say, I couldn't say. I wanted to make him understand what he'd done. But all I saw was a frail, dying, sick man.

In the course of their conversation, Mackle recalls,

I started to realise that here was a man who was himself a victim. A victim of the Church. He'd been shifted from pillar to post to protect the good name of the Catholic Church. He was their scapegoat.

Taylor spoke. He said: 'It wasn't just me.' He went on about Penney. He was in contact with Penney – a circle of friends. I ended up feeling sorry for him. He was a victim of the Catholic Church because those who knew of his paedophilia in the 1960s and 1970s chose to do nothing.

In the end, Mackle felt it was the Catholic Church itself which bore moral responsibility for the brutality and suffering caused to so many children: 'They are the ones who should be looking at themselves and praying. They are the ones who should have been in prison.'[153]

• • •

By 1999 the exposure of failings in so many cases finally brought about the resignation of Archbishop Couve de Murville. Announcing his departure on 27 June 1999, the archbishop referred to his declining health: 'I feel that a younger man is needed to administer such a big diocese as ours. There are initiatives one cannot undertake at my age as health and strength begin to decline.'[154] But it was universally assumed that Couve de Murville was resigning because of the abuse scandal. A 'church insider' was quoted as telling the *Sunday Times* that 'it is widely known that the Archbishop has become weary and exhausted by the criminal proceedings which were taken against the priest. He is thought to have been worried by the prospect of long, drawn-out civil actions.' This seems to have been a reference to the trial of Eric Taylor, convicted in 1998.

The archbishop's successor, Vincent Nichols, seemed determined that the archdiocese would mend its ways. The early signs were good: in October 2000 a priest, Father Gerry Flahive, was investigated for abuse of young girls (he was subsequently convicted); sensibly, Flahive seems to have been placed on administrative leave as soon as the allegations came to light. But other events suggested that the culture of the archdiocese had barely changed. Even by mid-2001, as the Nolan process was underway, the archdiocese seemed incapable of learning basic lessons from years of scandal. In June 2001, a priest who had sexually assaulted a woman whilst working as a parish priest in Coventry was ordered to pay damages to his victim, but in an extraordinarily insulting public statement the archdiocese maintained that he should be permitted to remain in active ministry because 'the Catholic Church is in the business of forgiveness and reconciliation'.

Father Terence Fitzpatrick, formerly parish priest of St Osburg's Church in Coundon, Coventry (not far from Clonan's Church of Christ the King), admitted sexually assaulting a parishioner, Pamela Brown. In the late 1980s, Mrs Brown, herself a victim of earlier sexual abuse, had gone to Father Fitzpatrick for advice and support. Fitzpatrick had accompanied her to counselling sessions and then repeatedly sexually assaulted her between November 1989 and March 1992. The allegations had initially been investigated by West Midlands Police in 1993. Father Fitzpatrick claimed that she had consented to the relationship, and no criminal charges were brought. Mrs Brown, however, brought a civil claim against Fitzpatrick. In 2001, after many years of trying to defeat the claim, Fitzpatrick admitted liability and judgment was entered against him. He agreed to pay

damages, although he claimed that as a monk he had no money
to pay the claim.

By that time Father Fitzpatrick, a Benedictine, was living at
Douai Abbey monastery in Reading and was a priest to four
parishes in Berkshire. A spokesman for the Birmingham archdiocese, Peter Jennings, apologised for the priest: 'Father
Fitzpatrick is extremely sorry that he has let the Catholic Church,
his Benedictine Order and himself down. He wants the very
best for Mrs Brown.' But Jennings initially refused to answer
any questions about Fitzpatrick's future, and it soon became
apparent that despite admitting to sexually assaulting a vulnerable parishioner for several years, his ministry was to continue
uninterrupted. Whilst this would almost certainly have been a
decision of the Benedictines rather than the Archdiocese of
Birmingham, the archdiocese supported it wholeheartedly. Several
days after the first statement, presumably following considered
reflection, Jennings issued a further statement in which he
endorsed Father Fitzpatrick remaining as a parish priest:

> The Catholic Church is in the business of forgiveness and recon-
> ciliation. Father Fitzpatrick has admitted he has done wrong, he
> is truly sorry and is prepared to forgo his own reputation to save
> Mrs Brown from further trauma and distress. We abhor it when
> a priest breaks a trust someone puts in them but at the end of the
> day a priest is only human. The Church is standing by him and so
> are his order and his monastery.[155]

The statement – aptly described by the local newspaper as
'nauseating' – says much about the Church's default mindset in
abuse cases. Father Fitzpatrick had denied responsibility for his

own behaviour for years, only admitting what he had done as a trial loomed. But those many years of trauma and distress for Mrs Brown were somehow erased by Father Fitzpatrick's sheepish last-minute admission. The admission was cast as an act of nobility on Father Fitzpatrick's part, because he was 'forgoing his reputation'. It was the Church's right to forgive, rather than the victim's. And – despite being ontologically changed by ordination – priests who commit sexual assault are 'only human'. The statement was revealing: it suggested that even after many years of scandal, the archdiocese still had much to learn.

CHAPTER 6

GUIDELINES FOR AN EMERGING CRISIS

The Penney case forced the Catholic Church in England and Wales to develop, for the first time, formal procedures for the handling of abuse allegations. In 1994 a group led by Bishop Budd of Plymouth produced 'Child Abuse: Pastoral and Procedural Guidelines'. Interviewed for the BBC documentary *Breach of Faith* in 1993, Budd had been candid that the Church simply 'had no procedures through which to respond' to allegations of abuse. The document was a first attempt to grapple with the emerging crisis. The Pastoral and Procedural Guidelines acknowledged the central lesson of the Penney affair – that fear of public scandal and protection of the institution had created a conspiracy of scandal:

> Where … a priest … is accused of misconduct, there is a temptation to protect that person, and the Church, from the glare of publicity … Misguided loyalty … can breed more evil. Fear of public scandal is no reason for silence.[156]

These were fine words, but the real question was whether the document could establish a mechanism to enforce them, and to change the culture of the Church.

The composition of the team set up to develop the guidelines was a step in the right direction. For the first time it included expertise from outside the Church: the director of children's services at the NSPCC, and police officers. This brought a welcome new perspective, and the most significant feature of the document was its embrace of the paramountcy principle – the principle that the welfare of the child is the paramount consideration – which was the centrepiece of the secular model of child protection formalised in the Children Act 1989. In practical terms this meant recognising that, as Budd later explained, 'when a court doesn't convict someone, it doesn't necessarily mean you have no grounds for concern'.[157] Even if an individual is acquitted in the criminal court, or even if the case never reaches trial because the criminal standard of proof cannot be satisfied, the paramountcy of the child's interests means that child protection measures may need to be put in place, and that may happen even if the suspected perpetrator is innocent in the eyes of the criminal law. With an eye on recent cases, the document acknowledged that this approach needed to be adopted in the Church:

> Given the widely varying nature of child abuse, it is possible that there may be little or no little physical proof that the child has been abused because there is no physical evidence or third-party corroboration available. Abuse can involve unwitnessed behaviour in private circumstances. How to judge the truth of an allegation may depend on a judgement, a decision about whose word is to be believed; that of the assumed victim or the alleged abuser. This is not always an evenly balanced matter, especially in alleged child sexual abuse cases where it may involve the word of an adult, with an adult's experience, knowledge of the world and facility of

expression, all against the word of a child. Because of the nature of child abuse, it is not always possible to achieve a position of absolute certainty. Nevertheless, if children are to be protected, decisions will have to be made about whether abuse has occurred and about appropriate action to be taken in consequence. No one wants to misjudge an innocent person, but neither should we use the lack of certainty as an excuse for not exercising judgement to protect children. There is no escape from the exercise of prudential judgement.[158]

A paper appended to the guidelines examined the clash between the paramountcy principle and a more traditional view of natural justice in which it would be seen as unjust to remove a person from post before a secular trial or canonical process had been completed, and in which the outcome of a criminal trial would be seen as definitive – 'innocent until proved guilty'. The presumption of innocence, the document explained, should 'not be misunderstood': there may be any number of reasons why a criminal conviction cannot be secured but if the criminal standard of proof is not met, although the defendant is then acquitted this 'does not necessarily mean that he or she did not commit the act in question, or is morally innocent ... Crudely, "innocent until proved guilty" attempts to ensure that only the guilty are punished; it does not ensure that all the guilty are punished.'[159] Whilst recognising the serious consequences of a false accusation for an adult's reputation and career, the consequences for a child of having a true accusation dismissed would be most serious too, 'as will the consequences for other children who are being, or will be, abused'. This meant that the Church, in the interest of protecting the weaker party, would now sometimes have to act in a way which could be seen as peremptory, unfair or arbitrary – but this arises from the specific nature of child abuse, which is often accompanied by fear, shame, secrecy and lack of witness evidence, which may stand in the way of successful criminal prosecution. Judgements and decisions in a child protection context would have to be made on a lesser standard of proof, the balance of probabilities.

The practical implications of the paramountcy principle were clearly spelled out: 'administrative leave' – i.e. leave of absence for priests – would have to become standard practice where there was a reasonable suspicion which required further investigation:

> If reasonable suspicion of abuse follows preliminary investigation and consultation, then the Church authorities will have to place the alleged abuser on administrative leave with pay/financial support, until the investigative process has been completed. Administrative leave does not imply either guilt or innocence of the person under investigation, and is a recommended procedure for dealing with these allegations … In other words, the accused person, however strongly he/she protests innocence, will ultimately be forced to stand aside while investigations take place.[160]

The potential risk to children if abuse had been committed had to take precedence over the rights of the accused.

As the document also explained, the principle would continue to apply after criminal proceedings had been concluded, even if the prosecution was unsuccessful: 'Where a person is committed to trial for child abuse, but is found not guilty the matter does not necessarily end there. Strong suspicion may remain … It is essential that the paramountcy principle of protecting children is maintained.'[161]

Having enunciated these basic principles, the second part of the document proposed new 'structures and procedures'. There were detailed recommendations for investigation of allegations, involvement of statutory agencies and measures after sentencing if a cleric is found guilty. To put all this into effect a new role was created: each diocese was appointed a 'diocesan representative' to be the bishop's representative in dealing with issues of abuse; the person would undergo professional training and manage a small crisis team.[162] The representative would also be responsible for educating both clergy and laity. A communications officer would be appointed to supply information to the public. There was some discussion of pastoral support for survivors although this issue was largely deferred to a later date.

Many of the ideas in the document were sensible – indeed, would have protected many victims in the cases we have considered. But, as quickly became apparent after 1994, the guidelines were fundamentally ineffective. This is not really a surprise: a disease of this enormity, deeply rooted in the culture of the Church, was never going to be cured at a single stroke.

The document called upon the Church to embrace an approach to child protection – the paramountcy principle – which had become well established in secular law and thinking with the Children Act 1989 but which for the Church would be deeply countercultural. The document contained a clear-sighted and intelligent explanation of the paramountcy principle but, perhaps inevitably, underestimated the challenge this would pose to an institution where priests are placed on a pedestal. The backlash that the application of the principle would generate became clear even as the ink was barely dry on the 1994 document. In September 1995, Father Michael Hollings, a well-known priest of the Westminster archdiocese, was accused by the *News of the World* of having attempted to kiss and fondle a seventeen-year-old boy twenty-five years earlier.[163] The newspaper had 'wired up' the alleged victim and recorded his conversation with Hollings; during the conversation, Hollings had made an ambiguous admission of guilt and had asked the victim to 'forgive him'.[164]

Hollings, a decorated military officer who had a reputation as an unconventional priest with a wide circle of prominent friends, and who was lionised by many,[165] was placed on administrative leave, disappearing from his parish for six months, part of which he spent at Arundel Castle as the guest of the Duke of Norfolk. In February 1996, however, the police announced that they were taking no action against Hollings, and Archbishop Hume announced that Hollings would be returning to his parish 'with immediate effect'. Hollings had less than a year to serve until retirement at seventy-five, and died in February 1997.

The suspension of Hollings was condemned as a 'witch-hunt' by prominent Catholics, many of whom regarded Hollings as a personal friend. Paul Johnson, the Catholic journalist and historian, claimed that the matter had been so badly handled that 'the Spanish inquisition in its heyday would have made a fairer job of it'. Although the primary blame belonged to the *News of the World*, Johnson said:

> What made matters worse was the behaviour of the Catholic diocesan authorities, who are now quite hysterical about this kind of accusation and overreact in the most brutal manner without any regard to justice or the rights of the accused man. So the priest was suspended from his duties without inquiry or a word of explanation to the parish.[166]

Julia Stonor, a member of one of Britain's oldest Catholic families, was 'deeply disturbed and upset' by the treatment of Hollings:

> Like many other ordinary parishioners I'm horrified by this whole business – by the damage it has done to a wonderful priest, by the secrecy with which the diocese carried out its investigation, keeping the parish in the dark throughout, and by the lack of support Father Michael has received from the Catholic Establishment, people who in the past have been found singing his praises.

Some parishioners wondered if Hollings was being punished for supporting the ordination of women, married priests and intercommunion between the Churches – in effect, if the new child protection procedures were being used to settle old scores.[167]

Responding on behalf of the hierarchy, Nicholas Coote[168] acknowledged that there had 'been disquiet', but tried to explain the new realities: 'What has happened is that the clergy have up to now been in a special position, and it has come as a terrible shock to them to find themselves in the same vulnerable place as others like doctors, teachers and social workers.'[169] This was right. Hollings could not be treated differently because he happened to be popular or well connected. But the Catholic grassroots found it very difficult to accept that a priest should be treated just like any other professional with access to children.

Hollings had accepted his suspension. But what if a priest were to refuse? As the guidelines noted, the provisions of canon law relating to sexual offences by clerics do not 'cover the complex, and sometimes lengthy, period before the offender is actually found guilty'. Under canon law, administrative leave could not be imposed on a cleric unless the Church penal process has been initiated. The document optimistically suggested that this should 'not raise insurmountable problems', as an offer of administrative leave could be accepted voluntarily by an accused priest, but the document did not say what could or should happen if such an offer were to be rejected. That issue was left open, and the problem created by the higher burden of proof required in canonical proceedings – 'moral certainty' – was not even discussed. Given the steep learning curve on which the Church was now about to embark, the document probably went as far as it could in tackling these particular issues but, as a later chapter will show, the tensions arising from the adoption of the paramountcy principle would still be unresolved a decade and a half later.

But this was only one of the problems with the 1994 guidelines. There were other, more glaring, flaws. For one thing, the document did not convey an unequivocal message that allegations of abuse should be reported to statutory authorities. The document advised that information should be shared with 'responsible agencies' but suggested that before reporting, the bishop's representative should 'feel confident that an approach to these statutory agencies will not automatically initiate an inappropriate child protection investigation'.[170] That caveat was not really explained. But it was very dangerous, given that the Church had a long history of keeping allegations 'in house' and away from police and child protection agencies. Given the Church's lamentable track record of hushing up allegations, the guidelines needed to spell out a definitive obligation to report. The necessity for this was illustrated by debate around the Hollings case, when it became very apparent how fiercely the grassroots of the Church would resist the notion of cooperating with secular authorities. One priest observed that 'such a development would seem like the Church working hand in glove with the authorities. But it needs to preserve some independence of action if it isn't simply going to give the green light to anyone who wants to make life uncomfortable for their local priest."[171]

The guidelines also had little or nothing to say about how the Church should go about cleansing itself of past misdeeds. This was fatal. There were many cases already known to the Church where the paramountcy principle dictated that a priest should be removed immediately from active ministry. The guidelines adopted the principle and this clearly meant that cases of past suspicion or concern needed to be looked at again. But the guidelines proposed no mechanism by which those past cases would be systematically reviewed, even though the authors of the document had direct personal knowledge of such cases. Bishop Budd had himself been involved in the Crowley case (see Chapter 4). In 1987 he did a favour to the Bishop of Leeds by taking Crowley into his diocese and installing him as an assistant parish priest, supposedly under a behavioural 'contract'. But the contract was broken, and in 1990 Budd had sent Crowley back to Leeds, where he went on to abuse more children. The mistakes in this case were committed by the Leeds diocese, not by Bishop Budd, but Bishop Budd had knowledge of the case; similarly, Nicholas Coote, a senior Church official and one of the other authors of the document, had been involved in the Hill case (see Chapter 7). They would have known that the Church was littered with problem priests and that a comprehensive strategy for dealing with the past was urgently needed. But the document did not address this.

Most crucially of all, although the document proposed a new approach to child protection in the Church it was not underpinned by any proper enforcement and policing machinery. The new diocesan child protection representatives might do their job well or badly, but nobody would be checking up on them other than the bishops who had failed so woefully in the past. As Budd would have known from the Crowley case, some bishops were more conscientious than others, and the diocesan structure of the Church, in which a bishop was king in his own diocese, effectively meant that a bishop who breached the guidelines could not be held accountable. Nolan later attempted to address this problem by the creation of COPCA, the Catholic Office for the Protection of Children and Vulnerable Adults, but nothing of that kind was proposed in 1994.

The consequences of that omission were graphically exposed within a few short years. In 1998, Father John Lloyd was convicted and imprisoned in south Wales for child sex offences. Lloyd was a close colleague and adviser to the Archbishop of Cardiff, John Ward. The case laid bare the fundamental weakness of the guidelines whenever a bishop chose to ignore them.

Lloyd targeted altar boys for abuse, carefully selecting and grooming them. One victim later told the BBC *Panorama* programme 'Power to Abuse':

It was very natural the way he went about it. He used to spar and sort of have these play fights with all his altar servers. There was something quite endearing about that, a priest sort of bashing altar boys about. It was sort of a bit maverick and it sort of built up a friendship that you wouldn't expect usually from an authority figure … And from there, the physical contact had been established, he'd move on to the indecent assaults.

But concerns had been expressed by parishioners for some time about Lloyd's personality: not about sexual activity, but about bullying behaviour. They wrote to Archbishop Ward to complain. The letters were written in the strictest confidence, but, incredibly, rather than acting on them Ward simply passed them on to Lloyd. One local priest interviewed by *Panorama* explained that

> they were returned to Lloyd, which always struck me as being the most absurd situation, presumably for Lloyd to act on them. But what in fact happened ... was that Lloyd used them to terrorise the people who had written them. He'd wave these letters and he'd say 'I've told you, there's no point in writing to him because he sends these letters back to me' ... This madness was always accepted as the norm.

Ward's actions were a flagrant breach of the guidelines but there was nothing to stop him doing as he pleased.

Ward's handling of another case – that of Father Joseph Jordan, which also came to a head in 1998 – was even more egregious. Jordan was a serial paedophile whose past was littered with warning signs. In the late 1980s, some years before joining the priesthood, Jordan had been a form-master and English teacher in a school in Doncaster. An eleven-year-old boy in the class complained to him that his back hurt after playing rugby. Jordan lied and claimed he was a qualified physiotherapist. He suggested the boy come back to his house for treatment. Once at the house, Jordan subjected the boy to a violent sexual assault.

The boy went to the police and other victims came forward. But at trial, Jordan was found not guilty. The school decided Jordan was too much of a risk and refused to let him return. Jordan resigned but found another vocation: a few weeks later he turned up in Plymouth to apply to be a priest.

At the selection interview Jordan made a point of talking to them about the events in Doncaster. He tried, successfully, to turn the experience to his advantage. The accusations were false, he said, but had broken him and caused a spiritual renewal in his life. This explanation was accepted. Speaking to *Panorama* in 2000, Bishop Budd admitted that the selection board had made no effort to check the background to the case: 'I have a regret about him not being properly sussed out at that stage.' Budd denied that this was a major error. 'I wouldn't call it major. It was a lapse, I think, of diligence.'

Jordan was then sent to Rome as a student priest. Here, he quickly became known for his abusive manner. On one occasion, during dinner in the presence of the Rector, he introduced the topic of homosexuality into the conversation by referring to another student as a 'shit stabber'. A fellow student complained; Jordan was spoken to about his behaviour, but despite his evident unfitness nothing further was done to assess his personality, and his progress in the Catholic priesthood continued unhindered. He was allowed to carry out pastoral duties including working in schools in Rome. He befriended a number of boys between the ages of nine and thirteen, using his knowledge of football and computers to spark their interest. The seminary where Jordan was training knew about the abuse allegations but did not divulge them to the schools or to the parents.

The 1994 guidelines stated clearly that 'there must be a thorough check on all candidates who are being considered for work'. As we have seen, the guidelines also highlighted that 'when a person ... is found not guilty, the matter does not necessarily end there'.

Of course, it was Bishop Budd, Jordan's sponsoring bishop, who had headed the team which produced the guidelines. Reflecting again on Jordan's acquittal in a criminal case, he decided to send Jordan to a clinic which specialised in assessing paedophiles. 'I wanted to make sure that he wasn't a paedophile, that's at that stage, so it was the paedophile issues which I'd learnt a lot about. I'd learnt, for instance, that when a court doesn't convict someone, it doesn't necessarily mean you have no grounds for concern.'

This should have ended Jordan's career in the Church. However, at this point, by chance, Jordan met Archbishop Ward in Rome. At the meeting Jordan lied and told the archbishop that his parents were planning to move to Cardiff. He wanted, therefore, to become a priest there instead of Plymouth. Ward agreed to consider him.

Budd wrote to Ward setting out his concerns about Jordan. He explained that he was proposing to have Jordan assessed by a psychiatrist. Ward promised to 'put him through our screening'. But the 'screening' was something different; it did not involve an assessment by experts in paedophilia. However, Bishop Budd could not impose that on another diocese. Budd told Ward exactly what assessment had been arranged and where, so that Ward could proceed with it. But when Jordan presented himself in Cardiff for selection, the assessment had been cancelled. Incredibly, Ward told just one other person on the selection panel about Jordan's earlier court case. This person, Dr Harri Pritchard-Jones, was a local retired psychiatrist. Ward got him to assess Jordan. They met once for just over two hours.

It was not the thoroughgoing expert assessment Budd had

intended. Pritchard-Jones was never told about Budd's conclusion that Jordan should be assessed for paedophilia. Indeed,
Pritchard-Jones, by his own admission, had no expertise in that
field. Yet despite his lead role in child protection for the Church,
Budd could not insist that Jordan was assessed for paedophilia:
he simply had no jurisdiction in Cardiff. 'I don't think I could
have done more than I actually did in what I stated in that letter.
I was as strong as I could be without being impertinent,' Budd
later told *Panorama*.

Ward admitted to *Panorama* that he had been wrong not to
follow Budd's recommendation, but only 'with hindsight'. At the
time, said Ward, 'I didn't think it was necessary. I was satisfied
with the questioning he presented, and I was quite happy with
the results of that.'

Jordan – now sponsored by Archbishop Ward – returned to his
training in Rome. Ward then received complaints from Jordan's
fellow students about his bullying behaviour. But these were also
ignored, and in 1996 Jordan arrived in Cardiff. Even then, other
clergy complained about the speed of Jordan's ordination and
his suitability. Father Ambrose Walsh, who was suspicious of
Jordan, pointed out to Ward in a letter that 'we don't even know
him'. Ward never replied.

Jordan was ordained as a Catholic priest in early 1998.
Astonishingly, yet more concerns about him were raised. He
shared a house with other priests, and one spotted two boys
coming out of Jordan's room. On another occasion Jordan was
seen hanging around the showers of a sports centre used by
a local Catholic school. Both these episodes were reported to
another priest in the house, who passed the details on to Ward.
Ward's later explanation was that he 'just saw it as immaturity

on [Jordan's] part. I didn't see any danger signals there.' This was despite the earlier warnings from Budd and the persistent concerns expressed by fellow students in Rome.

By this time, unknown to his housemates, Jordan was also taking boys to football matches on his own, and had a new job, chaplain to Cardiff City Football Club. He also became parish priest at Barry in south Wales. Here he befriended some young boys and took them away on trips and to football matches on his own. He sexually assaulted the boys and one of them told his mother, who went to the police.

Word of the allegations reached Ward. Ward knew that Jordan was about to be arrested. But incredibly, the archbishop tipped off Jordan in advance of his arrest. This gave Jordan the opportunity to hide incriminating evidence stored on his home computer: hundreds of pornographic images of young boys downloaded from the internet. Jordan persuaded a friend to hide his computer and it took the police five months to track it down. Jordan was then charged with perverting the course of justice. Ward had expressly broken the 1994 guidelines by forewarning Jordan of the action which was about to be taken against him.

Jordan was found guilty both of sexual offences and of perverting the course of justice. He admitted a further count of abusing a boy a decade earlier, before he was a priest. Several of Ward's own parish priests called upon him to resign. One, interviewed for *Panorama*, was blunt:

This was a disaster that needn't have happened. This was something that needn't have happened if the information had been properly acted on. I think that [Ward] is a man who is way out of his depth and I think that basically he's shown on many occasions that he is incompetent. I think he's unfit for office.

But Ward brazened it out, seeing 'no reason' why he should resign.[172]

The two cases from Cardiff graphically exposed the flaws in the 1994 document. Ward did not understand the new principles and probably did not care about them. From Ward's perspective, the guidelines seem to have been nothing more than an academic exercise. He could act as he chose in his own fiefdom and ignore representations from a fellow bishop. There was nobody in the Church to hold him to account. Only the media would do this but the media only gets to learn of cases when a priest is convicted at a criminal trial. The whole point of the paramountcy principle is to act at an earlier stage, before the damage is done. By 1994 at least some in the Church had recognised this, but events proved that they did not yet have the means to make it happen.

CHAPTER 7

'YOURS SINCERELY, MICHAEL S. HILL'

The shock which galvanised the Church hierarchy into attempting a far more comprehensive reform of child protection was the case of Father Michael Hill. The impact of the Hill case was an accident of timing. The case was not significantly different from any of the other tragic sagas of child abuse which have sullied the Church, but it emerged into public view just as Hill's former bishop, Cormac Murphy-O'Connor, was appointed as Archbishop of Westminster, and thus as Catholic Primate of England and Wales. Once the facts of the Hill case were revealed, the pressure on the hierarchy became irresistible.

Michael Hill was a priest of the Diocese of Arundel and Brighton. Born in 1934, he abused children from the 1950s to his arrest in the 1990s. Hill was first convicted of sexual offences in 1997 and jailed for five years. Following that trial, some of his victims brought civil claims against the Church. These claims were settled in 2000 on the basis of strict confidentiality. But the settlements and the story behind them were revealed to the BBC a few weeks later, and this coincided with Murphy-O'Connor's appointment to Westminster. This was a 'catastrophe' for the Church, as Murphy-O'Connor suggested in an interview many years later; an unfortunate description, since the real catastrophe was the lifelong suffering of Hill's many victims. Hill's subsequent disclosures at the Wolvercote Clinic led to a second trial and conviction in 2001, when he pleaded guilty to further offences. In the course of the case many of the documents relating to it were leaked into the public domain.

Hill was a typical priest of his generation in that he decided on his vocation at a young age, probably before he had acquired sufficient personal and emotional maturity to comprehend the sacrifices involved. Hill was born and grew up in suburban southwest London, attending Wimbledon College, the leading Jesuit grammar school. A fellow student remembered him as 'charming, personable, likeable',[173] but many years later Hill hinted at a darker childhood. He entered seminary in 1952. Senior seminary followed in 1954, at St John's, Wonersh, in Surrey. Ordained in 1960, in the Diocese of Southwark, Hill's first appointment was as an assistant priest in Folkestone, followed in 1963 by a move to Hove. But Hill had displayed an early interest in child development and in 1966 joined the Southwark Diocesan Children's Society, initially in Wallington and then in Purley. At the same time, he kept his priestly career on track by ministering at St Peter's and St Paul's Church in Mitcham. One of his former parishioners in Mitcham, then a youngster, remembers him: 'Michael was a nice man, really nice. Very engaging. He made me think about joining the priesthood.'[174] Hill was evidently seen as 'good with children' and was keen to pursue a career in Catholic children's services. In 1969–70 he attended a one-year diploma course at Newcastle University Department of Education, receiving a Home Office 'letter of recognition in childcare'.

By the late 1960s Hill's child abuse modus operandi was well established: recruiting boys he was attracted to as altar servers, and befriending their parents so he could be alone with each boy, often in their own homes. Charming and engaging, Hill was very adept at using his position as a priest to gain the trust of parents. In many of the cases for which he was later imprisoned, Hill went to great lengths to insinuate himself into the victims' family: sometimes being invited on family holidays, sometimes organising holidays for boys on his own initiative so the parents could 'get a break'. A favourite technique was to read bedtime stories, all the while molesting the child under the duvet. Another was to encourage a boy to have a haircut so he needed a shower afterwards, with Hill in close attendance. Hill realised he could obtain sexual gratification most easily by molesting disabled children; there would be no risk of complaint, and the child itself might not even understand what was being done. So he abused children he came into contact with through the Southwark Children's Society, children he met at a local swimming pool in Crawley (where he enjoyed seeing children undress), children he met through ministering at Mitcham on Sundays, and children he met in Newcastle whilst attending the childcare course there. All of Hill's admitted victims were boys, although in later criminal investigations the complainants included one woman who alleged that she was sexually abused by Hill in her early teens when he was an assistant parish priest in Folkestone, offences Hill denied.

After three further years as an assistant priest, Hill was granted his own parish – St Teresa's in Merstham, Surrey. This was part of the Diocese of Arundel and Brighton, a new diocese created by the Holy See in 1965 from a slice of the much larger Diocese of Southwark. 'I consider myself very privileged to have been offered so challenging a parish with such a nice church and comfortable presbytery. I pray that I will not betray the trust you have placed in me,' wrote Hill to his bishop in September 1973.

Hill's targeting of vulnerable boys abuse continued. Victims included boarders at a non-Catholic prep school, The Hawthorns, where Hill attended a weekly evening class. Many years later one boy described what happened: 'I began altar serving at St Teresa's. I was between the ages of eight and twelve. After washing me down in the shower [Hill] would then make me masturbate him in his bed.'[175]

When were the first complaints made about Hill? During litigation in this case I was contacted by a Mr B who lived with his family in Merstham between the 1960s and the 1980s. A parishioner of Hill's and a regular attender at St Teresa's Church, he ultimately left the Church due to suspicions about Hill. At that time Hill was cubmaster of the local Cub group, so Mr B came into contact with him through both activities.

It became obvious to Mr B soon after he got to know Michael Hill that he had 'a strong preference for the company of boys. It was such an obvious preference; it set alarm bells ringing in my head.'[176] Mr B's concerns deepened when a friend told him that 'Hill was taking children on their own back to his house at night-time, cutting their hair, bathing with them and playing with them on his bed'. It became apparent that

> Hill was doing this with various children amongst the local Catholic community; he'd take them from their home on the basis that he was giving them instruction. Amongst the children involved were the children of the [Z] family. My wife knew Mrs Z was a member of the church. Our children and the Z children were friends with each other.

Mr B was very worried: 'I felt his behaviour was unnatural and unhealthy and I didn't think it was something he should be doing.' One of the normal safeguards was absent – unlike his predecessor, Michael Hill did not have a housekeeper at the presbytery. 'Frankly, I was concerned that children were at risk of abuse.'

Mr B remembered:

I confronted Michael. I told him I didn't like what he was doing, I didn't want to see it happening. Hill denied any impropriety. Following that conversation, Hill terminated his contact with my family, he stopped visiting us at home. He also told my wife that he did not want her involved in Cubs and her involvement ceased at that point.

Mr B was reluctant to let the matter rest. 'I was very unhappy about the situation. I wrote to the then bishop, Bishop Bowen, at Storrington House.' Mr B recalls that this was 'in or around 1976': 'To the best of my recollection, his secretary telephoned to ask for more information and I said it was not something that I was prepared to discuss on the telephone. I made an appointment to see Bishop Bowen. We had a face-to-face meeting, just the two of us.'

Mr B set out his concerns:

I said that Hill's behaviour was unnatural and not befitting of a priest. I said I was very concerned that children were at risk of abuse. But Bishop Bowen told me that Michael Hill was a priest. Priests don't behave in that way and as far the bishop was concerned there was no substance to my complaint.

Mr B recalls:

> I told him in no uncertain terms that I did not believe that priests should be bathing young children and cutting their hair, or be alone with them at night-time in this way. It was an awkward meeting, quite frankly. I said I wanted the bishop to take some action about Hill. Bishop Bowen refused. Following that meeting I was very dissatisfied with the situation. I felt Hill had to be moved and taken away; his behaviour was not the behaviour of a normal man.
>
> However, since Bishop Bowen was not prepared to do anything, my family and I stopped attending St Teresa's Church and we joined the congregation of a different church, some miles away.

For Mr B – a devout Catholic then and since – Bishop Bowen's 'failure to take action gave Hill the green light to carry on the abuse. Bowen as bishop was supposed to be the shepherd of his flock and care for them but he cast the lambs to Hill to ravage them.'

So Hill remained at Merstham. After five years in charge he was transferred to St Edmund's, Godalming, as parish priest. This was in June 1979. When the twists and turns of Hill's career came under the spotlight many years later, Bishop Murphy-O'Connor,[177] the then Bishop of Arundel and Brighton, maintained that Hill's move to Godalming was 'part of a routine transfer procedure which takes place after a priest has been in a certain location for a period of time'; and indeed there is no information to suggest otherwise. However, we do know that more complaints were starting to be made. During his time in Godalming, Hill sexually assaulted boys at a local residential school, St Dominic's in Hambledon. The school was run by nuns belonging to a Roman Catholic religious order, the Sacred Heart Sisters, and sought to 'provide pupils with a Roman Catholic education in a setting which nurtured such faith and values'. Hill had the task of taking a newsletter up to St Dominic's one evening a week, and befriended boys whilst watching TV with them and chatting to them in their dormitories. One of his victims later described being touched under his bedclothes: 'He started to fondle me. I felt helpless and trapped. I froze and after a few seconds I started to cry. He must have heard me sob 'cause he stopped.'[178]

Interviewed many years later, one of the boys at St Dominic's at that time said he complained about sexual assaults by Hill to one of the sisters there. He was told he was lying: Hill 'would not have done this as he was a man of God'. The boy's family were not told; no further inquiries were made; it was 'pushed under the carpet'. The boy remembered that following the complaint Hill stopped coming to the school.

Bishop Murphy-O'Connor has always denied that he was aware of any complaints in respect of Hill's behaviour at St Dominic's during his time in Godalming, and there is certainly no evidence that the sister passed the complaints on. But other complaints seem to have been lodged with Church officials. On one occasion a boy told his parents of the abuse by Hill, and the boy's father threw Hill out of their home; he says he also informed another parish priest, although it is unclear who that might have been.

We know for certain, however, that a very detailed complaint was made to Bishop Murphy-O'Connor in late summer 1980. Belinda (not her real name) and her husband were parishioners at St Edmund's Church in Godalming when Hill was parish priest; Belinda's two sons were altar boys, and Hill sexually abused them. Hill befriended the family and visited them at home. He had a habit of going upstairs to be with the boys at bedtime.

After a long period, this and other matters aroused Belinda's suspicions. She decided she 'had to act'. In August 1980 the family went on holiday and Hill joined them for part of the time. He insisted on being close to the boys at night-time. Belinda remembers: 'Shortly after our return from holiday, my husband and I had a meeting with Father Hill and confronted him with what had happened. The meeting took place at his home. The meeting lasted about four hours. Father Hill didn't deny our allegations, but he didn't elaborate either.'

Subsequently Hill wrote a letter apologising for what had happened. Belinda has retained the letter, which I publish here with her permission. Dated 24 August 1980, it read:

Dear Mr and Mrs —,

I am writing to you because I cannot bear to wait any longer to tell you how very sorry and ashamed I am for my behaviour. As you know I tried to see you on Thursday 14 August and I called you on my return to Godalming on Friday last, only to find that you were away. I cannot justify nor excuse my behaviour, which was grossly wrong. I have asked God to forgive me and to restore me to his friendship. I do not expect you to restore me to your friendship after such a betrayal, but I do beg your forgiveness.

I am going away for a few days, hoping and praying that the rest will help me to rededicate my life to God in whatever way he now wants me to serve him. I can't help thinking of the words of the psalmist:

With all my voice I cry to the Lord, with all my voice entreat the Lord. I pour out my heart to Him. I call him all my distress while my spirit finds within me. For O Lord know my path ... I cry to you, O Lord, I have said: 'You are my refuge, all I have in the land of the living. Listen, then, to my cry for I am in the depths of distress ... bring my soul out of this prison and then I shall praise your name. Around me the just will assemble because of your goodness to me.'

Please pray for me as I will for you and your family. Believe me it aggrieves me to think I have hurt you and your family as much as I have hurt God. It aggrieves me to think about what I have done when both God and you have done so much for me with your generous and sincere love.

When I was quoting the psalmist, I left out some of his words. They are: 'There is no one who takes my part. I have no means of escape, not one who cares for my soul.' I left that out because I know God understands me and cares for my soul. I know there is someone else who does, and I desperately hope that you do too. Because, believe me, I do love God and his church and his people and I have tried desperately hard, though often not hard enough, to prove my love for twenty years as a priest and I still wish to do so, however heavy my cross may be.

Pray for me.

Yours sincerely, Michael S. Hill

Belinda preserved her diary from that period and was able to tell me that after some initial uncertainty she made some enquiries of the Church:

I had a meeting in a car park in Henley with a Mr Coote. He was something to do with the Church ... This meeting took place on 3 September 1980. We sat in the car with him and told him about what had happened. He told us that we had to bring this to the attention of the Church locally.[179]

On 13 September 1980, Belinda and her husband had a meeting with a Monsignor McConnon, a diocesan official.

We told him about what Father Hill had done. Initially we didn't mention names. At the end of the meeting, however, he told us he had to know who was involved if he was going to be able to do anything about it. I gave him a copy of the letter from Father Hill in which Father Hill apologised for what had happened. Obviously he immediately realised that it was Father Hill. I remember him saying when he saw Father Hill's handwriting: 'You don't have to name him – I know who it is.' He told us that we had to go and see the Bishop, so we made an appointment to go and see Bishop Cormac.

The meeting with Bishop Cormac took place on 16 September 1980. We showed the Bishop the letter from Father Hill. Bishop Cormac said that he would have to do something. He accepted that the abuse had occurred. Basically, his attitude seemed to be that he was going to move Hill to a new parish.

From Belinda's detailed account, it seems very likely that both Monsignor McConnon and Bishop Murphy-O'Connor were aware Hill had sexually abused Belinda's sons and had admitted doing so. However, the question of involving the police was never discussed.

Belinda was able to confirm to me, from her diary, that there was a parish meeting on Friday 3 October 1980, and that at this meeting it was announced that Father Hill was going to a different parish. 'Everybody was aghast that Father Hill was leaving us so soon. They obviously were not aware of what had happened.' It seems that at that stage, it was unclear where Hill was actually going; he was not allocated to a new parish, Heathfield, until early 1981.

Was Hill moved in order to cover up the allegations of abuse? The moving of paedophile priests from one parish to another to hush up complaints has been a persistent feature of the worldwide Catholic abuse scandal and, unsurprisingly, it is the charge which senior clerics are most anxious to refute. Bishop Murphy-O'Connor has repeatedly denied that he moved Hill in response to sexual allegations. When the scandal broke in 2000, he was adamant:

In some media reports the implication has been drawn that I was aware at the time of the offences of Father Hill that have since come to light and responded by moving him from parish to parish. This is simply not true. After Father Hill had completed a normal term at Merstham, he was appointed to Godalming. Following a period of disagreement and unrest in the parish (wholly unconnected with any question of child abuse) I realised that this was not a good appointment and in January 1981 moved him to Heathfield.[180]

Belinda, who was active in parish life at the time, disputes that there was 'unrest in the parish', recalling that Hill was 'a popular priest. In fact, when it was announced he was going to a new parish, parishioners who were unaware of the sexual abuse got up a petition saying he should remain.' In fairness to Bishop Murphy-O'Connor, his claim that there was unrest in the parish was corroborated in 2000 by Father Jim Maguire, curate at Godalming when Hill first arrived in June 1979. He told *The Tablet* that Hill very quickly alienated members of the parish with a plan to divide it in two. 'He upset everybody with his dictatorial style. He was unfriendly, argumentative, contentious. If they went to see him he would give them short shrift ... [Hill] could not work with the parish and the parish could not work with him.'[181]

However, the claim that Hill's move had nothing whatsoever to do with Belinda's complaint is difficult to accept. Hill himself said many years later that he had been moved from Godalming because of complaints of sexual misconduct; he was never directly confronted by the bishop about it, but he got moved from Godalming to Heathfield because of it. That, of course, may simply have been Hill's incorrect assumption; we cannot know. But the detailed evidence of Belinda's complaints to Coote, to McConnon and then to Murphy-O'Connor, and the timeline of events, seems to bear him out. Bishop Murphy-O'Connor said later that there was no explicit complaint of sexual abuse, simply that Hill had 'taken too much interest' in a boy. But Belinda remembers otherwise:

> We gave him the facts of what was going on in a very cool, calm way. Why else would we have gone to see the Bishop? We told him that he had befriended us and had been putting his hands in my boys' beds and down their sleeping bags and we showed him the letters from Father Hill.[182]

And she must be right, because in July 1981 Hill was sent for counselling explicitly related to his sexual misconduct. Hill attended the Dympna Centre for therapy between July and September 1981, where he was seen by Father Louis Marteau. In one of the many letters from this saga later leaked to the press, the bishop wrote to Father Marteau in July 1981:

> As you will have gathered from our conversation on the phone, the matter is very serious, and I would be most grateful for a full report from you when you have finished the examination and consultation with him. It is a question of not only what continuing care he needs, but also whether he should have the pastoral care of a parish at the present time.

'The matter is very serious': of course, at that time Hill did have the pastoral care of a parish, Heathfield, where Bishop Murphy-O'Connor had installed him in January 1981. Either the serious matter was Belinda's complaint, or another complaint had come to light by July 1981. It was almost certainly the former: in 1997, the Vicar-General of Arundel and Brighton, Monsignor John Hull, told the police that Hill was referred to the Dympna Centre as a direct result of Belinda's complaint.[183]

In any event, the chronology strongly suggests that Hill was moved away from Godalming because of the events involving Belinda's sons. Hill wrote his letter of apology to Belinda and her husband on 24 August 1980; they met with Mr Coote on 3 September; they met with Monsignor McConnon on 13 September and showed him Hill's letter; they met with Bishop Murphy-O'Connor on 16 September, and recalled him saying that Hill would need to be moved to a new parish; and the public announcement of Hill's departure from Godalming came on 3 October, just over two weeks later. It seems that Hill did not actually start ministering in Heathfield until January 1981, confirming the impression of a departure from Godalming in indecent haste. In the light of that timeline, it is hard to believe that Hill's departure was unconnected with Belinda's allegations. In fact, when he was interviewed by Jeremy Paxman on BBC *Newsnight* many years later, the now Archbishop Murphy-O'Connor seemed to concede this, stating that 'with Michael Hill, I took him out of a parish after allegations made against him, sent him for therapy...'[184]

What happened next? After seeing Hill, Father Marteau reported back to the bishop that Hill was cooperative in interview; Father Marteau concluded that Hill's sexuality

has really not caused him any major problems for the first twenty years of his priesthood so the question which now poses itself is why now? ... My own feeling about sexuality, both physiologically and psychologically is that it has to do with the creative instinct in human nature. It would seem in some way his creativity ... is in some way blocked...

Father Marteau's analysis seems amateurish; no proper attempt was made to unpick what Hill had really been doing, and his claim that his sexuality had been dormant for twenty years was accepted at face value. It reflects the otherworldly belief of a conservative Catholic therapist that sexuality can simply be switched off or buried. The outcome of the therapy is unclear, although Bishop Murphy-O'Connor subsequently asserted that 'at the completion of the sessions, the Dympna Centre assessed Father Hill as being suitable to have the pastoral care of a parish'.[185] Given the poor quality of the medical advice, that seems entirely possible.

And so Hill was back in Heathfield, where he resumed his sex offending. But again, he fell foul of some of his victims' parents. In or around January 1983, John Sullivan, the Dean of Eastbourne, received a complaint from the mother of a boy that Hill behaved inappropriately with her son. The mother remembered the meeting thus:

> He accepted that sexual abuse had taken place. He said it showed that Father Hill was a very lonely man. He promised to 'deal with it' but he told me that the whole legal process would be very upsetting and it would not be in our interests for the police to be contacted. He wanted no more to be said about it, and suggested that if the police got involved it would be terrible for us.[186]

At this point, it seems that Hill was referred to a local Catholic psychiatrist in Chichester, who concluded that he was not suffering from any major psychiatric illness:

> He has a psychosexual disorder in that he identifies himself 'as a homosexual', with young males as his preferred choice of sexual partner. He acknowledges that the overt sexual behaviour/ relationship is inappropriate, but feels that his homosexuality is an integral part of himself and not intrinsically abnormal. He acknowledges numerous episodes of sexual behaviour with young people over the last few years. These generally occur when he is tired; low in spirits and lonely. The young people are frequently those who he recognises as being possibly unhappy, often missing their father, who may not be in the family.

The psychiatrist concluded that Hill needed 'to learn' to avoid the specific situations which led him to abnormal behaviour. 'It would be inappropriate to try and help him require more appropriate sexual partners as he has chosen a life of celibacy.' The psychiatrist warned that 'the prognosis and situation such as Father Michael Hill's must be very guarded'.[187]

On 10 February, Hill left St Catherine's, Heathfield, to start a therapeutic course at the Servants of the Paraclete Clinic in Stroud.[188] He underwent sessions with a psychotherapist, Father Hilary Clark. But within four months Hill had discharged himself, telling Bishop Murphy-O'Connor in a letter dated 24 June 1983 that he was not benefiting from the programme and that remaining there would be 'completely counterproductive'.[189]

Soon afterwards another psychotherapist at Stroud, Father John Murphy, wrote to the bishop emphasising that Hill could reoffend. Although Hill had now 'gained some insights into his paedophilia', Father Murphy cautioned that it was 'very difficult to assess to what extent he has really come to terms with his own sexuality and is prepared to make necessary changes in his behaviour so as to safeguard any further repetitions'. He concluded:

I must say I am wary about another assignment for him … Your Lordship does not need me to point out that there is still a risk that Father Hill will act out again. In fact, no one could give any moral certainty that he would not, especially when he is reported to have said that he believes the children enjoyed their experience with him. While wishing to be just and charitable in Father Hill's regard, I must advise Your Lordship that my thinking is directed towards the good of the faithful and that a high risk does pertain in this case.[190]

One of Father Murphy's medical colleagues, a Dr Spencer, also expressed concern at the risk of Hill committing 'further pederastic acts': 'I am sure he does need to be steered in some direction of a therapeutic nature if you are to avoid further scandal emanating from Michael in the future.'

But Hill did not re-enter therapy; at that point he seems to have withdrawn from ministry for a period, living for some months with a fellow priest in Cranleigh, doing a course at Farnborough College and renting his own house in Crawley (from the mother of one of his victims), presumably paid for by the Church. In August 1983 he was seeking secular employment and between September 1983 and March 1984 he was on a training course for accountancy technicians; this was followed by his employment as an accounts clerk.

So by that time Hill's direction of travel was clearly towards a secular, civilian life. It would have remained so had Bishop Murphy-O'Connor not agreed to bring him back into the ministry. It seems that Hill pleaded with the bishop for another chance: he wrote to Murphy-O'Connor on 1 February 1984, shortly before his fiftieth birthday, that he was saddened 'to think I will not be celebrating it as a practising priest. But I still hope and pray that one day I may have the privilege of serving God and his people as a priest because, though I failed him, I've never wanted to do anything else.'[191]

Eventually, Bishop Murphy-O'Connor gave in to these pleas. 'He begged me on his knees to find something for him,' recalled Murphy-O'Connor. 'I looked up the recommendations, [which said] that he shouldn't be sent back to a parish but he could go to a place where there weren't any children. Unfortunately for me, Gatwick was vacant.'[192] And so, in early 1985, Hill was offered a 'limited ministry in a non-parochial setting as chaplain at Gatwick Airport'. Bishop Murphy-O'Connor has always acknowledged that this decision was a 'grave mistake', whilst also maintaining that he acted at least in part on expert advice. Looking back, Murphy-O'Connor has analysed it thus:

> I think that most of the mistakes that bishops have made have been through being too kind ... the priest is meant to be your brother. Clearly it was a bad mistake and I should have taken counsel. I should have handed him over to the police. But you are talking about the early 1980s. No bishop would have handed a priest over to the police in those days.[193]

A serious mistake it undoubtedly was: the chaplaincy at Gatwick gave Hill access to many vulnerable families, including immigrant families, who desperately needed his help and were easy prey. One of his victims was a disabled boy who arrived with his mother at Gatwick from the USA, homeless and hungry. Hill arranged temporary accommodation for them and gained the mother's trust. He subsequently offered to take the boy on a trip to France, an offer the mother joyfully accepted. Hill and the boy (then aged thirteen and wheelchair bound) started the holiday at Hill's home in Crawley. A later summary of this case recounted:

> During the evening Hill suggested that X take a bath which he ran for him. While in the bath, he discussed the size of X's penis with him and got him to measure it. After the bath, Hill towelled X dry and went with him into the back bedroom of the house, where he started to talk to him about masturbation. Initially, X

was nervous about talking about such things to Hill as he was a priest, but after being reassured by him, the matter was discussed. Hill subsequently got X to get an erection and proceeded to masturbate him, putting Vaseline on his finger and slipping his finger into X's anus as he did so. He masturbated X to ejaculation and gave him some tissues to clean himself up with. Following this Hill lay next to X, pushing his right front tight up against X's back. He then rubbed his erect penis in between X's buttock cheeks until he ejaculated … this also happened on the following day when Hill and X returned from Dieppe. He took X home the following day, but before dropping him off told him not to tell anyone what they had done together.

X was devastated by the abuse: in adult life he started to abuse drugs and alcohol and developed strong feelings of guilt and shame over what happened to him. His sexual and emotional development was affected and he had problems defining his own sexuality. He found it difficult to form and maintain relationships and to trust people, and suffered from anxiety attacks when on his own and bouts of paranoia when outside.[194]

Bishop Murphy-O'Connor's decision to send Hill was made against the backdrop of Dr Clark's assessment in July 1983. Dr Clark observed:

Michael has a particular sexual profile as a homosexual who is attracted to pre-adult teenagers. He has a history of behaviour which has caused retribution and reactions from others. This makes him a difficult man to place in ministry for there is a need to protect his pastoral contacts, the good name of the priesthood and, not least, himself from worse consequences of his behaviour, e.g. police involvement.

We considered Michael's problem in the light of its compulsive nature and the reputation this difficulty has for being recidivistic despite the best of treatment.[195]

The phrase 'the reputation this difficulty has for being recidivistic' is interesting here: the Catholic Church has often argued that the risk of recidivism in paedophiles was not understood in the 1970s and 1980s, but this letter confirms otherwise. And of course Dr Clark was not the only medical expert who had made such an observation about Hill: exactly the same point had been made by Father Murphy and Dr Spencer. We do not, of course, know precisely what information Dr Clark had regarding Hill's offending and the allegations against him, but all of the experts seem to have proceeded on the basis that Hill had an extensive sexual history involving minors.

Dr Clark set out three options. First, that Hill be given a limited ministry that would preclude him from potentially dangerous situations. 'This is a weak possibility. Michael is young, vigorous and enthusiastic and one would find an emasculated ministry frustrating and demeaning. Anyway, external control is a poor guarantee of prevention.' An alternative was restoration to full active ministry:

This is the option that Michael would love to have. He feels that his experience at Graylingwell and Brownshill [clinics] has given him the opportunity to deal with many repressed negative feelings that gave power to his compulsive behaviour. Michael says he has a positive accepting attitude towards his sexual orientation and that his sexual drive is well under control. Add to this the vindictive consequences of his ever acting out again and he feels he has an array of defences to keep him both happy and safe in active ministry. My comment on this option is that here we are asking Bishop Cormac to take a calculated risk on a contractual basis, i.e., one offence and Michael is out of the ministry. Can such a risk be taken to give Michael a second chance, and how would Michael feel under the threat of such a contract?[196]

The third option was 'that Michael take a leave of absence for an indefinite period and seek further treatment'. This was the option Dr Clark seemed to recommend, although the letter is not totally clear; the recommendation was implicit rather than explicit and the remainder of the letter was taken up with 'Michael's anxieties' about option three and how they might be addressed.

In his press statement of 19 July 2000, Bishop Murphy-O'Connor responded to criticism of his decision to send Hill back into ministry at Gatwick:

I have stated openly and clearly that some issues regarding Father Hill's behaviour were raised with me prior to 1983. My reaction was to challenge him and require him to undergo assessment and counselling. It was only in 1983 that allegations of a specific and more serious nature were made and I immediately took action: removing Father Hill from the parish, and ensuring he received further professional assessment and, later, therapy. In the light of the assessment I withdrew his licence to work in a parish and for eighteen months he worked in a commercial office. The advice I had received in 1983 included an option that he might work in some restricted pastoral role outside of a parish. In 1985 I decided

to follow this option and he was offered an industrial chaplaincy.
Of course it is true to say that if the strict procedures for child
protection that are now in place in Arundel and Brighton diocese
had been in operation then, the matter would have been handled
differently. I maintain that with the facts then known to me the
decisions made at that time in his regard were not irresponsible.

He went on:

It is always quite difficult to look back over twenty years or so
and to recall attitudes to child abuse that were commonplace at
that time. With hindsight, what still surprises me is the amount
of genuine ignorance that there was, not only among bishops
and priests, but also in society at large, including the medical
profession, about the compulsive nature of child abuse. To my
knowledge, no direction or instruction on this matter was given
in seminary formation at that time, and doctors and psychiatrists
to whom I have spoken have also admitted their comparative
ignorance, at that time, of these issues. This is not to excuse but
rather to explain the inadequate measures taken in times past, not
only for child protection but also for truly confident and accurate
assessment by professional people. It is now clear that child abuse
is not rarely encountered in the community at large and this
distressing fact is now more openly recognised.

In the context of the advice received from those who had treated
Hill, this seems unconvincing. It is true that Dr Clark's letter did
not categorically recommend any particular option, and to that
extent the medical evidence was not unequivocal. However, the
industrial chaplaincy at Gatwick was characterised by Dr Clark

as a 'weak possibility' because 'external control is a poor guarantee of prevention'. But, most importantly, given what we know of the medical evidence in this case, it is impossible to accept Murphy-O'Connor's claim that there was 'genuine ignorance ... not only among bishops and priests, but also in society at large, including the medical profession, about the compulsive nature of child abuse'. Dr Clark had specifically highlighted 'the risk of recidivism', and the other experts had repeatedly made the same point; this risk should have been obvious as the Church was aware of several allegations against Hill by this time, and Hill himself had admitted multiple sexual episodes with children. The suggestion that mistakes in the Hill case can be blamed on the lack of medical understanding of paedophilia at that time is refuted by the documents.

Hill remained in his post at Gatwick, living in a diocesan house – and continuing to abuse children – until retirement in October 1996. Either at the time of or shortly after his retirement, Hill was cautioned for an indecent assault on an adult in Slough. But his retirement coincided with the police investigation into his activities many years earlier and he was eventually convicted and jailed in 1997; Belinda's sons were amongst those who gave evidence against him. Hill was convicted of ten specimen counts of sexual assault on minors whilst a priest of various parishes between 1978 and 1985.

At that stage, Hill maintained that his offending was limited to a few years from the late 1970s to the mid-1980s. Later, following treatment, Hill admitted to a much longer list of offences extending over a period of nearly forty years. But following the 1997 trial there were already suggestions that the Catholic Church had been complicit in covering up Hill's behaviour. Several victims

wrote to Cardinal Hume to point out that 'his perversity operated within the context of his pastoral relationship and thus his
victims were subject to repeated assaults by a man placed in a
position of trust and authority by the diocese',[197] and to suggest
that the Church had long known more about Hill's proclivities
than it cared to admit. Cardinal Hume simply passed the letter
to Bishop Murphy-O'Connor, who expressed his 'great sadness
and grief over this whole matter' but resisted any suggestion that
the Church might be culpable. In 1998, legal proceedings were
commenced against the Diocese of Arundel and Brighton and
against Bishop Murphy-O'Connor personally, alleging that

> they failed to report their knowledge of the evidence of abuse
> against Father Hill to the police; failed to take away Father Hill's
> pastoral licence and permitted him to continue to work as a
> priest; and failed to warn the claimants or their parents of Father
> Hill's past record of sexual abuse of children.

These proceedings were resolved shortly before Bishop Murphy-
O'Connor was announced as Hume's successor.

How should we assess the Church's handling of the Hill case?
The most egregious fault in the case was the failure to involve
the police at any stage; in fact, it was worse than that because
there is evidence that families – such as the mother who saw
the Dean of Eastbourne in 1983 – were actively discouraged
from going to the police. This was in a context in which there
had been numerous complaints about Hill dating back to 1976,
starting with Mr B's approach to Bishop Bowen and continuing
with a series of detailed complaints from anguished families;
in a context in which Hill himself, in treatment, had admitted

numerous sexual episodes with minors; and in a context in which medical experts warned about the risks of recidivism. These failings were disastrous and avoidable: not all of them were the fault of Bishop Murphy-O'Connor. The best that can be said in the bishop's defence was that medical input was sought at an early stage of his own involvement in the Hill saga; in this sense, the case is probably unusual at that time as allegations were often hushed up without medical advice being obtained. But the medical advice was that Hill was a serial sex offender who was likely to reoffend, and it did not support the return to ministry at Gatwick. As we shall see in the next chapter, when those facts became publicly known, the pressure on the Catholic hierarchy became overwhelming.

CHAPTER 8

NOLAN

When Basil Hume died in June 1999 he was Britain's most popular religious leader. Lionised by press and public, the Archbishop of Westminster was barely touched by the abuse crisis. In 2005, six years after his death, questions started to be asked about his handling of complaints at Ampleforth.[198] But even then, little of the scandal seemed to taint Hume personally. His biographer, writing in 2006, claimed that Hume was fortunate in that there were no scandals during his watch over the English Church comparable to those in Scotland and Ireland.[199] This is not really true. But Hume was a canny media operator. He adopted a low profile whenever the abuse issue hit the headlines, only commenting publicly on events in own diocese.

Hume was able to sidestep difficult questions partly because the Archbishop of Westminster's role in the national Church is ambiguous. The archbishop is often referred to as head of the Catholic Church in England and Wales. This is not quite right: although the Archbishop of Westminster is undoubtedly *primus inter pares* amongst his fellow Catholic bishops,[200] he does not, at least as archbishop, have any authority over the other English dioceses. In the 1990s, faced with the allegations emerging from Birmingham and elsewhere, Hume hid behind the fact that every Catholic bishop has exclusive jurisdiction in his own diocese, and is accountable only to the Pope. In 1997, responding to a letter from victims of Father Michael Hill, Hume did not even pretend to address the broader questions raised by the case: 'Every diocese in this country is independent of another. I have no jurisdiction ... I cannot involve myself when I have no power to do so.'[201] He had nothing further to add. His answer was technically correct, but to remain silent on the wider lessons of the case was an abdication of leadership. Child abuse was, after all, the foremost challenge confronting the Church. In fact, Hume did have a measure of executive authority over the whole of the English Church, not as archbishop, but as President of the Bishops' Conference.[202] His successor used that position to drive through the Nolan reforms. But Hume, who, as Paul Johnson observed, was ever alive to his standing with the chattering classes, took care to ensure that he was only ever going to be on the hook for Westminster. He was lucky; scandals which might have blotted his reputation remained hidden until after his death.

His successor, Cormac Murphy-O'Connor, was appointed in February 2000. Approaching seventy, he was a surprise choice. In twenty-two years as Bishop of Arundel and Brighton he had almost never been in the spotlight and could appear otherworldly in dealing with the media. Unfortunately for the Church, within three months of his appointment the Hill affair had turned into a media firestorm. An investigation by the BBC Radio 4 *Today* programme exposed leaked documents relating to the Hill case and revealed that litigation against Murphy-O'Connor by several of Hill's victims had been settled just a few months earlier on conditions of strict confidentiality. The legal claims alleged that Murphy-O'Connor had been negligent in his handling of Hill from the early 1980s onwards. In effect, embarrassing allegations against Murphy-O'Connor had been quietly buried in readiness for his new job. Only a few months into the post he was facing calls to resign.

Murphy-O'Connor's public performances during this period were sometimes clumsy but his response to the crisis was far more decisive than Hume's; he used his authority as President of the Bishops' Conference to announce the establishment of an independent commission under Lord Nolan with a wide-ranging brief to transform child protection in the English Church. Of course, Murphy-O'Connor acted under intense pressure from victims and the media, but his genuine determination to implement comprehensive reform should be acknowledged. In creating the Nolan Commission, a majority of whose members were non-Catholic, Murphy-O'Connor acted unilaterally, without consulting his fellow bishops and effectively presenting them with a fait accompli which, given the frenzied media atmosphere, they were powerless to resist. Explicit in Nolan's remit was a 'one Church' approach; legal niceties about the jurisdiction of this or that bishop were to be set aside in favour of a comprehensive national strategy. Although this has proved difficult to implement in practice, Murphy-O'Connor deserves credit for trying and his approach was unique amongst Catholic leaders worldwide; others would have done well to follow his example. He was unable, however, to persuade some Catholic orders like the Benedictine Congregation to participate, a refusal which has returned to haunt the Benedictines, who have featured heavily in the abuse scandal in the post-Nolan period.[203]

Nolan's final report was published in September 2001 and was unanimously endorsed by the Bishops' Conference. 'A

Programme for Action' set out comprehensive new procedures and structures for dealing with abuse in the Church. Rather ambitiously, the report began by asserting that the Church in England and Wales should become 'an example of best practice in the prevention of child abuse and in responding to it'. To achieve this would require a unified, 'one Church' approach: 'It is crucial that the policies and practices we recommend are implemented throughout the Church and are, therefore, adopted both by bishops and their dioceses and by religious superiors and their orders.' This, Nolan acknowledged, would not be straightforward, since

> each diocesan bishop exercises his power autonomously though not in a totally independent manner ... In canon law, every diocesan bishop has equivalent status, and only the Holy See has the power to control and limit the exercise of the bishops' power. Religious orders are governed by their own specific law and constitutions and, in general, the diocesan bishop has no capacity to intervene in their internal affairs.

Nevertheless, Nolan was confident that 'by acting together in the best interests of children and of the Church, bishops and religious superiors can put in place arrangements which are effective and can restore confidence'. This, however, would only be achieved through several fundamental reforms:

> A single set of policies, principles and practices based on the paramountcy principle ... effective and speedy implementation in parishes, dioceses and religious orders ... an organisational structure in the parish ... a national capability (the National Child

Protection Unit) which will advise dioceses and orders, coordinate where necessary, and monitor and report on progress; and the provision of adequate resources to support these arrangements.

Nolan was right to identify all these features as being critical to a successful child protection strategy; he did not foresee how controversial they would prove to be within the Church. With the benefit of ten years' hindsight, we can see more clearly that many aspects of Nolan, whilst straightforward in secular terms, constituted a radical departure from previous Catholic norms. For example, one of Nolan's demands was that the lay voice must be heard through the appointment of a lay child protection representative (PCPR) in every parish with the responsibility 'to ensure that diocesan policies and procedures are known and followed, that awareness is raised, and that principles are worked through into everyday practice'. This seems unexceptional from a secular perspective, but the notion that clergy would take orders from laity (particularly women) was alien to the Catholic Church and in practice would meet significant resistance.

Similarly, the idea that the reforms would be centrally coordinated through the establishment of a National Child Protection Unit ran counter to the devolved diocesan structure of the Church, particularly as the unit would be policing the implementation of Nolan and using compulsion where necessary. Nolan said:

The unit should bring any apparent failure in diocesan or religious order arrangements immediately to the attention of the bishop or religious superior and make regular reports to diocesan bishops and religious superiors on the effectiveness of arrangements in

each diocese and order. It should also make annual reports, which
should be published, to the Bishops' Conference.

This name-and-shame function constituted a wholly new level
of external oversight of diocesan behaviour; an entirely necessary and justified one given the lamentable history but, as events
would prove, a very difficult change to implement successfully in
the face of resistance on the ground.

Nolan did not comment on specific cases but they clearly
influenced the commission's thinking. The committee presumably had the Jordan case in mind when recommending that
'bishops and religious superiors should not overrule selection
boards where reservations are expressed about a candidate's suitability for ordination on the grounds of possible risks to children'.
Diocesan independence was no excuse:

> We have heard of cases where there has been inadequate sharing
> of information between one diocese and another, or where those
> in charge of a candidate's formation in the seminary have not
> had access to information known to the selection board. In some
> cases, this has produced situations in which children have been
> exposed to serious harm … we regard it as essential that those
> who are involved in advising on or making decisions about the
> formation and ordination of candidates should have access to all
> the necessary information.

Hence, 'the Church should maintain a single national database
of information on all applicant candidates for ordained priesthood … and decisions should not be made by selection boards,
bishops or religious superiors without reference to it'.

Getting then to the heart of the issue, Nolan set out that 'disclosures and suspicions should always be investigated and acted on swiftly'. Nolan was clear that there would be no excuse for not sharing information with the authorities:

When there is a disclosure, the statutory authorities should be brought in straight away, without any process of filtering, to take the lead in investigating and assessing the situation ... when there is or was only a suspicion, the CPC (Child Protection Coordinator) should arrange for an initial assessment to be made to discern simply whether there are concerns that should be acted upon. If there are any such concerns, then the statutory authorities should be brought in.

The paramountcy principle meant:

Following the initial risk assessment, the person against whom allegations have been made may need to be withdrawn from any contact with the child concerned or possibly any other child. This removes risk to the child, allows the investigation to proceed and safeguards the rights of the alleged abuser.

This would apply to clergy just as much as laity:

We can see no grounds for treating clergy differently from lay people in this respect. The importance of removing risk to the child, allowing the investigation to proceed and safeguarding the rights of the clergy is just as great. Our clear view is therefore that, on the recommendation of the CPC and his/her team, following consultation with social services and the police, any priest or deacon should be required to take administrative leave (the nearest equivalent for a priest of suspension for a secular employee) at a location to be determined by the bishop.

On the conflict between the paramountcy principle and canon law in these circumstances,[204] Nolan was circumspect:

We are aware that 'administrative leave' is provided for in canon law within the context of a judicial trial initiated by the Church. But we underline the necessity for the Church to have satisfactory administrative procedures to achieve the withdrawal of the priest or deacon from contact with children in those circumstances where a judicial procedure has not been, or cannot be, initiated by the Church. It is well understood in professions such as teaching that suspension in these circumstances does not imply guilt.

Of all aspects of Nolan, none has proved more controversial within the Church than this. Priests do not see themselves as comparable to other professionals and have tried to insist that canon law should prevail.

Nolan considered what would happen if an allegation is not proved but suspicions remain:

After an allegation has been investigated, the case may be dropped or the alleged perpetrator found not guilty. In these cases, a thorough risk assessment should be made. Desirably, this assessment will be undertaken with the statutory authorities, or at least with the benefit of relevant evidence collected by them in the course of their investigations. The outcome of this risk assessment should always be acted on so that a person is not placed in any role that might put children at risk.

Precisely what this meant would prove to be controversial in practice although at the time Nolan could not sensibly do more than enunciate a general principle.

Where an allegation is proved, Nolan adopted the secular principle that a person who has been cautioned or convicted of a serious offence against children should no longer be allowed to hold any position that could possibly put children at risk: 'The committee believes, in accordance with the paramountcy principle, that the Church should adopt and implement a similar principle. The bishop or religious superior should justify any exceptions to this approach publicly (for example, by means of a letter to be read out in churches at Mass).' Nolan conceded that 'implementation will … need to be done in a way that accords with the structures and processes of the Church'. So far as lay workers are concerned, 'the position of the Church is substantially the same as that of many other organisations'. However, 'the position of clergy is more difficult. Most posts to which priests might be appointed are likely to involve some contact with children. Nonetheless, the general principle needs to apply in their case too.'

This begged the question of whether convicted priests would automatically be laicised (i.e. dismissed from the clerical state). As Nolan acknowledged, most people would assume that laicisation is 'the appropriate penalty whenever clergy are convicted or cautioned of a child abuse offence'. Here, however, the Nolan Committee slightly pulled its punches, noting:

Laicisation is the most serious perpetual penalty that can be imposed by the Church. Normally it can be imposed only after a formal judicial process involving a collegiate tribunal of three judges. Furthermore it can be argued that clergy can be much better supervised if they remain as clergy than if they are laicised (because it is argued that in the latter case the Church will have no further relationship with them, and no role in their supervision).

Nolan concluded that 'laicisation is an extreme step which is not always appropriate. Our report covers the whole range of child abuse, not only sexual abuse, and laicisation will not be a proportionate response in every case.' However,

we believe that the principle to be applied is that laicisation should be considered appropriate where (in the words of a comparable decided case) 'all right-thinking members of the public, knowing all the facts, would feel that justice has not been done by any other course'. We suggest, therefore, that if a priest or deacon is convicted of a criminal offence against children and is sentenced to serve a term of imprisonment of twelve months or more … then it would normally be right to initiate the process of laicisation. The period of twelve months is the minimum period adopted by statute for the compulsory disqualification of adult offenders from working with children…

Nolan was well aware of the problems this would present in terms of canon law and custom and practice in the Church, where laicisation would need Vatican approval, might take years and might be impossible in any case because of canonical time limits:

We say 'initiate' because we are aware that laicisation (except by consent) is the decision of a tribunal at the end of a legal process. We also appreciate that in cases where the events took place some years ago the normal canon law process would not be available because of the statute of limitations. However, we understand that even such cases can be taken forward by reference to the Holy See.[205]

In the decade since the publication of Nolan, the failure to laicise convicted priests in accordance with its recommendations has become a major controversy. Given subsequent events,[206] it is important to note that Nolan explicitly rejected the excuse that laicisation could be counterproductive for managing clerical sex offenders because it would necessarily sever the connection between priest and Church: 'Laicisation does not mean that the Church has no further part to play in relation to the abuser. As with lay worker abusers who are no longer employed by the Church, the Church may nonetheless be able to assist with the rehabilitation and pastoral needs of the individual.'

Nolan then went on to address the critical issue of past (or 'historic') allegations:

It is sometimes suggested that cases where the allegation is of abuse that took place some years ago can be handled differently, and by implication with less urgency or rigour, from those that are current. We do not take this view. The evidence is that those who have abused in the past may still represent considerable risks in the present. It is for this reason important to treat such allegations in the same way as current allegations ... By extension, it is our view that there may be current risks arising from cases in the past that are known to the Church but, in the then state of knowledge about child abuse, were not acted on or not acted on fully at the time.

This meant that 'bishops and religious superiors should ensure that all such cases are the subject of an assessment as soon as possible and that there is appropriate follow-up action'. Old allegations would be reopened; the stables would be cleansed.

The weakest sections of Nolan concerned vulnerable adults and pastoral support for survivors. The issue of vulnerable adults was largely ignored as being outside the committee's remit and expertise.[207] In relation to survivors, the report retreated into vague platitudes about making a 'support person' available. There was no information on how such people would be recruited, their qualifications and experience, their precise role and how they would be funded. In truth, and contrary to the pleas of many survivor groups, Nolan's expectation was that future support would mostly come from outside the Church: the National Child Protection Unit would compile and maintain a 'database of services to meet the needs, including the spiritual needs, of survivors and their families'. The commission's assumption was that, irrespective of their wishes, the needs of survivors would be met by external organisations, not by the Church which had harmed them: they would be shuffled off as someone else's responsibility. Nolan did not really bother to listen to the detailed submissions from survivor organisations.[208]

That was a significant failing. But much of the rest of Nolan represented – at least on paper – a decisive break with the past, and a compelling prospectus for a better system of child protection in the future. Of course, the Church had already committed itself to upholding the paramountcy principle in 1994.[209] But what was new was an explicit 'one Church' approach, a policing mechanism, and a commitment to face up to past allegations in the same way as new ones. Nolan was endorsed unanimously by the Bishops' Conference. However, the real question was not whether the Church wanted to be seen to change, but whether it could and would actually do so in practice.

• • •

The publication of Nolan and the creation of a new child protection apparatus did little to stem the tide of media hostility. In his first three years as Archbishop of Westminster, Cormac Murphy-O'Connor was subjected to a sustained assault on his record: speaking in 2012, he described it as 'relentless' and his 'most difficult period as a bishop'.[210] Several factors contributed. The confidentiality agreements in the Hill claims fostered the impression of a cover-up. Murphy-O'Connor was accused of having tried to 'silence' the victims. Technically, the confidentiality agreements only prohibited the victims from speaking about the financial settlements, not about the abuse itself, or about the Church's handling of Hill. Nevertheless, this prohibition was significant, because the payments were an implicit acknowledgement of Murphy-O'Connor's mistakes. At that time, a claimant seeking compensation had to prove negligence. Although the cases were settled without any formal admission of liability, in paying the claims, Murphy-O'Connor was effectively acknowledging fault (as he later did publicly). The confidentiality agreements were interpreted by the media, perhaps not unreasonably, as an attempt to conceal his culpability.

The Hill case also kept reappearing in the news. In 2002, Hill received a second jail sentence after pleading guilty to further charges of indecent assault. The publicity which followed the first prosecution had emboldened other victims to break their silence, and Hill himself had made extensive further disclosures in the course of treatment. As it became clear that Hill had abused many more children than he had originally admitted, some journalists inferred that Murphy-O'Connor had other things to hide, and set about investigating other cases in Arundel and Brighton.

Some of these cases – uncovered by the BBC Radio 4 *Today* programme's Angus Stickler – begged uncomfortable questions, and the Church's response was often shaky and unconvincing. A Father Tim Garrett had been convicted of taking indecent photographs of boys during the 1980s, but had been permitted to move from the Diocese of Portsmouth to take up a new role in Arundel and Brighton whilst Murphy-O'Connor was bishop. Interviewed in the *Daily Telegraph*, Murphy-O'Connor admitted:

> I think in the light of Nolan I wouldn't have accepted him today. I do think, however, that the decision that I took to accept the priest at the request of the Bishop after the professional assessment was not unjustified. In fact, since that time there has never been any complaint against that priest.[211]

Clearly, however, the case raised the question of whether a priest who would not be accepted after Nolan should remain in post: notwithstanding Nolan's promise of a comprehensive trawl of historic cases, the Church's position was unclear.

Even more seriously, one of the cases exposed by the BBC raised fundamental questions about the Church's ability to manage clergy who might pose a continuing risk. At a news conference in December 2002, Murphy-O'Connor and his successor at Arundel and Brighton, Bishop Kieran Conry, were questioned repeatedly about Father Christopher Maxwell-Stewart, who was alleged to have molested children in the early 1980s when he worked in Chichester. Father Maxwell-Stuart was charged in 1996 with indecent assaults on three children but the case was dropped for insufficient evidence. A professional assessment conducted by a hospital in the United States had concluded that Father Maxwell-Stewart should not have primary responsibility for ministry to children but that he was not a paedophile. In a *Newsnight* interview a few weeks earlier, Murphy-O'Connor had given assurances that Father Maxwell-Stewart 'had been put in a situation where in fact he was away from children' and had been placed under a contract restricting his activities.[212] But *Newsnight* discovered that Father Maxwell-Stuart was living in a house in Deal, Kent, overlooking the local primary school; had been celebrating Mass once a month for the previous four years at the Church of the Sacred Heart at Walmer, Kent; and had instructed children in the faith. He was openly flouting the restrictions imposed upon him. Pressed on this, Bishop Conry claimed that the Church was powerless to act because Father Maxwell-Stuart had not been convicted of any crime. The Church could do nothing to force Father Maxwell-Stewart to abide by the terms of his contract because 'he hadn't broken the law in terms of the civil law or the Church's law. The point of a contract is that two people agree with it. If one person breaks it, we have no sanctions.'[213]

Bishop Conry's comments were completely at odds with the whole thrust of Nolan. In any case, surely in these circumstances a bishop could withdraw a priest's faculties?[214] Canon lawyers disagreed with Conry:

> When a priest is ordained, he is entrusted with the duty of providing pastoral care. If a risk assessment concluded the priest posed a risk to children, he would no longer be able to fulfil this obligation ... A priest is bound by his promise of obedience to his bishop. If he is in a restricted ministry and he fails to keep to the terms of that, he is failing in his duty as a priest. There are a series of steps that could be taken, ending in dismissal from the priesthood.[215]

The bishop may have misspoken in the heat of a press conference. Or he had misunderstood the legal position or, worse, had unwittingly acknowledged a serious obstacle to the implementation of Nolan; neither explanation inspired confidence. Conry's answer suggested that even senior bishops who were responsible for implementing Nolan were uncertain about the new ground rules. Responding on the issue, Eileen Shearer, the new head of COPCA, the Catholic Office for the Protection of Children and Vulnerable Adults, acknowledged 'a serious gap' between referral for investigation to the statutory agencies and ultimate laicisation. 'What goes on in between? While we are developing the national policy on this, with consultation, we are likely to have different practice in different places.'[216]

Murphy-O'Connor attempted to restore his reputation by sending files on all allegations against priests in the Arundel and Brighton diocese to an external solicitor for 'independent' review. This backfired when it transpired that contrary to public assurances, Murphy-O'Connor had put ten cases forward for review but had 'forgotten' about an eleventh.[217] In any case, the review was not truly independent: it was conducted by a solicitor instructed by the Church, and the terms of the instruction were never publicly revealed. So it did little to restore public confidence. Later, Murphy-O'Connor was himself investigated by the police in relation to his mismanagement of the Hill case. A member of the public claimed that he had committed a criminal offence, and a file was sent to the CPS. The outcome was no further action. Whatever Murphy-O'Connor's other mistakes, this was entirely predictable. In the absence of a mandatory reporting law it is difficult to see what crime he could have committed.[218]

The most serious accusation made against Murphy-O'Connor during this period, however, was an outright lie. This was the claim, made by the *News of the World*, that he and a fellow bishop had attempted to bribe Hill into silence. In January 2003 the *News of the World* ran a story headlined 'Cardinal's £50,000 bribe to silence beast priest'. It claimed that Murphy-O'Connor had sent Bishop Howard Tripp of Southwark to visit Hill in prison and offered him a bribe 'to keep his mouth shut and not embarrass the Church any further'; in addition, it claimed that Tripp offered Hill a house and any care he might need. The story was based on a 'transcript' of the alleged conversation between Hill and Tripp.[219] The story was a hoax, and the 'transcript' was a forgery. Murphy-O'Connor complained to the Press Complaints Commission and seven months later the *News of the World* apologised: 'We now know this story to be untrue, although it was based on what we believed at the time to be convincing evidence.'

At the time, Bishop Conry described the story as 'another deliberate attempt to discredit the Cardinal and to force his resignation', but emphasised that this 'is not a media plot. Someone is passing around stories to journalists that are maliciously false. There is no malice on the part of the journalists. They are simply treating information seriously which they believe they are receiving from a reliable source.'[220] In fact, the *News of the World* almost certainly knew at the time of publication that the documents were forged. Two weeks before the story was published, the documents were sent to me. The sender claimed to be in possession of confidential information from a source in Murphy-O'Connor's office, and confidential police and prison documents. Implausibly, he also claimed to be working for the security services. He claimed the security services wanted to damage Murphy-O'Connor – although he did not really explain why. Projects to achieve this end included leaks about the Hill affair and, latterly, the Tripp documents. The security services, he claimed, had also been 'irritated' by Cardinal Hume's saintly reputation; however, they had had a 'hold' over Hume because they had compromising information about his private life – specifically, proof of homosexual liaisons – and Hume knew it, so they 'had him on a leash'.

When this person sent the Tripp documents to me, I strongly suspected they were forgeries: there were several telltale signs and when I questioned him about their provenance I found his answers unconvincing. The forgeries were clearly targeted at Murphy-O'Connor personally. Murphy-O'Connor has always maintained that he did not meet Hill until 1978, and there is no reason to disbelieve him. The forged documents included a 'report' to the police purporting to be from a person who encountered

Hill and Murphy-O'Connor together at the Catholic Children's Society in 1966. This document, which read like a badly written John Grisham novel, was clearly designed to suggest, falsely, that Murphy-O'Connor and Hill had been close friends since the 1960s. The aim was evidently to insinuate that Hill and Murphy-O'Connor had been implicated together, since that time, in some vast criminal conspiracy.

Shortly before publication of the story I was contacted by the *News of the World* for comment. I told them that the Tripp story was a hoax, and that they should have nothing to do with it. The *News of the World* elected to publish anyway, despite telling me privately that they doubted the authenticity of the material. It seems that more responsible media outlets came very close to running the story, but backed off at the last minute.

• • •

Some prominent Catholics, including Murphy-O'Connor himself, have complained that news reporting of the abuse scandal during this period was not only unfairly biased against the Church, but was fuelled by anti-Catholic prejudice. Is this justified? The 'beast priest' article was certainly shoddy and dishonest. However, the *News of the World* was never exactly a byword for responsible journalism, and Murphy-O'Connor and Tripp were just two of its many innocent victims. But the more serious accusation is that, in common with much of the British Establishment, the BBC and the quality press was – and still is – riddled with anti-Catholicism, 'the last acceptable prejudice', to use Philip Jenkins's phrase.[221] It was also suggested that Angus Stickler was recruited to the *Today* programme specifically to 'cause trouble' for the Catholic Church.[222] John Wilkins, a prominent Catholic journalist who edited *The Tablet* during this period, and who is respected for his independence and objectivity, thinks there 'undoubtedly was a bit of malice' against the Church in the coverage of the abuse scandal. Wilkins acknowledges that, at least in part, this was an inevitable reaction to the Church's self-proclaimed moral superiority: 'A Church which sets itself up in judgement on others, which has an iron grip on the flock, which wants to control sex, it becomes an irresistible target.'[223]

Murphy-O'Connor certainly became the whipping boy for systemic failings in the institution, even though he probably did more than anyone at a senior level in the Catholic Church to tackle clerical abuse. The media focus on individuals is inevitable and at times Murphy-O'Connor got the tone wrong, seeming to focus on the damage to the Church rather than the damage to victims – a stance that unsurprisingly reinforced media hostility. In November 2002, facing repeated calls to resign, he asked priests in his Diocese of Westminster to read out a personal statement to thousands of worshippers at morning Mass:

> As you know, not only I personally but the whole Catholic Church in England and Wales has been under attack from some quarters during these past days ... For myself, I deeply regret any damage that has been done following a mistaken decision in the past ... Failure of course has to be acknowledged, but we also recognise the gift of the Lord's forgiveness.[224]

The phrase 'any damage that has been done' and the trope about forgiveness were doubly unfortunate, since as more than one newspaper pointed out, a very great deal of damage had been done to victims, and only they could decide whether to forgive. Paeans from senior Catholic clerics about forgiveness – at around the same time Archbishop Conti of Glasgow made similar off-colour remarks – have been, for victims, a particularly repellent feature of this scandal.

As lawyer acting for victims, I could see that media coverage of individual cases was sometimes oversimplistic. One case unearthed by the BBC concerned a Father Love, whom the *Today* programme described as having 'assaulted two young boys in Glasgow' in the 1980s and who was then transferred to Arundel and Brighton from Glasgow in 1991. *The Tablet* pointed out that Father Love had always denied the allegation of inappropriate behaviour, that a police investigation had resulted in no further action and that the Glasgow archdiocese had sent Father Love for a professional assessment which had concluded there was no reason to prevent him returning to a parish. *The Tablet* concluded:

Murphy-O'Connor is entitled to feel deeply indignant at the way he was treated by the BBC ... No one who listened [to the *Today* programme] could have failed to be struck and touched by what the families concerned were saying and the pain of their experience. It is entirely understandable that they might complain to the media if they felt the Church and the statutory authorities had failed them. But there is then a corresponding duty on the media to hear the Church's part of the story and present it fairly. Archbishop's House were never told what the allegations in the *Today* programme were to be, and so never had any chance to check the facts. Much of the programme consisted of the reporter interviewing actors pretending to be members of the public who apparently had a grievance against the cardinal. Names and voices were disguised, places concealed, 'to protect identities' so it was said, a device which made answering the charges – or even judging their inherent plausibility – almost impossible. But at the heart of the programme came the admission, undermining its entire drift, that 'parents, victims and parishioners concede that the church authorities appeared to follow the letter of their law, but not the spirit'.[225] The Church had indeed followed the letter: in all the new cases cited the allegations had been reported to the police and child protection authorities and, after an investigation with the Church's full cooperation, no further action was recommended. There was no acknowledgement by *Today* that it is the task of the bishop in such circumstances to assess the risk. The clear sense of the commentary, backed up by further anonymous voices, was that the priests concerned were nevertheless guilty, and that the Church knew or ought to have known that and yet kept them in post where they had contact with children … What are church authorities to do when allegations are made but not proved, even after extensive police and social services investigations? Many priests feel that the principle enshrined for everyone else – innocent till proved guilty – no longer applies to them … But the *Today* programme did not stretch to such real and interesting questions.[226]

There is some merit in these points: black-and-white media coverage of abuse cases often obscures difficult legal dilemmas and problems of risk management. But is this fuelled by anti-Catholic prejudice? Having acted in abuse cases for twenty years I can recall countless of examples of media misreporting or oversimplification of complex issues. These failings apply to reporting of abuse in a whole range of institutions: care homes, schools and hospitals, as well as religious organisations. The quality of media reporting may well be declining as traditional press and TV try to outdo each other with ever more lurid stories in a shrinking market. Stories always focus on, and exaggerate, the element of individual culpability as opposed to systemic failure; it makes for better copy.

That said, the whiff of anti-Catholic prejudice cannot be entirely denied. Philip Jenkins maintains that anti-Catholic sentiment is rife in the news media and popular culture, and something of that was undoubtedly present during this period: Margaret Kennedy, then head of the clerical abuse survivors campaign group MACSAS (Ministry and Clergy Sexual Abuse Survivors), recalled that when she was telephoned by reporters, they only wanted to know about Catholic cases: 'I tried to tell them that it [abuse] was a problem in all the churches, but they were only interested in the Catholic ones.'[227] Kennedy felt that some of the coverage was 'definitely malicious'.

However, the point should not be overstated. Jenkins was writing during the papacies of John Paul II and Benedict XVI. His thesis may be undermined by the media's lauding of Pope Francis and maybe the simple truth is that there was much that was wrong with Pope Francis's predecessors. Similarly, it is indisputable that in its reporting of this scandal the media shone a light on evils which would otherwise have remained hidden. Without Angus Stickler's exposé of the Hill saga on the *Today* programme, Nolan would simply never have happened.

Even at the height of the hostile coverage this fundamental truth was rightly acknowledged by some Catholic bishops. In an open letter to his parishioners in December 2002, Crispian

Hollis, Bishop of Portsmouth, accepted that media criticism of the Church was justified:

> We must not forget that we are in the relentless media spotlight because children have been sexually abused and we have not always handled this matter in a proper way ... We are at fault for our mistakes, however uncomfortable and unhappy that may make us feel. The Church is not the victim in all this — the children are.[228]

The *Catholic Herald* attacked Bishop Hollis for disloyalty, but Bishop Conry made the same point: 'I can quite understand the emotional response of someone who has taken the brunt of this. But a more rational response is to say that if we have done wrong we deserve to be scrutinised and castigated.'[229]

CHAPTER 9

AFTER NOLAN

In January 2002, Eileen Shearer, an experienced child protection social worker and non-Catholic, was appointed to head COPCA, the new Catholic Office for the Protection of Children and Vulnerable Adults. COPCA was to oversee policy implementation on a national basis. Shearer was confident of success: 'The Roman Catholic Church has listened to Lord Nolan's recommendations and intends to implement them. The Church takes these measures extremely seriously.'[230]

Shearer, however, had limited resources: at the time of her first interview with *The Tablet*, five months into the job, she still had no office and was working mainly from home.[231] And from the very start, she encountered resistance. The early years of Nolan saw two developments: a spike in the number of historic allegations,[232] probably as a result of increased publicity around cases like Hill, and a concerted push by COPCA to collate, document and act on past allegations which had been buried in Church archives, or, if not documented, were known to the clerical community. Because the Church had mishandled cases in the past, allegations that had previously been dismissed or buried had to be looked at anew. The paramountcy principle meant that anyone accused of child abuse had to be removed from contact with children whilst an allegation was investigated. In the case of parish priests, this usually meant suspension from active ministry; this in turn would generally mean that the priest must leave the presbytery, which was usually his home. Where the case was not pursued, Nolan recommended that a risk assessment should be undertaken if any concern remained; this could also result in the priest remaining suspended.

This was too much for many priests, who claimed they would now be easy prey for malicious allegations. 'Someone could say that twenty-six years ago I abused them and I would not have a leg to stand on. My reputation would disappear overnight and nothing the Church could do would help me get it back. We are sitting targets,' said one.[233] Priests simply refused to accept that they should be put under the same legal regime as teachers and other professionals working with children. Arguing for a kind of clerical exceptionalism, they claimed that they were different from professionals in the secular world.

There were, they maintained, several reasons why they were different. One was that they had no organised representation: 'If I was part of a professional body, such as that representing social workers or teachers, I would have an organisation behind me. The National Conference of Priests does nothing.'[234] In fact, Nolan had urged that a 'support person' should be available to those against whom allegations are made, to provide advice and ensure legal representation if necessary. Many priests, however, said that this was too vague and demanded that dioceses should be obliged to pay for a specialist solicitor. They were also different from other professions because the consequences of losing one's job were so much worse: 'Priests are a special case because we are living in a tied cottage. If we lose our job we lose our home. Teachers in the same position may lose their jobs but they don't lose their homes.'[235]

But, most of all, priests asserted that they were different from secular professions simply because canon law made them so. Dusting off the code, which had been ignored for years in child abuse cases, they demanded that their canonical rights be respected. The Code of Canon Law, for example, does not recognise any right on the part of the diocesan bishop to 'suspend' a cleric from active ministry pending any form of investigation, other than a full penal trial. Hence, there is no provision in the Code itself for a priest to be placed on 'administrative leave'[236] during an initial investigation – as may be required by the application of the paramountcy principle. At a meeting of the National Conference of Priests in 2003, a Father Francis Marsden proposed a motion that canonical process should be observed to the letter before any priest is placed on administrative leave. He cited cases of priests who had been forced to leave their presbyteries with notice ranging from thirty minutes to a few hours. 'Under canon law, a preliminary investigation must always precede administrative leave. The accusations must be in writing and the accused must have a right to counsel and a right of appeal.' His motion was carried overwhelmingly.[237]

The priests found support from canon lawyers, who emphasised that Nolan's recommendations had not yet received the *recognitio* (formal endorsement) of the Vatican: unless and until this was secured, 'Bishops of England and Wales are bound to follow the norms set out in the universal law of the Church, contained in the Code of Canon Law and in *Sacramentorum Sanctitatis Tutela*'.[238] Hence: 'At present then, the recommendations of the Nolan Report are precisely what they claim to be, recommendations, not obligatory norms.' They should therefore be adhered to only 'in so far as this can be done, and provided that they are compatible with canon law'.[239] On the administrative leave point, whilst the diocesan bishop had certain 'executive powers' he could exercise against a priest facing an allegation, 'such moves do not amount to a *carte blanche* imposition of administrative leave'.[240] In the absence of a formal penal process, the bishop 'does not have the power to forbid the celebration of Mass or the sacraments, but only to restrict the circumstances'; nor could he 'prohibit or impose places of residence, or restrict movement'.[241]

These arguments, even if technically correct, missed the fundamental point: priests really had no substantive grounds for demanding exemption from normal child protection principles. Priests did not argue – they could not sensibly argue – that as a profession they had much less contact with children than teachers or social workers, or that the contacts they did have involved less risk. They were not different in that sense, so their argument – I paraphrase – was essentially that Nolan was trying to overturn their agreed terms and conditions of service, as set out in the Code of Canon Law, and that this was not permissible, legally or morally, because canon law was the governing law of the Church and the basis on which they had been ordained. Of course, some of their fears for reputation and job security in the face of COPCA's desire to 'cleanse the stables' were understandable. And some felt that after years of mishandling cases, the bishops were now turning tail and dropping them in it: one priest complained to me that after Nolan, with all the media glare, 'the bishops were running round like headless chickens. They were terrified of their own shadow.'[242] But looked at objectively, these fears were really an argument for priests to acquire employment rights and trade union representation, not for rejecting Nolan. In the demand for special treatment there was a whiff of clericalism.

As we saw in Chapter 2, the belief that the priesthood is set apart, special, on a higher plane than the laity is ingrained in Catholic theology: ordination is said to change the priest ontologically, to transform the nature of his being so that he becomes different from a lay person. The argument that clergy are a special case amongst professionals working with children and therefore entitled to more favourable treatment was, I believe, essentially a clericalist argument masquerading as a legal one.

However, this demand for special treatment was repeated *ad nauseam* in the years following Nolan. Writing in 2007, the Catholic commentator Austen Ivereigh saw the treatment of priests as fundamentally unjust:

> Ever since Caiaphas observed that the destruction of an innocent man was justified to save a nation, the law of Christian countries has upheld the presumption of innocence and the need for hard evidence to convict. In the Church's legal tradition, this is known as *favor rei*: the accused enjoys the benefit of the law. Due process and individual rights, Pope John Paul II said in 1979, should never be sacrificed for the sake of the social order. Yet this is precisely what has happened through the implementation of the UK Catholic Church's child-protection regime.[243]

In Ivereigh's view the Church, by embracing the paramountcy principle, was making the mirror image of the mistakes which had led to the abuse crisis in the first place:

> It was the bishops' failure to follow canon law in the 1970s and 1980s which in many ways lay behind the clerical sex-abuse crisis. Sexual abuse of minors is one of the most serious offences in

the 1983 Code (as it was in the earlier 1917 Code), one of the *gravora delicta* for which penal sanctions, up to and including dismissal from the clerical state, are demanded. The purpose of those sanctions, as the code puts it, is 'the reform of the offender, the reparation of scandal, and the restoration of justice'. In the 1970s and 1980s the failure to repair scandal and restore justice through penal sanctions left the victims, and the wider Church, indignant and angry. When the media storm broke, the bishops, under pressure to restore confidence, opted for policies that effectively renounced their responsibilities under canon law, to be implemented by quasi-judicial bodies such as COPCA...

Now, claimed Ivereigh,

the paramountcy principle means that any accusation, however vague, spurious or old, results in the priest's instant dismissal from his parish – in most cases, indefinitely. If the police do not consider it worth investigating, if the evidence is inconclusive, and even if the charges are thrown out in court, the priest does not return to his parish but must undergo 'risk assessment' by a psychological expert whose best verdict can only be that a priest is 'low risk'. This small window of uncertainty can be used by bishops to keep a priest on administrative leave for years, for fear that a reinstated priest might later abuse and the bishop face legal claims and calls for his resignation.[244]

Similarly Father Paul Bruxby, one of the Church's most respected canonists, told a meeting of priests that 'in the Church in England and Wales, which preaches justice in and out of season, a man is no longer innocent until proven guilty but guilty until proven innocent'. Bruxby maintained that, per the Code of Canon Law, a canonical 'preliminary investigation' (with counsel and right of appeal) should be completed before a priest is placed on administrative leave; to remove before a full investigation was effectively to assume guilt. Moreover, in line with canon law, there must be 'moral certainty' about an accusation – 'not least because some accusers are mentally disturbed'.[245] It was abhorrent, said Bruxby, that priests' rights should be cast aside for the sake of the safety of children; both are paramount.[246] According to a report of the meeting, Archbishop Nichols – the archbishop in charge of COPCA – 'sat thunder-faced' during Father Bruxby's comments.[247]

Bruxby and Ivereigh are both respected commentators but their argument that a penal trial should take place before administrative leave, and that the standard of proof in such investigation should be 'moral certainty', was unrealistic and flawed given the realities of child abuse and the Church's history. Child protection requires that a possible perpetrator be removed from contact with children right away. A higher standard of proof than the civil standard would inevitably result in many perpetrators remaining in ministry.

In any case, as Shearer pointed out, arguments such as Bruxby's are based on the false premise that untrue and malicious allegations are commonplace. Psychological factors make priests resist the thought that friends and colleagues are capable of such behaviour. 'The children who make these allegations are unknown to them. They are faceless, whereas the priests are their best friends and it is difficult to believe they could behave like this.'[248]

False allegations, Shearer explained, are statistically rare. 'In one particular diocese, the child protection coordinator is very experienced. He has been doing this since 1994 and has received 150 allegations. Of those, only two have proved to be unfounded after investigation.' She questioned the idea that priests' lives could be ruined by a minor indiscretion committed decades ago. An accused person claiming that an assault was a one-off 'moment of madness' should not be believed:

> All sex offenders will say 'That was a one-off, I've never done it again.' No one knows if it has happened again except them. That's the problem. What we know about paedophilia is that it is addictive, repetitive behaviour and that without treatment it does not stop. It is never a one-off.

Shearer rejected the claim of widespread miscarriages of justice arising from the accused person's difficulty in disproving an allegation, particularly if it dates back decades. Historically the scales had been weighted heavily against abused children. 'Some years ago a child telling his parents he had been abused by the priest would have got a clip round the ear, even though he was telling the truth.' She had no difficulty about the removal of a priest from active ministry, even where there is insufficient evidence to take his case to court. It was only done when police and social services had investigated and decided that abuse had taken place although they could not prove it. 'You must understand that very, very few cases ever get to court, because the witnesses may refuse to go, it may be too damaging to the child to give evidence or a child may be too young technically to give evidence.'[249]

• • •

Shearer also ran into other difficulties. Nolan had enunciated a series of principles to govern child protection in the Church. But as became apparent when Bishop Conry was questioned about the Maxwell-Stuart case, many in the Church had little grasp of how to implement these principles in practice. For decades the default setting in the Church was 'believe the priest', and a failure to appreciate the recidivistic nature of child abuse. Changing this default setting amongst those charged with delivering child protection on the frontline would not happen easily, as was highlighted by the case of Father William Hofton. Hofton was sentenced in August 2004 for sexual offences against two teenage boys in the early 1990s. He had been guilty of 'persistent and ongoing sexual harassment' of the two brothers over a five-year period.[250]

Hofton's diocese, Westminster, had not known of these offences until his arrest. But it had known that Hofton might pose a risk to children. In 2002 Hofton, at that time a priest in Borehamwood, Hertfordshire, had admitted to abusing a different boy at Allen Hall seminary in 1986. His victim had been seventeen at the time. Applying Nolan, the Westminster diocese called in the police, removed him from parish duties and sent him for independent psychiatric assessment. The assessment concluded that he presented only a 'low risk' to minors and he was sent to work as an assistant priest in Kentish Town. This was supposedly under condition of no unsupervised access to young people, although his church was connected to a school. No one but the parish priest was told of his past history, and thus the burden of supervising him fell entirely on that priest. The local child protection representative was not informed. In late 2003 the two brothers came forward with new allegations relating to

Hofton's behaviour towards them in the 1990s, matters Hofton had not disclosed. But parishioners remained in the dark until Hofton was charged in July 2004.

The news was devastating for many parishioners. At a parish meeting attended by Bishop Bernard Longley, Anne Wixstead, the retired head teacher who held the voluntary post of parish child protection representative, and who was never told about Hofton's offence at Allen Hall, expressed her fury: 'I feel betrayed by the diocese.' She was, she said, 'hurt and very, very angry'. Parishioners at the meeting accused Longley of 'making excuses' and 'talking like a civil servant'. It was 'just common sense', said one, that 'if someone comes to you and says "I have abused a child" you should not put him in a parish'. Longley was contrite: 'It may sound hollow but we are still learning and have a lot to learn.'[251]

The risk assessment had been carried out by Donald Findlater's team at the Wolvercote Clinic, but the decision to put Hofton back into ministry was made by the Westminster diocese's Child Protection Commission. The decision seems to have been naive. Hofton had portrayed events at the seminary in 1986 as a homosexual relationship with a seventeen-year-old boy who looked 'older than his years', and thus Hofton claimed he had believed he had been dealing with an adult. A spokesman for the diocese stated of Hofton that 'I think people privately concluded he was a homosexual but not a paedophile and this gave them a false sense of security'.[252] The diocese admitted that this had been a mistake, but tried to suggest that the mistake only became apparent in hindsight: 'In the light of what was subsequently revealed, it was not right for him to have been sent back to a parish.'[253]

Findlater explained that 'there is nothing foolproof about risk assessment. In this case we concluded that Father Hofton posed a low but continuing risk to children that required careful management by the church.'[254] In Hofton's case, that 'careful management' does not seem to have happened; in breach of Nolan, the local child protection representative was not informed about Hofton's past history.

The case raised the broader question of whether it could ever be safe to allow a priest to return to active ministry if he was known to have committed sex offences, even minor ones. Eileen Shearer, the head of COPCA, was clear: 'I find it hard to understand how a priest can act even as an assistant priest in a parish and not be treated as a trusted adult by parishioners.'[255] Accordingly, Shearer was in no doubt that a single offence should ordinarily result in the priest being removed permanently from active ministry: in effect a 'zero tolerance' policy. Margaret Kennedy, speaking for survivors, also argued for zero tolerance: 'Low risk is not good enough when we are talking about young children. We have had too much of this now.'[256]

Donald Findlater argued for a less black-and-white approach: in his view, if the Church adopted a 'zero tolerance' or 'one strike and you're out' policy this might increase risk. The Church, Findlater argued, could never eliminate risk altogether:

Even if the Church dispenses with every single priest where there is a whisper about them, the risk posed by that individual to children in that context may not be minimised. The Church will never extinguish risk and I am not sure I would want to live in a society that believed it had achieved this.[257]

That was a reasonable point, but approaching the issue of risk on that more nuanced footing could only work if one could be certain that proper risk management measures would always be put in place in the Church and fully enforced. The Hofton and Maxwell-Stuart cases suggested otherwise: the detail of effective risk management procedures had clearly not been properly considered, let alone instituted. In that context 'zero tolerance' was much the safer option.

• • •

Given the way allegations had been mishandled in the past, one of COPCA's priorities was to deal with 'current risks arising from cases in the past that are known to the Church but ... were not acted on or not acted on fully at the time'. Nolan had recommended that bishops 'should ensure that all such cases are the subject of an assessment as soon as possible, and that there is appropriate follow-up action'. But this proved very difficult. Whether by carelessness or design, many Catholic dioceses and orders had not maintained documentary records of past allegations. So getting a true picture of past allegations would depend on the willingness of both clergy and laity to disclose all they knew. But at grassroots level there was a reluctance to inform on fellow priests, especially where the allegations dated back many years.

This was highlighted by the case of Father Neil Gallanagh. Gallanagh joined the Diocese of Leeds in 1960, having transferred from Derry in Northern Ireland, where he was ordained. The switch was very unusual: a move from one diocese in England to another would be rare enough, but a move from one country to another was even more so. The reason for the transfer came to light nearly five decades later: in 1960 Gallanagh had been convicted of sexually assaulting a nine-year-old boy on the Isle of Man. The assault seems to have been committed during a day trip to the island.

At the time of the 1960 offence, Gallanagh told police that 'it was a horrible thing to do'. He went on: 'I have been worried with this sexual trouble for some time and recently it has become an obsession with me.'[258] At his 1960 trial, Gallanagh promised to seek treatment, and was let off with a fine. He was quickly transferred to Leeds. In 1960, the Roman Catholic Bishop of Leeds was George Dwyer. In 1965 Dwyer became Archbishop of Birmingham. We have no way of knowing whether Bishop Dwyer informed his successor, William Wheeler, about Gallanagh's 1960 conviction, and what documentary records existed of it in the diocese, but no mention of it appeared in Gallanagh's personnel file when this was disclosed in civil proceedings many years later.

Self-evidently, the worst place to put a convicted sex offender was a school where most children could neither hear nor speak, but in 1973 the Leeds diocese moved Gallanagh to St John's School for the Deaf in Boston Spa. He worked there until 1987. During his time at St John's, Gallanagh sexually abused vulnerable pupils there. His offences started to come to light in 2002. By that time, Gallanagh was working as a parish priest in Horsforth, north Leeds. In 2005 Gallanagh stood trial and was convicted: he received a suspended sentence. The sentence reflected offences against two boys, but he is likely to have been more prolific: a further eleven charges were left to lie on file, and Leeds Social Services concluded that Gallanagh had abused pupils for most of his time at the school. Gallanagh's 1960

conviction was apparently unknown to the Leeds diocese even
at the time of his criminal trial in 2005, at which point the Nolan
process had been underway for over three years, and Gallanagh's
crimes had been extensively reported. It was only discovered
later, by a journalist working with MACSAS, the clergy abuse
survivors group: they tracked down an obscure newspaper article from 1960 about Gallanagh's conviction in the Isle of Man.
Asked to explain why the Church had no record of the conviction, a diocesan spokesman said that 'records were sparse'.[259]

The Gallanagh case raised many questions; after Gallanagh's
earlier conviction was exposed, MACSAS demanded a full
explanation from COPCA, who referred the request to the
diocese, who in turn sent it to their solicitors. No response was
ever received. In their submission to the Cumberlege inquiry
MACSAS urged that 'transparency should prevail and that
enquiries should be responded to in the spirit of openness, not
a spirit of defensiveness and secrecy'.[260] Exactly who knew what
about Gallanagh's 1960 conviction within the Leeds diocese
has never been established, but it seems scarcely credible that
nobody knew anything. The fact that it took a journalist and a
campaigning group to unearth the truth did not inspire confidence that the Church, left to its own devices, would put its house
in order.

• • •

The Nolan reforms were the subject of a comprehensive review
by Baroness Cumberlege in 2007. Some claimed that her report
was watered down before publication. But even if it pulled its
punches on some issues, the report was a penetrating and in many

ways disturbing critique of the post-Nolan era. Cumberlege found that since 2001 there had been some changes for the better. There were now national policies and procedures. Most allegations of abuse were being reported to the statutory authorities. But overall, Cumberlege concluded, implementation of Nolan had been seriously flawed, and the pre-Nolan mindset remained widespread. COPCA's achievements had been mainly at the national rather than the local level; its reach had not extended sufficiently to the grassroots. COPCA had suffered from staff shortages, and was overly dependent on volunteers. Resourcing of child protection varied from one diocese to the next, as did the quality of personnel: 'Some at diocesan level have little or no experience in this complex and demanding work so it is perhaps unsurprising that the achievement of consistently good practice is proving an elusive goal.'[261]

Some child protection posts remained unfilled. The Church continued to be very poor at dealing with past cases, which were the majority of disclosures. Too little attention had been paid to vulnerable adults. Cumberlege confirmed that Nolan had compelled the Church to work in unfamiliar ways – dioceses working with each other, and in external partnership with secular agencies. The Church was still struggling to adapt to ways of thinking that had been second nature for most secular organisations for many years. Changing systems, it was apparent, was only the first step; cultural change was taking much longer. Child protection, it was clear, still needed to be embraced, not simply tolerated, by both clergy and laity. The paramountcy principle was still not widely accepted within the Church. The report concluded: 'The task is far from done. If the tensions that have come to the fore in this review are left unaddressed by those in the Church with the authority to deliver, we believe they risk a serious reversal of some of the important gains made to date.'[262]

The reaction to Cumberlege from some in the Church confirmed this somewhat bleak view. Cumberlege recommended that 'Bishops and congregational leaders should apply the civil standard of proof (the balance of probabilities) in the investigation and determination of any matter relating to the abuse of children and vulnerable adults'.[263] This was implicit in Nolan, although Nolan had not spelled it out; it simply reflected the secular position. However, it was at odds with the 'moral certainty' required under canon law, and again generated furious opposition from priests. Father Paul Bruxby argued that Cumberlege's recommendation would 'mean that anyone who works for the Church, priest or lay person, may be removed from office on the basis of information that could have at least two and possibly many more interpretations'. Christ, said Bruxby, was condemned by Pontius Pilate on the balance of probabilities:

> Some would say that those who serve Christ in the Catholic priesthood should be willing to emulate their Lord in accepting injustice for the sake of the common good. I disagree. We do Christ no service in allowing the priesthood to be sullied by anything less than hard evidence.[264]

Father Bruxby is an eminent canon lawyer, experienced in prosecuting alleged abusers as well as defending them. But the obvious retort to his comments is that family courts up and down the country make decisions about child protection every day of the week on the 'balance of probabilities': children suspected of being at risk of abuse are removed their parents on precisely that basis. And so it has to be; to do otherwise would be to condemn thousands of children to preventable abuse. There is no good reason why priests should be entitled to special treatment, as Shearer explained:

> Why should the Church be any different from other organisations that work with children and vulnerable adults? If it claims to be, it risks not only its finances, but also its credibility and its reputation ... It is not helpful to argue that clergy should be treated differently from others in the secular world whose work is closely involved with children or vulnerable adults, and to whom exactly the same principles and standards of proof apply. This approach reinforces the idea in the public mind that the Catholic Church does not understand the issues or take them seriously enough.[265]

• • •

The publication of Cumberlege was preceded by Eileen Shearer's resignation. Announcing her departure, Shearer said that:

> The Catholic Church leaders in England and Wales have undoubtedly risen to the challenge of implementing A Programme for Action. Their serious and consistent commitment to developing sound national structures, policies and practice is very clear, and safeguarding vulnerable people is increasingly woven into the fabric of the Church.[266]

The media saw it differently: *The Guardian* claimed that Shearer had had 'an enormous battle to engage with the Church' over the issue of sexual abuse.[267]

Shearer has rarely spoken about her time at COPCA and her few public comments have been mixed. Writing in *The Tablet* she complained that the media had focused unduly on the negative aspects of Cumberlege:

> If the report had been solely positive, not only would it have been (rightly) perceived as a whitewash, it would also have been less than helpful in pointing the way forward. Changing culture and attitudes in a complex institution like the Church (which operates collegially rather than through line-management structures) is a long-term and very challenging project. This is especially so when fundamental principles of safeguarding the vulnerable require an unaccustomed accountability and transparency in how these matters are handled. In this situation long term means at least ten to fifteen years. There is no quick fix, no easy short cuts. Instead there has to be a determined effort to create a culture of safety, vigilance and renewed confidence at local level. The Cumberlege Report shows us the next steps we need to take to do this.[268]

Shearer highlighted the achievements of the first five years: allegations were being reported to the authorities; Criminal Records Bureau checks were being systematically undertaken; thousands of clergy and laity had received training; strong partnerships with local and national statutory and voluntary agencies in the field had been put in place and 'some progress has been made towards achieving that most difficult challenge – a "one Church" approach'. Moreover, COPCA annual reports now publicly recorded how allegations were dealt with: 'There is no cover-up of the level of abuse reported, and the Church is unique in demonstrating this level of public accountability and openness.'

Shearer denied that her resignation betrayed frustration over lack of progress. In October 2007, however, she was more critical, according to *The Tablet* expressing the view that 'the bishops of England and Wales had failed to fully grasp what was involved in child protection and the changes that needed to be made'. Interviewed on Radio 4 *Woman's Hour*, she gave vent to some of her frustrations: 'It's true, in part, that there was a tolerance rather than an embracing of this issue. It's an incredibly difficult issue to deal with for people who haven't experienced at first hand the devastating effect of child abuse, especially sexual abuse.' She went on: 'We were desperately short staffed [and] the pay-scale was not attractive to the market I was seeking to recruit from. For two years I wasn't able to recruit any child protection staff and that undoubtedly meant some of what I wanted to do didn't get done.'[269]

• • •

In the course of writing this book I have spoken to several current and former diocesan child protection officials from various parts of the country. None was prepared to be quoted on the record. But some common themes emerged.

They confirmed that Shearer's attempts to roll out national policies had encountered considerable resistance. Views about her approach were mixed; one official suggested that she 'struggled to understand how the Church worked'. A 'top down' approach, issuing policies in the form of a central diktat and expecting them to be implemented, was never going to work. One felt Shearer had a 'quasi-Stalinist' mentality: 'Name and shame if you don't do it.'

But there was agreement that the Church's structures presented Shearer with a serious problem: dioceses were used to autonomy; there was 'nothing between a bishop and the Pope', so dioceses could look at policies and just decide to ignore them.

Whether dioceses embraced Nolan or not was critically dependent on the personality and attitude of the individual bishop. If a bishop was supportive of COPCA's agenda it would be followed; if a bishop was sceptical or downright resistant, it would be stalled or even ignored: 'Shearer wanted people to dance to her tune. The power of Nolan was supposed to be that every bishop agreed to it. But Vincent Nichols had no power over a bishop.' One official complained that their bishop constantly 'had to be pushed'.

This meant that in some dioceses two things in particular either didn't happen or took a very long time to happen. One was reporting back: dioceses supplying figures to COPCA. There was a real dislike of having to account to a body outside the diocese.

The other was historical trawls. One official explained that 'Eileen really wanted us to look at absolutely every priest's file in the diocese; she was determined to deal with the historical stuff'. This led to the realisation that documentary records of past allegations were often extremely poor or non-existent: 'Even where we knew there had been an allegation in the past, invariably there was nothing on the file.' Diocesan child protection officials were often given admission to the secret archive only to find that there was very little of value in it. [270]

Surprisingly, personnel files often lacked even the most basic information: qualifications, documents relating to when the priest was incardinated, a biographical outline. 'There might be a little bit of information from when they declared they wanted

to be a priest, but not much else.' This rings true: from dealing with historical allegations of abuse in the context of civil
claims I can confirm the paucity of record keeping in many
dioceses. This, of course, was a serious problem when it came
to tracking down and acting on historical allegations. Diocesan
officials had to fight to ensure every priest had a criminal record
check – this would ensure, at least in theory, that they then had
to disclose past allegations against them, but of course it was
not failsafe.

The process of cleansing the stables was often shocking – one
official described unearthing a 'den of iniquity'. It involved a lot
of detective work: if there was a self-disclosure by a priest of
some past misdemeanour, diocesan officials would interview and
make a recommendation. But this could become bogged down in
legal problems: 'I believed that because bishops had signed up to
Nolan it was going to happen. But the canon lawyers were saying
you can't do this. You can't hoof someone out of the priesthood
without a canonical trial, and this comes up against time limits.'

Shearer, one said, was unpopular, other than with Archbishop
Nichols, who shared her agenda. But the official was blunt:
'Eileen was unpopular because she was on the side of the victim.'
Priests felt that their rights were being eroded. Old-fashioned
misogyny and clericalism came into play: 'Many of the priests
didn't like being told what to do by a lay person, a social worker,
a woman.' The paramountcy principle was not accepted: 'The
attitude was, well, if the police aren't interested, why should we
be? You are innocent until proven guilty.'

Risk assessment became a battleground: Shearer wanted a
facility for risk assessment independent of the Church.[271] And
she was against putting people back into circulation even if low

risk. But 'you'd come up against a lot of resistance from priests: "What about forgiveness?" This was very deep-seated.'

Priests 'didn't like CRB checks, they couldn't see why a house-keeper or an altar server should have a CRB check. They thought it was a witch hunt.' The Church, one official noted, is culturally resistant to formal procedures and paperwork, a point acknowledged by Vincent Nichols in 2006:

> During these five years I have become accustomed to the place and importance of the detailed procedures which have been introduced into my ministry as a bishop ... Often I have found these procedures to be both impersonal and unforgiving. That is the nature of objective procedures. But, in my experience, they do not sit easily with the patterns of faith and responsibility in the Church, which have formed me.[272]

Of course, secular organisations can also feel crushed by the weight of paperwork in child protection, but officials felt that the Church found this particularly difficult, both because it was countercultural and because Nolan was forcing the Church to embed in only a few years principles and practices which had taken secular organisations many decades to develop.

• • •

More than half a decade on from Cumberlege, child protection in the English Catholic Church remains fraught with controversy. At the time of writing the Nolan reforms have yet to win the formal endorsement of the Vatican. Writing in 2007, Father Paul Bruxby thought it 'inconceivable that the Holy See will permit derogation from the universal law of the Church so that the bishops of England and Wales are the only ones in the world who may allow the dismissal of a priest on the "balance of probabilities"'.[273] And he seems to have been right. In one of her central recommendations, Cumberlege had tried to take that issue head on, urging that the Nolan reforms be given official Vatican recognition. Noting the 'possibility of conflict between the procedures recommended by Lord Nolan, and those called for by canon law', she proposed that the English Church draw up 'a general decree for England and Wales to be sent to the Holy See for *recognitio*'. This, explained Cumberlege, 'would enable our recommendations to become part of the particular law of the Church in this country'. Of the Vatican *recognitio*, Cumberlege said:

> It should specifically recognise the 'paramountcy principle'; ensure that the evidential standard of proof in matters relating to the welfare of children and vulnerable adults is the civil test of the balance of probabilities; endorse the possibility of the temporary withdrawal from ministry of a cleric as a precautionary measure when this is considered necessary; and recognise the right of victims to have recourse to higher authority when the procedures have not been followed.[274]

But as of 2014 no such 'recognition' has been secured from the Vatican. That silence is telling: the English Church is uneasily poised between those who favour the Nolan, secular model of child protection and those who insist that canon law should prevail, but the canonists seem to have the backing of Rome. The lack of Vatican *recognitio* means that many aspects of Nolan still do not have legal force: they remain 'recommendations, not obligatory norms'.[275]

Other aspects of Cumberlege have been even more controversial. Survivor groups felt that Cumberlege's diagnosis was right in many respects, but that her medicine was wrong: her central proposal – to abolish COPCA and put final responsibility for child protection back with the bishops – was especially badly received. Implemented in 2007, it put the bishops back in charge of the very area in which they had failed so disastrously in the past. Cumberlege believed that it was the only way properly to engage bishops and congregational leaders in the challenge of child protection, but the new bodies – the National Catholic Safeguarding Commission (NCSC) and the Catholic Safeguarding Advisory Service (CSAS) – have struggled to gain public confidence.

In January 2012 Baroness Scotland resigned as chair of the NCSC after only ten months in the post. Her resignation was welcomed by survivor groups, who said that she 'never seemed to understand the systemic nature of the cover-up of abuse in the Church'.[276] That year saw multiple resignations in the Clifton diocese: Roger Bird, the chairman of the diocese's safeguarding commission, Jane Dziadulewicz, the safeguarding coordinator, and Eugene Gallagher, the safeguarding officer, all resigned following a dispute over the treatment of a priest in the diocese who was convicted of handling child pornography. The same priest was later accused, but not convicted, of breaching the terms of his sex offences order. Bird, a retired judge who was chair of the Clifton Safeguarding Commission for eleven years, also resigned from the board of the NCSC. According to the *Catholic Herald*, 'Friends of the priest had complained to the police that Mrs Dziadulewicz had treated him unfairly after he was accused of breaching the terms of his sex offender order. An internal diocesan grievance procedure found against Mrs Dziadulewicz but a second one cleared her of wrongdoing.'[277]

The newspaper also reported that Mrs Dziadulewicz, who had worked in safeguarding for twenty-three years, had begun legal action against the diocese for constructive dismissal, alleging that she was not properly supported.

The Church describes the NCSC as 'an independent organisation'. But its independence has been questioned. Survivors see an organisation whose membership 'is dominated by bishops, priests and members of religious orders and whose chairs are appointed by the Catholic Bishops' Conference and the Congress of Religious'.[278] One commentator pointed out that the panel which shortlisted candidates to replace Baroness Scotland was dominated by clergy:

> The rhetoric is of 'independence', but the reality is that the panel was appointed by the two presidents of the Bishops' Conference and the Congress of Religious: Father Marcus Stock, General Secretary, Brother Tom Campbell, Bishop Lang and Sister Jane Bertelsen, the other vice chair of the NCSC. There appear to have been no members who were not bishops, priests or members of religious orders and no representatives of survivors' organisations.[279]

The Catholic Church has long been criticised for dealing with the problem of child abuse 'in house'; given its supposed commitment to breaking with that legacy, the apparent lack of independence of its safeguarding commission remains a serious cause for concern.

• • •

The same complaint – lack of independence – has been made about the Church's systems for assessment of suspected sex offenders. After the independent Wolvercote Clinic closed in July 2002, the locus of assessment and treatment of offenders moved to Our Lady of Victory Clinic in Stroud. This clinic had been established by the Servants of the Paraclete, a Roman Catholic religious order dedicated to supporting priests with alcohol abuse or sexual problems. The Stroud facility dealt primarily with addiction problems: porn, gambling, drugs. But from 2002 to 2004 it became the primary centre for treatment of clerical sex offenders; at that time, although a Paraclete facility, it was run by the widely respected, and independent, specialist Donald Findlater.

In 2004, however, Our Lady of Victory was closed. Psychological assessments were moved in house and since 2004 have been undertaken at St Luke's in Salford. Findlater strongly opposed that decision, arguing that given past history the Church needed to use external expertise in risk assessment and it would be dangerous to close the only programme offering this; Shearer is believed to have shared his concerns. 'Both from a PR perspective and from a substantive perspective, it was profoundly unwise to rely on a Church-driven assessment and treatment model,' Findlater told me. 'There was a risk of lack of sharing with statutory agencies and a risk of lack of proper risk assessments.' Indeed, Findlater questions whether the Catholic Church could ever be the right place to do risk assessment:

In order to properly assess individuals who have been involved in abuse you have to assess human sexual fantasies and talk about

them with the priest. But the Church doesn't want to discuss
this. If an individual who is involved in abuse can't talk about his
sexual thoughts then how are you going to get him to manage it?
There is, within the Catholic Church, a denial of sexual identity
and a refusal to admit problems and these are then left to fester.

That, says Findlater, is one of several compelling reasons why
assessment and treatment should be done externally, but the
Church disagrees.[280]

• • •

Another ongoing controversy – and one which the Church seems
notably reluctant to discuss openly – is the failure in many cases
to laicise convicted priests. Laicisation ('de-frocking') is removal
of a priest from the clerical state: a permanent return from
clergy to laity. It is seen in the Catholic Church as an extreme
step, because it reverses ordination, and ordination of course is
believed in Catholic theology to change a man's very essence.

The debate over laicisation dates back decades: Father Gerald
Fitzgerald, the founder of the Servants of the Paraclete, was an
early proponent of immediate laicisation of priests convicted of
sexual offences. Father Fitzgerald, who was ordained a priest in
Boston in 1921, established the Servants of the Paraclete in 1947.
In 1962 he wrote to the Holy See urging laicisation as a solution for priests who sexually abused minors. These priests, he
argued, should 'be given the alternative of a retired life within
the protection of monastery walls or complete laicisation. We
have the former in most cases, for laicisation is at best the lesser
of two evils.' In August 1963, Father Fitzgerald had an audience

with the newly elected Pope Paul. He told him: 'Where there is indication of incorrigibility, because of the tremendous scandal given, I would most earnestly recommend total laicisation.'[281] Father Fitzgerald argued that any priest who sexually abused a child should be laicised even if this was against his will. The then Pope, however, did not accept his view. The priesthood was seen as a sacred calling; the Pope considered the notion of taking it away from an ordained man to be an unacceptable violation of his right to remain a priest, no matter what he had done. This attitude is deeply rooted in the Church and has persisted down the years.

The issue was then specifically addressed by Nolan:

> As a general rule, clergy and lay workers who have been cautioned or convicted of an offence against children should not be allowed to hold any position that could possibly put children at risk again. The bishop or religious superior should justify any exceptions to this approach publicly (for example, by means of a letter to be read out in churches at Mass) ... If a bishop, priest or deacon is convicted of a criminal offence against children and is sentenced to serve a term of imprisonment of twelve months or more, then it would normally be right to initiate the process of laicisation. Failure to do so would need to be justified. Initiation of the process of laicisation may also be appropriate in other circumstances.

Nolan accepted that laicisation is 'an extreme step', but recommended that it be done according to the principle that 'all right-thinking members of the public, knowing all the facts, would feel that justice has not been done by any other course'.

As Phillip Gilligan points out, this is more than simply a

matter of risk management.[282] By his very status, if a priest wishes to commit child sex offences, he will find it easier to do so than if he were a layman.[283] This was a point implicitly recognised by Lord Justice Longmore when he analysed the Church's legal responsibility for a priest in the *Maga* case (see Chapter 13):

> For centuries the Church has encouraged lay persons to look up to (and indeed revere) their priests. The Church clothes them in clerical garb and bestows upon them the title Father … It is difficult to think of a role nearer to that of parent than that of priest.[284]

But more than this, many Catholic victims of abuse find comfort and safety in their faith; therefore the failure to act against priests who have been convicted of sexual offences may be regarded (and indeed is regarded) by victims as a betrayal.

Recommendation 78 of Nolan's final report said that in cases attracting a sentence of twelve months or more it would normally be right to *initiate* the process of laicisation: as Nolan explained, the word 'initiate' was used because ultimately the decision may not rest with the Church of England and Wales; it may rest with Rome, after a canonical process. But it should be initiated. Nolan, therefore, was clear as to what was expected in relation to laicisation. Since 2001, the Church has repeatedly reaffirmed its commitment to the Nolan principles, and the Cumberlege Report was clear that 'there can be no going back to a pre-Nolan mind set; no relinquishing of the values implicit in Nolan; no reversing of the thrust of the work in this challenging area'.[285]

Despite these emphatic words, Nolan's clear recommendations about laicisation seem to have been consistently flouted.

Not only have a significant number of convicted priests not been laicised, but by carefully parsing Church documents Gilligan has identified a subtle but significant shift in Church policy away from Nolan's original recommendation.

Gilligan notes that Cumberlege, curiously, did not specifically address laicisation, nor did she comment on the implementation of Recommendation 78. But the CSAS manual (most recently updated in December 2010) states:

> As a general rule, clergy or religious who have received a police caution or conviction for an offence against a child or vulnerable adult should not be allowed to hold a position that could possibly put children and/or vulnerable adults at risk again i.e. he or she must be removed from active ministry.

The same section then states that when a bishop or congregational leader decides not to follow the stated policy, they 'should be prepared to justify any exceptions and record their reasons on their individual's personnel file'. However, this is clearly very different to the requirement in Nolan's Recommendation 77 that 'the bishop or religious superior should justify any exceptions to this approach publicly (for example by means of a letter to be read out in churches at Mass)'. As Gilligan points out, between 2001 and 2010, the requirement that exceptions should be justified *publicly* appears to have disappeared entirely.

Elsewhere in its 2010 manual, the CSAS states that laicisation 'will be considered following every conviction or caution for an offence against a child and/or vulnerable adult'. But, contra Nolan, the manual does not say what outcome should normally be expected.[286] In comments reported in *The Tablet* in 2010, Adrian

Child, the director of CSAS, seemed to confirm this subtle shift. Child emphasised the benefits of managing offenders within the Church community: 'This is more effective than brandishing them on the wider community, which evidence suggests could lead to more offending.' But Nolan made clear in 2001 that laicisation and managing an offender within the Church community were not mutually exclusive, so the argument is a red herring.

This change between 2001 and 2010 – effectively dropping Nolan's recommendation on the quiet – has never been publicly admitted by the Church. But in the light of it, it should come as no surprise to discover that many convicted priests have not, in fact, been laicised as Nolan stipulated. Determining precise numbers is difficult as there is no single and publicly available source of information on the point – indeed the absence of one may itself be very telling. But in 2010 the journalist Anthony Barnett tried to piece together the available data. Barnett identified thirty-six priests who had been convicted of sexual offences between 1993 and 2009. Twenty-two of these thirty-six had been sentenced to twelve months or more – the Nolan threshold for initiating the process of laicisation. Of these twenty-two, eight (i.e. 36 per cent) had been laicised by September 2010; fourteen (64 per cent) had not been laicised. Numerous individual examples can be cited; flicking randomly through the *Catholic Directory* for 2008, I see that Fathers Gregory Carroll and Piers Grant-Ferris, convicted in 2005 of serious sexual offences at Ampleforth, were still listed as priests of England and Wales three years after their conviction and imprisonment. Father Neil Gallanagh, referred to earlier, escaped being laicised despite his conviction in 2005. The Bishop of Leeds decided that Gallanagh's laicisation was unnecessary; it would be sufficient to stop him from exercising his ministry. 'He is not in good standing with the Church as a priest,' said John Grady, the bishop's spokesman. 'He is not allowed to exercise ministry of any kind. He has observed these restrictions to the letter.' The diocese did not refer the case to the Vatican until 2007, two years after Gallanagh's conviction, and even then did not ask for laicisation. 'Bishop Roche took the view that Neil had had his faculties removed at the time of the disclosure – he had not acted as a priest or worn priest's dress – and still does not.' But again, this was contrary to Nolan.

Why has the Church reneged on Nolan's recommendation? Since the change has not been publicly admitted, no explanation has been given. Either what Lord Carlile, the Liberal Democrat peer and lawyer who investigated abuse at St Benedict's, described as 'backsliding tendencies'[287] in the English Church have gained the upper hand, or the problem lies in Rome, or a mixture of both. In 2010 the local press in Wigan and Manchester highlighted the case of Father William Green, who was jailed in October 2008 for twenty-six sexual offences against boys at St Bede's College. His laicisation, according to the Diocese of Salford, was 'ongoing' but it was also 'out of their hands': like all such applications, it rested with the CDF in Rome.[288] And the wheels of the Vatican move notoriously slowly: as the then Cardinal Ratzinger once famously said: 'The art of *soprassedere*, of postponing ... can prove to be positive, can permit the situation to become less tense, to ripen and therefore to clarify itself.'[289] The institutional inertia of the Vatican bureaucracy may be one reason why laicisations take so long, but we can only guess: the English Church's unwillingness to explain itself openly on this point has become yet another reason for survivors to doubt its good faith.

CHAPTER 10

MONKS AND BOYS TOGETHER

'Monks and boys together': monasticism has long been a draw for parents seeking a traditional Catholic education. But it may also explain why schools associated with the English Benedictine Congregation have featured so prominently in the abuse scandal. These schools – Ampleforth, Downside, St Benedict's Ealing, Buckfast Abbey, Belmont Abbey and Worth – have educated many of Britain's most distinguished Catholics. The English Benedictine Congregation has a long and proud history; destroyed in England by the dissolution of the monasteries under Henry VIII, and exiled to continental Europe, the present congregation was restored in England under the Stuarts. But it really took off in the early 1800s, as monks persecuted in Europe following the French Revolution established successor houses – and schools – in England. But over the past two decades the Benedictine 'brand' has been sullied by a succession of scandals. Some of these date back many years, but others, such as those at Ealing, post-date the Nolan reforms. Stonewalling seems to have been a persistent theme. In 1992 Father Michael Creagh, formerly deputy headmaster at Douai Abbey School in Berkshire, pleaded guilty to the indecent assault of a twelve-year-old boy at the school; in the court hearing a police officer complained that Benedictine monks at the school 'closed ranks'

to protect Creagh.[290] In 2013, the Benedictines were back in the
news with revelations of abuse at Fort Augustus, the congregation's Scottish outpost, and the congregation's President, Richard
Yeo, floundered as he tried to justify why known abusers had
been sheltered there.[291] Monasticism without oversight, out-
dated and unacceptable governance and a failure to embrace the
Nolan principles: for all these reasons the Benedictine ethos has
been badly damaged, and may take many years to recover.

• • •

The official history of Ampleforth explains its origins: 'The boys
were sent to Ampleforth because there were monks there (something which has remained true ever since) and the monks were
there, to begin with, because they could not find anywhere else to
live after nine years of trying other places.'[292] The monks' search
was caused by the seizure of their monastery in revolutionary
France. Ampleforth in North Yorkshire was the successor house
to Dieulouard, a college modelled on the Jesuit system, intended
to be a complete educational establishment involving all ages
from seven to doctorates. Ampleforth College is academically
and socially elitist: many victims of abuse there are now successful professionals. Some hold prominent positions in the law and
the City, and one is related to a member of the royal family.[293]

Basil Hume, later Archbishop of Westminster, was Abbot of
Ampleforth from 1963 until 1976 and during that period was
responsible for running both the school and the abbey. His
personal philosophy was that 'those who made mistakes needed
help and guidance ahead of public condemnation'.[294] Hume died
in 1999 and during his lifetime the school appeared relatively

scandal free. In 1995, Dom Bernard Green, a housemaster at the college and a noted medieval historian, indecently assaulted a thirteen-year-old boy who was sleeping in a dormitory. The school initially stated that they intended to deal with the matter internally and did not expect it to become the subject of a police inquiry.[295] But Green was later arrested and pleaded guilty to indecent assault.[296] He was placed under restrictions 'designed to avoid any further problems with the young'.[297] At the time nobody suggested that the school had a systemic problem. In fact it did, but the real scandal emerged only after Hume's death, when two monks were convicted of historic offences.

In July 2005 Father Gregory Carroll, by then in his late sixties, pleaded guilty at York Crown Court to fifteen charges of indecent assault and gross indecency against boys. The charges spanned the period 1973–87. During that time Carroll had been a master at Junior House. Carroll 'showed no emotion and spoke in a firm voice as the allegations of indecent assault and indecency with a child were put to him'.[298] But his defence barrister claimed he had 'expressed his revulsion towards his behaviour and described it as grotesque'. He was, she said, 'naïve and unworldly. He did not have his first sexual experience until the age of thirty-four.'[299] Carroll, who in 2005 was living in retirement at Ampleforth Abbey, was jailed for four years.[300]

Later in 2005 another former monk and teacher at Ampleforth, Father Piers Grant-Ferris, was also convicted of serious sexual offences, pleading guilty to twenty counts of indecent assault on fifteen boys, all aged under twelve. The offences occurred between 1966 and 1975 when Grant-Ferris was a teacher at Gilling Castle, the Ampleforth prep school. Grant-Ferris, the son of a Conservative MP, had a rather strange reputation at the school. His sexual proclivities and enjoyment of corporal punishment earned him the moniker 'Pervy Piers' but he had also been regarded in a more heroic light in 1981 when he made a solo climb of Mount Aconcagua in the South American Andes. The expedition nearly turned to tragedy when he got lost on the way down, and was found dishevelled and exhausted nine days later by the Argentinian army.

Public statements from the school after these convictions offered an 'unreserved apology' but glossed over what had really occurred. Speaking after Carroll's trial, the Abbot of Ampleforth, Father Cuthbert Madden, alluded to the school's longstanding knowledge of his offences:

> Almost a quarter of a century has passed since these events took place, and a great deal has changed. In the world of education the requirements and safeguards of child protection today are almost unrecognisable from those applying in the past. Then, the focus was more on prevention than prosecution, and Ampleforth's action in immediately removing Father Gregory from the school on his first admission of inappropriate contact with a boy, although insufficiently robust by current standards of risk management, was not out of line with common practice at that time. Contrary to certain perceptions in media reports of the case we cooperated fully with the statutory authorities. Today a similar case would certainly be referred promptly to them.

The statement pointed out that Carroll's connection with the school 'ended in 1987'.[301] In relation to Grant-Ferris, Madden claimed that effective and immediate action was taken. That said, what was considered adequate in the world of education many years ago would not be viewed appropriate by prevailing standards today. What we can say with certainty is that the supervision and restrictions which disciplines of monastic life would allow to be placed on a monk who made an admission of this kind to his Abbot were effective in the cases under discussion.[302]

But these carefully worded statements did not acknowledge what had really occurred. The offences, or at least some of them, had certainly long been known to the school. In 1975, Grant-Ferris had admitted to Hume that he had molested boys. In 1987, Carroll had admitted to Hume's successor that he had enjoyed some sexual contact with a boy, but claimed that this was an isolated incident. On both occasions, to hush up the scandal, Hume and his successor had dumped the offenders in a Benedictine 'mission parish' in Workington on the Cumbrian coast. There, at least one of the men went on to abuse local children.

Their offences remained hidden until 1999, when Carroll told the then headmaster at Ampleforth that the 1987 incident was not isolated; there had been others, but he had been too afraid to say so at the time. Worried about how to deal with this in the new climate, the college decided to ask Dr Elizabeth Mann, an independent psychologist, to carry out a risk assessment. Carroll cooperated with Dr Mann and disclosed much more extensive abuse. But the assessment was never completed as the abbot was not prepared to release to Dr Mann papers relating to Carroll's history. Dr Mann then felt professionally compelled to report the abuse to the authorities, instigating a more wide-ranging police investigation.[303]

When the original admissions had been made by Grant-Ferris and Carroll, in 1975 and 1987 respectively, they were removed from the school and sent to minister in Cumbria. This was a shocking misuse of the mission parishes, particularly as no one in the area was told that they were sex offenders. The relationship between Ampleforth and its mission parishes dates back centuries. Generally in deprived areas, mission parishes were staffed by the Benedictine monks of the abbey, who would undertake good works. According to Ampleforth's official history, the missions 'played [a] large part, directly or indirectly, in the lives of all the monks'.[304] Missions tended to be industrial parishes of northern England, the 'dark satanic mills' with their rapidly growing populations of Irish Catholic immigrants: 'In these areas the fathers were therefore very familiar with poverty, crowding, poor housing and disease, as well as with remarkable and striking faith.'[305] At least until the late nineteenth century men joined the Benedictine Congregation with the clear expectation of going on mission, and a 'missionary oath' (only recently abolished) formed part of the monk's profession. From 1890 the missions were under the direct control of Ampleforth Abbey. Workington in Cumbria was closely linked to the Ampleforth community for many years: in the nineteenth century one monk from Ampleforth spent no fewer than forty-seven years there, and Ampleforth's official history tells us that 'his long residence and zealous labours in Workington earned him the respect, not only of his own flock, but of all the townsfolk and indeed of west Cumberland generally'.[306] The parish was staffed by monks of Ampleforth until 2009, when it was handed over to the Diocese of Lancaster.

Grant-Ferris was sent to Workington in 1975, where he was appointed as a parish priest at Our Lady & St Michael's. Carroll followed him there in 1987. They remained under the control and direction of the Abbot of Ampleforth. During his time in Cumbria Carroll certainly gained a reputation for good works in accordance with the Ampleforth mission philosophy, starting a credit union and setting up a home for released prisoners.[307] But the clergy in Workington and the Lancaster diocesan authorities were not told about either man's past history. Both men had free contact with children and other vulnerable people. Grant-Ferris was appointed chaplain at St Joseph's RC High School in Workington, where he was supposed to carry out pastoral work with the pupils. Given his own office, he took confessions from children in private.[308] Carroll worked as chaplain at the local infirmary. They were there for many years: Grant-Ferris served in Workington until 1989, Carroll until 2001.

The consequences were calamitous but entirely foreseeable. My former client Mr T grew up as a child in Workington and attended Our Lady & St Michael's Roman Catholic Church. By the late 1980s Carroll was a priest at this church and became friendly with Mr T's family. Mr T – at that time nine years old – decided that he would like to take on the role of altar boy and as part of this carried out chores in the church.

Initially nothing happened but after a while Father Gregory began to have conversations with me of an adult nature ... I recall the first actual case of indecency happened when I was nine years old. This was in the church itself. There was a rear room/vestry that was used for people to get ready.

Mr T went on to describe a succession of incidents of indecent assault: Carroll masturbated him, inserted a finger into his anus, and lay on top of him simulating intercourse.

> It was around this time that my mum asked me if something was happening, she asked me if Father Gregory was doing anything he shouldn't be doing with me. I did not tell her of the assault but stopped going to the church, giving the excuse that I was bored with it.

For many years later Mr T suffered confusion, guilt, shame and psychiatric problems: depression, anxiety and relationship difficulties. Twenty years later, he frequently became distressed talking about what had happened, which – given Ampleforth's knowledge of Carroll's proclivities – had been entirely preventable.

Given the facts of these cases, it is difficult to make sense of Abbot Madden's statement in 2005 that 'we cooperated fully with statutory authorities'; that cooperation only came after Dr Mann found herself professionally compromised by the school's unwillingness to disclose relevant records, and went to the police. Although Carroll's 'connection with the school ended in 1987', he remained under the Abbey's control during his time in Workington. The claim that 'supervisions and restrictions' were 'effective in the cases under discussion' is equally bemusing: it does not seem that any such restrictions were placed on the priests in Workington. The abbot's statement is true in the sense that the removal of the priests from Ampleforth protected pupils there from further abuse. But it did so only by putting vulnerable children in the mission parishes at risk, and at least one of those children is still paying the price today.

• • •

St Benedict's School in Ealing is a private Benedictine day school, founded in 1902 by monks from Downside who, five years earlier, had established Ealing Abbey. Alumni of the school, known as 'Old Priorians', include prominent figures like Lord Patten (chairman of the BBC Trust) and the comedian Julian Clary. The presence of a monastic community is central to the school's ethos and at least until recent revelations has been an attraction for Catholic parents; monks have supplied many of the school's teaching staff. For many years the abbey and school effectively operated as one: as a former pupil who attended St Benedict's in the 1970s explained to me: 'The abbey and school were really a single site. Monks wandered through the school freely and boys wandered into the abbey church.'[309] Until 2007 St Benedict's was boys-only from ages three to sixteen, although girls were accepted into the sixth form from the 1970s and the school became fully coeducational in 2008.

The school's mission is to

> develop young men and women who will aspire to success at school and beyond, understand and live by gospel values, be happy in their personal and family lives, make a distinctive contribution to society and take with them, throughout their lives, a sense of belonging to the community of St Benedict's and that they have learned how to live.[310]

But St Benedict's has been plagued by abuse scandals which persisted for many decades and have continued well into the post-Nolan period. Father David Pearce was convicted in 2009 of offences covering the period 1972–2008. John Maestri, a former priest who worked as a lay teacher at the school, was convicted of sexual offences in 2003, 2005 and 2008. Father Laurence Soper, a former head, bursar and abbot, was indicted for sexual assaults on boys but jumped bail and is believed to be hiding abroad. Allegations have been made against four other members of staff. Lord Carlile of Berriew, the Liberal Democrat peer and lawyer who was commissioned in 2010 to carry out an independent inquiry into abuse at the school and abbey, found 'lengthy and culpable' failures in child protection.[311] Carlile identified a culture of opaque governance and weak management and recommended major structural overhaul. The problems in the school, it was clear, had deep roots in the monastic tradition: as Carlile concluded, primary fault for the abuse lay with the abusers but

> secondary fault can be shared by the monastic community, in its lengthy and culpable failure to deal with what at times must have been evident behaviour placing children at risk; and what at all times was a failure to recognise the sinful temptations that might attract some with monastic vocations.[312]

Carlile issued a call for witnesses and was contacted by around 100 individuals wanting to give evidence. Some complained about corporal punishment with a sexual undercurrent:

> Most of the complaints I have received, some against individuals who are now deceased, related to forms or methods of what purported or was represented at the time to be chastisement and physical punishment. It is clear to me that some of those

'punishments' were carried out in entirely inappropriate ways and circumstances, and on many occasions with a sexual motive. Such a motive was not always overt and indeed often may have been sublimated, in the sense of the person responsible channelling impulses regarded as unacceptable, especially sexual desires, towards an activity that appeared to him to be more socially acceptable, the punishment of children.[313]

A former pupil I spoke to endorsed this analysis but felt that corporal punishment also played a conditioning role:

Equally important in the beatings was making people feel guilty, engendering a sense of guilt. Pupils were told that they were very privileged that they had been let in. Their parents were making sacrifices for them. That instilling guilt was clearly a control mechanism when I look back on it.[314]

The Carlile inquiry focused on allegations made since the 1990s and did not delve further back, but the history of sexual abuse at St Benedict's goes back many decades and may be more extensive than described in the Carlile inquiry. Father Kevin Horsey joined the Ealing monastic community in 1942. In 1948 he seems to have sexually abused a boy in the local Ealing Scout troop. By the mid-1960s he was master of the middle school. A former pupil recalled being sexually abused in his first year of middle school by Father Kevin:

This took place in the old gym during PT lessons. Father Kevin organised team games and the 'resting' team sat on the edge of the stage alongside Father Kevin. He sat you on his lap, and within minutes he would place his hand inside your PT shorts and fondle your genitals. This occurred frequently during PT lessons, and to many boys. I did not know the significance of his actions at the time but I have never forgotten them. I would say that my main feelings have been of shame and anger. I never mentioned this to anyone [until 2010].[315]

Horsey died in 2006 without being prosecuted but was named by the *Daily Mail* as a prolific abuser; his obituary was removed from the Old Priorians' Association website, and a school building named after him was renamed. It seems likely that in 1965, a boy's parents complained to the then abbot, Dom Rupert Hall, about a sexual assault on their son. Father Kevin was removed from the school to parish work, but the precise details have never been confirmed by the school.[316]

Most prominent in accounts of sexual abuse at St Benedict's are David Pearce, a monk, and John Maestri, a lay teacher. The two overlapped. In 1969 Pearce, who had been a pupil at the school and gone on to train as a dentist, joined the abbey as a novice. Maestri joined the school as a teacher a year later. Pearce was ordained in 1975 and was appointed to the teaching staff in 1976, mainly teaching RE. Carlile referred to him as being 'known to the boys by a nickname' which 'did not imply abusive behaviour as such, but should have registered an alert'.[317] This moniker was 'Gay Dave'. A former pupil who attended St Benedict's from 1975 to 1982 confirmed that Pearce was hiding in plain sight:

The boys never had any qualms about calling him 'Gay Dave' in front of staff. The staff didn't react if you said that. Everyone knew that underneath that stone, there was something nasty. He had this Cheshire cat grin, the expression on his face was the one he wanted and rarely reflected reality. Everyone knew he was sexually interested in boys. On one occasion the boys put up a joke notice on a noticeboard, asking boys to report to his office with a jar of Vaseline and four short lengths of rope. Everyone knew he was a paedophile, it was common knowledge amongst the boys and staff. At a camp in Cumbria somebody said within earshot of him: 'I wonder where that fucking queer priest is hiding.' Pearce said: 'I'm over here.'[318]

There was only one occasion this former pupil recalls when a boy got into trouble for insulting Pearce: 'One boy said to him in class, "Sir, you're a fucking queer." He took this lad into his office, and he was expelled a month or so later, allegedly for having a crew cut. But nobody gets expelled for having a crew cut.' Pupils inferred that this boy had crossed an unwritten line. But this was rare:

Once I challenged him by quoting from the Bible (Luke 17: 2): 'It were better for him that a millstone were hanged about his neck, and he cast into the sea, that he should offend one of these little ones.' I did that in 1978 or 1979. I just did it to annoy him. I did it deliberately. I believed, everyone did, that he was a nonce. He just laughed.

This former pupil was in no doubt that staff turned a blind eye to Pearce's behaviour: 'There were plenty of reasons for senior members of staff to dig around – they didn't, they knew what they would find.' Lord Carlile agreed: Pearce's 'notoriety was

ubiquitous in the school over years'[319] and 'it is difficult to concep-
tualise a situation in which other monks were not suspicious of
or at least alerted to the possibility of abusive or inappropriate
behaviour'.[320]

In 1972, Pearce committed the first offence for which he was
later convicted. Further sexual offences followed throughout the
1970s but Pearce was promoted to head of the junior school in
1984. In 1992, Pearce 'retired' from the post of junior school head
teacher, possibly following complaints of abuse. It seems that the
complaints were not followed up at the time by the complainant's
mother due to the death of the boy's father. Pearce was moved to
the role of bursar of the school, and was succeeded as head of the
junior school by Martin Shipperlee (the current abbot). In 2004,
Pearce was appointed novice master. But in the same year, another
former pupil of the school made a complaint to Shipperlee that he
had been sexually assaulted by Pearce from 1989 to 1993.

According to this ex-pupil, Shipperlee (who had been a monk
at the abbey when the boy was at the junior school) told him that
he had 'known of rumours about Pearce and of his reputation
before Pearce had ceased to be headmaster at the junior school'.[321]
In 2005 the ex-pupil, anonymised as C in court proceedings,
initiated a civil damages claim against Pearce and the school. C
said that Pearce had touched his genitals whilst drying him with
a towel after swimming lessons, had videoed him whilst he was
taking a shower, and on another occasion had fondled his penis.

In 2006, C's action was heard by Mr Justice Field.[322] During
the trial Pearce denied sexual assaults. The judge found C to
be 'an entirely convincing, reliable and credible witness' whose
evidence 'was clear and unmistakeably had the "ring of truth"'.[323]
Pearce, by contrast, was 'an unconvincing witness'. His evidence

'lacked spontaneity. It appeared to me to have been carefully rehearsed.' C's allegations were upheld, and he was awarded damages of £43,000. During the proceedings, Pearce had been granted anonymity, but at the end of the trial the judge removed this in the public interest: 'The public should know not only that C was sexually abused but also the identity of his abuser and the school where it happened.'[324]

Following that court decision, Pearce was placed on something called 'restricted ministry'. This apparently meant that he was not to have any public ministry, was to celebrate Mass only in private within the monastery, and was to have no contact with children. The reason given publicly by Abbot Shipperlee for these restrictions was 'to protect Father David from unfounded allegations'.[325] This was after a High Court judge had concluded, without any ambiguity, that Pearce was a paedophile.

Pearce's ministry was not restricted enough. Between 2006 and 2008 he sexually assaulted his final victim, a pupil of the school who came in to the monastery at weekends to wash dishes. The boy was aware that Pearce was subject to restrictions but neither knew what they were nor why. Pearce befriended and then abused him.

Complaints from the boy triggered an extensive police investigation. Pearce was arrested in 2008. He was eventually charged with over twenty offences against several different boys, all pupils or former pupils of the school, over the period 1972–2007. He pleaded guilty to ten offences of indecent assault and one of sexual assault, and in October 2009 was sentenced to eight years in prison (later reduced on appeal to five years) and placed on the sex offenders' register for life. It was clear from the words of the prosecuting barrister that Father Pearce...

got himself into a position of trust and authority and then used that position to prevent his victims from speaking up, and to prevent them for a long time from being believed even when they did speak up. One victim was even estranged from his own parents for a time as they found the accusations to be unbelievable.[326]

The abuse had had a devastating effect on the lives of the victims; impact statements read out in court talked about how Father David 'was everywhere' in their lives.[327] In mitigation, Pearce's barrister tried to argue that Pearce 'had also done much good in the world, that he had been a good and effective teacher, that he had partici-pated in and led a great many out-of-hours school activities, and that many pupils had benefited from the education he had had a part in providing'.[328] Many people came forward as character witnesses for Pearce, including pillars of the local community. But the barrister's claim that Pearce had 'not acted as a predator' ('the crime career of a sexual predator classically involves an escalation in the seriousness of offences over time, which didn't happen in this case') was roundly rejected by the judge.[329]

Abbot Shipperlee was not present at the sentencing, but later issued a statement:

The crimes perpetrated by David Pearce were a betrayal of the trust placed in him as a teacher and priest. His exploitation of the most vulnerable was brought to an end by the courage of those of his victims who came forward and revealed what had been happening. I would like to apologise in every way I can to the victims and to everyone else who has been affected by this case. I will remember in my prayers all those whose lives have been troubled by David Pearce's actions.[330]

The abbot said he was launching an independent review into the case 'to examine what there is to be learned to ensure that there can never be a recurrence of this situation'. He added: 'David Pearce's future as a priest will now be reviewed by my superiors in accordance with the child protection procedures of the church.'

The statement was aptly described by campaigners as 'weaselly' – after all, some of the offences committed by Pearce occurred *after* the school had paid damages to one of his victims following an unequivocal court decision that Pearce had molested him, and *after* he was supposedly placed under restrictions which would prevent him having contact with boys. This was the kind of situation that in an American courtroom would risk a jury finding of gross negligence and a multi-million-dollar punitive damages award; in England, Abbot Shipperlee could get away with promising an independent review. In fact, by this time multiple inquiries were already underway. In July 2006 the Charity Commission had opened a statutory inquiry into Ealing Abbey, following an anonymous complaint. The complaint pointed out that Pearce had been accused of paedophile activity and that damages had been awarded to the victim, and alleged that funds of the Order of St Benedict Ealing, i.e. the school's charity, had been misappropriated to pay Pearce's legal costs to defend the case. The commission had concluded that the use of funds for this purpose was arguably within the remit of the charity but that the Charity Commissioners ought to have been consulted first, and was about to publish its report when Pearce was arrested in February 2008. Instead it delayed publication and instigated a second inquiry, this time to examine 'how the charity's trustees exercised their duty of care to the beneficiaries of the charity (i.e.

pupils) in the light of Pearce's recent arrest'.[331] Not surprisingly, the commission concluded that

despite assurances from the trustees, they failed to implement the restrictions placed on [Pearce] whilst on charity premises and the Commission is extremely critical of the trustees in this regard. One of the terms of [Pearce's] continued role in the charity was that he was to have no access to children and young people on the charity's premises – the trustees failed to ensure that this was the case.[332]

One of Pearce's lay colleagues on the teaching staff was John Maestri, who taught at St Benedict's from 1970 until his departure in 1984. Maestri was not a monk although he seems to have previously been a priest in Scotland, having been ordained in around 1964. At St Benedict's, Maestri taught maths. A former pupil remembers him as 'an engaging fellow, extrovert, a clever man, he played music in class and was always up for jokes and amusements'. But he left the school quite suddenly in 1984. He was due to be made headmaster of the middle school but a former pupil believes that 'the school secretary intervened – "if you make that man headmaster I will go to the police"' – and Maestri simply disappeared. In evidence at his most recent trial in 2011,[333] Maestri stated that he left St Benedict's in 1984 because of complaints about him. Maestri went on to teach at a girls' convent school in Berkshire.

In 2003, Maestri pleaded guilty to sexually abusing pupils at St Benedict's and was sentenced to two and a half years. He was convicted again in 2005, and given a community service order; and then convicted for a third time in 2008 and given a suspended prison sentence. In August 2010 Pearce and Maestri were arrested on further allegations of abuse, but this time both were acquitted at trial in 2011.

In the meantime, another suspected abuser at St Benedict's had fled abroad. Laurence Soper (a monastic name: his real name is Andrew Charles Kingsdon Soper) is an Old Priorian who was appointed master of the middle school in 1982 and rose to become abbot (an elected position) in 1991. As master of the middle school, complaints were made by parents about his conduct, but to no avail. A former pupil recalls that 'there were rumours about him beating boys, taking down trousers, this sort of thing'. Immediately after his retirement in 2000, Soper departed to the Benedictine headquarters at Collegio Sant'Anselmo, a monastery outside Rome. This was normal: it is a Benedictine tradition that after retirement an abbot will spend a year away from the house he led in order to allow his successor to establish himself. But Soper never returned. Indicted on various sexual offences, he skipped bail and by 2011 was 'believed to be living in an Italian monastery'.[334] A European arrest warrant has been issued for Soper, and speaking at the press conference on the publication of his report, Lord Carlile urged him to turn himself in:

> He may feel he owes a personal and ethical duty to answer whatever questions are put to him. I regret the difficulties he has caused the inquiry process. I hope ... that everybody who has, and has had, contact with Soper should inveigh upon him very strongly to surrender himself to the British authorities.[335]

It seems that despite being a fugitive from justice, Soper remains a Benedictine priest; he has not yet been laicised, although it was announced in September 2012 that his licence to practise as a priest had been revoked.

The roll-call of suspects at St Benedict's does not end there. In December 2011 Stephen Skelton was convicted of two indecent assaults, one against a St Benedict's pupil in 1983, one at another school in 1993. Skelton left St Benedict's after only one or two terms following a parental complaint, but went on to teach elsewhere. When arrested he was working as a volunteer at a children's railway in Hampshire. In March 2010 Ealing Social Services started an investigation into allegations of past abuse by another priest who had taught at St Benedict's. He resigned as a trustee, and was also placed on restricted ministry.[336] Finally there was Father Stanislaus Hobbs; in 2005 a complaint was made regarding abuse by Father Hobbs twenty years previously. He was arrested and resigned as a trustee. In 2007 he was acquitted, but in taped police interviews admitted to being sexually attracted to boys, and admitted to assaulting a boy whilst supervising a school trip to Italy. That offence in Italy could not be prosecuted in England at the time. Hobbs was placed on restricted ministry, and barred by the Secretary of State for Education under Rule 99 from any contact with children. Under pressure from the Department for Education, Abbot Martin Shipperlee eventually moved Hobbs out of the monastery to a care home outside the Diocese of Westminster. However, all the former pupils of St Benedict's I have spoken to described Hobbs as blameless, and were adamant that he was never the object of suspicion during his time at the school; and many worshippers at Ealing Abbey also felt that Hobbs, alone amongst those accused at the school, was the victim of an injustice.

In April 2010, the Independent Schools Inspectorate (ISI) made an unannounced inspection of St Benedict's, concentrating on safeguarding issues; the report which resulted was described by one parent as 'devastatingly bad'.[337] The rising adverse publicity led to the appointment of Lord Carlile. By this time, Jonathan West, a local anti-abuse campaigner, had started a detailed blog itemising failings at the school; the headmaster, Christopher Cleugh, used his prize-giving day speech in September 2010 to attack West and others, claiming that criticisms of the school were anti-Catholic:

> There have been failures here in the past and quite rightly those involved have been or are being exposed and punished. The school continues to cooperate with all the relevant authorities. I absolutely refute that anyone associated with St Benedict's School has misled the inspectors or protected offenders – such allegations are at best misguided and at worst deliberately malicious. Recent media and blog coverage seem hell-bent on trying to discredit the school and, at the same time, destroy the excellent relationship between school and monastery. Is this part of an anti-Catholic movement linked to the papal visit? I do not know, but it feels very much as if we are being targeted.[338]

In fact, all West was really asking for was a clear and unambiguous safeguarding policy – a not unreasonable demand after the events of the previous sixty years. By October 2011, the school's reputation was sufficiently battered for Rome to become involved: the Congregation for the Doctrine of the Faith ordered its own inquiry (an 'Apostolic Visitation'), conducted by Bishop John Arnold. He was initially accompanied by Abbot Richard Yeo, the English Benedictine Congregation President. Yeo, however, offered his resignation from the Visitation after Lord Carlile protested about his obvious conflict of interest. One of the criticisms of the school Yeo was investigating was that Pearce had been kept at the abbey on restricted ministry. But Yeo had done the same thing as the Abbot of Downside (see below) – allowing Richard White to remain at the monastery even though he had admitted to abusing boys at the school.

The Carlile Report, published in November 2011, focused on the school's governance, which Carlile concluded was 'wholly outdated and demonstrably unacceptable ... In a school where there has been abuse, mostly (but not exclusively) as a result of activities of members of the monastic community, any semblance of a conflict of interest or lack of independent scrutiny must be removed.'[339] The trustees were 'drawn from too narrow a group of people'.[340] Carlile confirmed what many pupils had long known – that management of the school had often been amateurish. As a former pupil told me:

> There was no control over what the teachers and monks were doing. It was not the super grammar school that people imagined. The head in my time, Father George Brown, was in decline and appeared to be suffering from dementia. He would occasionally appear at assembly. On these occasions it was a bit like Leonid Brezhnev appearing at the Kremlin Wall.[341]

In the case of Father Pearce, Carlile found that the 'St Benedict's rule of love and forgiveness appears to have overshadowed responsibility for children's welfare'.[342] The abbot, said Carlile, now accepted that 'another dwelling has to be found for any member of the monastic community' who posed a risk to children.[343]

As Carlile observed, a 'backsliding tendency' remained in the school and 'there can be almost no limit to the level of vigilance required'.[344] The Carlile Report focused on governance rather than the fine detail of safeguarding, but when the school announced a new safeguarding policy in November 2011, Carlile endorsed it. However, in the eyes of campaigners that policy was still flawed, primarily because of the 'wriggle room' it continued to allow staff in terms of reporting child protection concerns to the authorities. Campaigners wanted a policy without any ambiguity. In September 2013, after four years of stalling by the school, they got it. West observed: 'It could have been done in four weeks rather than four years. It *should* have been done in four weeks. But after exhausting all other options, the school has finally done the right thing.'[345]

• • •

Other schools in the Benedictine Congregation have also been beset by scandal. At Downside, an abuse victim and former pupil alleged that the school was 'infiltrated by paedophiles at all levels'.[346] His comments followed the jailing in 2012 of Richard White (also known as Father Nicholas White), a monk of Downside Abbey who formerly taught at the school. His abuse was known about by monastic and school staff at the time but he evaded criminal charges for more than twenty years. White was jailed for five years for gross indecency and indecent assault on a pupil in the late 1980s. White had been allowed to continue teaching after he was first caught abusing a child in 1987, merely being restricted from teaching the very youngest boys; and was able to go to assault another pupil in the school. After the second incident – involving a pupil named Rob Hastings – White was sent to Fort Augustus Abbey, the Benedictine outpost in Scotland. He returned to Downside in 1998. Once back there, he was placed, like Pearce, on restricted ministry. But the police were not informed of the allegations, and White was not arrested, until 2010.

For eight years of that twelve-year hiatus, White's abbot at Downside was Richard Yeo, now President of the English Benedictine Congregation. Yeo was certainly aware of White's history. The issue was touched on obliquely in the recent BBC documentary *Sins of Our Fathers*, about abuse at Fort Augustus, which was aired in September 2013. Much of the programme concerned paedophile monks who were relocated to Australia rather than the police being informed, and how neither the civil nor the Church authorities in Australia were warned about the people they were receiving – a story, of course, with echoes of what happened at Ampleforth. Yeo was amongst those interviewed. After apologising for 'any abuse that may have been committed at Fort Augustus', Yeo was pressed on the Australian aspect: 'That is unacceptable, I'm not defending that.' Asked whether he had spoken about this to Father Francis Davidson, the headmaster of Fort Augustus at the time, Yeo then said that he was 'not prepared to talk about specific cases'. Later in the programme, linking the scandal at Fort Augustus with events at Downside, Yeo was asked whether he had met Richard White at Fort Augustus, and admitted that he had, in 1997. On being asked whether he knew White was a paedophile, he said he knew there had been serious allegations made against him which had not been passed to the police. But the BBC reporter seemed to have been unaware that Yeo was elected Abbot of Downside in 1998, and was in charge there when White was permitted to return from Fort

Augustus, and continued to live at Downside, unbeknownst to the police, until his arrest in 2010.[347] Documents made available at White's trial indicated that the school had sought legal advice as to whether they were legally obliged to report the allegations to the authorities at the time; of course the school was not obliged to do so, because of the absence of any mandatory reporting law.[348] So no report was made, and the police stumbled across the case by accident during a separate investigation.

Two other Downside teachers, both monks, received police cautions. In total, seven monks with links to the school have faced police investigation over child sex and pornography offences. In a letter to parents, Yeo's successor, Abbot Bellenger, said four had faced police action and two, against whom allegations 'were founded', had restrictions imposed on their ministry. The seventh was cleared and allowed to return to monastic life. One of the monks receiving a caution was a former senior member of the school staff. OFSTED summarised their concerns in their 2010 report on the school: 'There are significant failings in how the school keeps boarders safe. There is poor and inconsistent practice in respect of staff recruitment and in how the school manages risk. These procedures are not sufficiently robust to ensure boarders are protected from harm.'[349] But the changes demanded by OFSTED were slow in coming: six months later, a follow-up report by the ISI was even more damning, complaining of 'serious mismanagement' of safeguarding and quoting the head as telling the governors that in this respect, Downside was 'effectively in special measures'. The ISI report observed:

The school is aware that its procedures and practices have not been, and are still not, up to the standard required in all respects, despite the steps taken since the inspection and safeguarding audit. Given that six months have passed since the inspection, the expected sense of urgency is not particularly apparent, and such progress that has been made has generally been slow and, in some cases, still not compliant.[350]

The school's longstanding practice of inviting pupils from the school into the monastery for 'overnight retreats' was only stopped in 2011 at the ISI's insistence, since the monastery contained monks who were on restricted ministry because of the risk they posed to children.

At Buckfast, Father William Manahan was convicted of eight charges of sexually assaulting pupils; Father Paul Couch was also found guilty of thirteen counts of sexual/indecent assault. At Belmont, which closed in the early 1990s, Father John Kinsey was convicted in 2005 for a series of assaults on boys, grooming and attacking victims during bell-ringing lessons and altar service duties. At Worth Abbey, a Father Andrew Brenninkmeyer was exclaustrated in 1995 following sexual allegations; one victim said Brenninkmeyer 'repeatedly asked him to strip naked when he approached him for confession'.[351] To cap it all, the individual delegated by the Diocese of Plymouth to investigate some of these allegations on behalf of the Church was then jailed for child pornography offences: Christopher Jarvis, a former social worker, admitted twelve counts involving indecent images. The judge said children who had confided in Jarvis would feel 'sullied and let down'. Jarvis had access to confidential Church files on abuse cases, particularly on Benedictine schools in the south-west. As a member of the Devon and Cornwall Multi-agency Safeguarding Team, he worked with police officers and social services. He was arrested after uploading images of pre-pubescent boys to a social networking website; more than 4,000 pornographic images, mainly of boys aged ten to twelve, were found by police on his Church-supplied computer and memory stick. David Pond, chairman of the Plymouth Diocesan Safeguarding Commission, said Jarvis's crimes had been 'a great shock to the many people who had placed their trust in him and worked with him to protect vulnerable children and adults'. But he claimed that 'this particular incident was not a systemic issue in the Roman Catholic Church. It is about an individual who had got himself into a position of trust.'[352]

• • •

To what extent are these appalling failings a specifically Catholic, indeed Benedictine problem? A former pupil who attended St Benedict's between 1975 and 1982 sees the issues at the school more in terms of an institution fighting to protect its standing and income stream rather than as a Catholic issue: 'In a sense the Catholicism is almost incidental, it was much more about an organisation seeking to protect its reputation.'[353] Similarly, the Catholic journalist Elena Curti, who worships at Ealing Abbey, observed that

behaviour of the kind described by Lord Carlile at St Benedict's was not unusual in many boys' schools at that time. Could the central problem have been that it was emulating the English public-school caricature of hard work, hard play, harsh punishment, rather than the fact that it was run by celibate men? Quite apart from St Benedict's I have lost count of the number of men

over fifty who have told me about schoolteachers who were either
sadistic thrashers or over-tactile and to be avoided.[354]

There is some force in that point: amateurish management,
corporal punishment and a cavalier attitude to child protection
characterised many fee-paying schools in the 1970s and 1980s.
And indeed there have been several high-profile cases involving non-Catholic schools in which school management knew
of child protection concerns but did not disclose these to the
police. But the cases cited in this chapter also highlight features
unique to Benedictine institutions. The geographical reach
of the congregation led to the dumping of paedophile monks
in missions or abroad. Monasticism in practice meant monks
having freedom and no oversight, and at St Benedict's that was
compounded by poor governance. As another former pupil at
St Benedict's said of one abbot: 'Many were surprised when he
was elected but in retrospect it is precisely because of his weakness that he was elected by the paedophile monks. They knew
that he could not properly oversee them nor strongly protect the
students.'[355] As Carlile commented, OFSTED were concerned
at reporting and governance issues both at St Benedict's and at
Downside.[356] But the governance structure is much the same
at all the Benedictine monasteries and their remaining associated
schools: Ampleforth, Downside and Worth have all rejected the
separation in governance between school and monastery which
has now been implemented at St Benedict's.

Perhaps most importantly, as we saw in an earlier chapter,
the Benedictines failed to engage fully with the Nolan process.
The consequences are apparent in the way Pearce was allowed
to continue having access to children despite a damning court

decision in 2006, and in the way Richard White was sheltered at Downside until 2010. Decisions of this kind were common and systemic in Catholic institutions until the Nolan changes, but are utterly unforgivable in the very recent past: in the months following White's arrest and conviction, both OFSTED and the ISI issued excoriating reports about safeguarding shortcomings at Downside and the lack of progress in addressing them. What seems most striking about events both there and at St Benedict's is the persistent stalling involved – even in the face of endless inquiries, pressure from campaigners and dreadful media headlines over several years, St Benedict's resisted a clear and unambiguous safeguarding policy until finally conceding it in September 2013. That speaks of a deep reluctance, more marked even than in other Catholic dioceses and orders, to embrace the new realities of child protection. It will likely take many years to restore confidence: the Benedictine 'brand' may recover, but only when the lessons of the past few decades are fully acknowledged and understood.

CHAPTER 11

AN IMBALANCE OF POWER

Media reporting of the Catholic abuse scandal has focused on the sexual violation of children. The sexual exploitation of adults has been largely ignored. But in reality adult abuse is a significant problem – not only of adults with learning disabilities who fit the traditional definition of 'vulnerable adult', but also of women who seek help from clergy in times of crisis and whose emotional vulnerability exposes them to sexual exploitation by priests. Research by Margaret Kennedy identifies a widespread but shockingly underreported scandal of abuse and sexual exploitation of adult women in all the mainstream churches.[357]

Legal redress for victims is rare, but occasionally perpetrators have been held to account in the criminal courts. In November 2000 Robert Deadman, a Cistercian monk who offered 'counselling and spiritual healing' to women at his monastery, was convicted of indecently assaulting four women and jailed for six years. Deadman sexually assaulted the women after 'anointing' their bodies with oil. The assaults were carried out in or near the confessional or in the guest retreat at St Bernard's Abbey in Coalville, Leicestershire.

Joan[358] was one of Deadman's victims. Her experience illuminates how offenders like Deadman can so easily operate with impunity. Brought up as a devout Catholic, her childhood was 'totally ruled by religion' and she was raised to believe that 'the Church dictated how we led our lives'.[359] Joan was never allowed to play out on a Sunday and went to a convent school; 'my family were totally tied to the Catholic faith'. The priest was a very powerful figure to her; she was brought up to believe that priests could do no wrong. Criticising a priest was blasphemous. As an adult Joan continued to fear anyone connected with power in the Church. She went to Mass every Sunday morning: 'I was convinced that to miss Mass meant that I would go to hell.' Joan went through a difficult time in the early 1980s, with the disintegration of her marriage and the death of a loved one. Isolated and desperately in need of emotional guidance, she was directed to meet Father Deadman, who advertised himself as providing 'spiritual counselling'. The services at St Bernard's were free, and anyone would be accepted for help. The abbey was an attractive place to visit, the grounds were peaceful and beautiful and 'one could have a relaxed, warm and therapeutic feeling being there'. Joan was introduced to Father Deadman on her first appointment at the abbey. He seemed friendly and warm; he embraced her at their first meeting, which she felt happy with. She was unused to physical affection, especially from a priest, but she liked it.

Over a two-year period Joan saw Father Deadman once a week or once a fortnight. At first she looked forward to going to see him; he was someone who would listen to her and made her feel important. She found him very comforting to talk to. They sat and talked, and he would hold her hand, and her emotions came flooding out. He was willing to listen. Within Joan's own family, it had never been considered acceptable to express emotions. This was a new experience. As a result she became very trusting of him:

I knew that my family loved me but this was always shown through fear. Nobody ever hugged each other. My father was always terrified this would bring shame to the house. This was a very emotional time for me and I was very vulnerable. Father Deadman was extremely devious, but very smooth, clever and subtle all the same. He groomed me.

Father Deadman was an extremely popular figure at the abbey, particularly amongst women. He had a huge following. When he did his faith healing sessions there would be 'an enormous crowd in the room, like a cult'. But after a few months, Joan began to feel uncomfortable in Father Deadman's presence. He would hug her with one arm round her and one arm stroking her soothingly. She remembers him saying she was like an 'elusive butterfly'. Sex was emphasised in meetings and presented as curative; the sexual assaults started soon after.

It took Joan a long time to properly understand what was going on. Christian expectations and humility framed her response: 'Basically, I excused everything he did because he was a priest. I thought he couldn't help it because, although he was a priest, he was also a man.' Joan gradually began to understand that what he was doing to her was wrong. Even though she knew this there was nobody she could tell. She had been brought up to treat the priest as her confidant so she was left with no one. She was unable to tell her husband as she feared his reaction. She still needed to visit the guesthouse to study as she had her own room there and it was the only place where she could work in peace. If she managed to avoid Deadman, she would breathe a sigh of relief, but he knew she was there, he would seek her out and make arrangements for her to see him. She tried to see him less but he could show his anger if he was not pleased and she felt threatened by him. She was under his power and authority; she couldn't escape him. Eventually she stopped visiting the guesthouse. She left England and at the same time Deadman was moved away from working at the guesthouse. She was told that he had been sent to Stroud; she had no idea why.

The assaults were devastating for Joan, but she assumed she was a lone victim. In 1999, she heard out of the blue that Deadman had been accused by other women of indecent assault. The news, she recalled, 'burnt a hole in me'. She was frightened but agreed to help the police, and give evidence in court against Deadman.

The trial took place in October and November 2000. Joan remembers the whole experience as 'incredibly traumatic'. Deadman pleaded not guilty. Giving evidence, Joan was very scared: 'It was hellish.' She was fiercely cross-examined by Deadman's barrister on the issue of consent. But it was worthwhile: the jury, satisfied that Joan had never consented, convicted Deadman of indecent assault.

• • •

Joan's experience was typical of many women who have been sexually exploited by clergy to whom they went in times of crisis or distress. Duped by a priest who was supposed to be offering pastoral support and counselling, it took her a long time to see clearly that she was being harassed and assaulted. Yet in one respect her case is not typical at all: the law came to her aid. Deadman was eventually punished for his behaviour. The prosecution was successful partly because Loughborough police sought expert advice on vulnerable adult abuse from Margaret

Kennedy of MACSAS and Jenny Fasal of POPAN (Prevention of Professional Abuse Network). This was very unusual. The prosecution of Deadman is unique; no other English Catholic priest has been prosecuted in a criminal court for the sexual abuse and exploitation of adult women.

There are several reasons why. For one, the scale of the problem is not understood. Undoubtedly, more research is needed on the prevalence of sexual exploitation of adult women by clergy. Studies of sexual exploitation by professionals have tended to focus on therapists, examining the extent to which therapists sexualise their interactions with female patients. Other studies have examined sexual contacts between doctors and patients. These studies have typically found around one in ten doctors admitting to sexual interactions with patients.[360] But clergy have not been studied to the same extent, in part reflecting an assumption that clergy are not 'professionals'. Kennedy's research examined the experiences of a sample of 100 women sexually exploited by clergy as adults, and other studies have examined the prevalence of domestic violence in Christian communities. But there is as yet no definitive research data on the frequency of sexual molestation of vulnerable adults by the clergy from whom they seek help. However, the available data suggests that the problem is extensive but significantly underreported.

That underreporting stems from a widespread prejudice that classifies the sexual exploitation of vulnerable adult women by priests not as assault but as an 'affair'. Richard Sipe, an American psychotherapist and former Catholic priest, estimates that around 10 per cent of priests are sexually active with adult women.[361] These women are typically seeking help in the context of personal crises and many are themselves victims of child abuse. But because the majority of women groomed in such situations technically have the legal capacity to enter into a sexual relationship with the priest – even if in reality that consent is compromised by their vulnerability – they are generally not seen as victims of exploitation or abuse. Indeed, the women themselves, even where groomed and manipulated into sex, may – at least in the early stages – see what has occurred as more akin to a 'relationship' than a form of abuse.

Reflecting widely held social attitudes, media coverage of such cases typically tends to focus on the 'affair' from the point of view of the priest, who is seen as the victim of an out-dated and inhumane doctrine of celibacy.[362] Typical of the public stereotype was the case of Bishop Roddy Wright in Scotland. In 1996 Bishop Wright fathered a child with a woman he was pastorally 'helping'. This was portrayed by the media as an 'affair', a human failing not a pathology – a perception fostered by Wright's later presentation of the scandal as a love story in his autobiography *Feet of Clay*.[363] Indeed, as Kennedy shows, the 'normalising' language used to describe sexual exploitation of adult women by priests helps to 'reconceptualise clergy misconduct into a discourse that obfuscates' what is actually occurring. This false 'naming' by the Church – 'mistakes', 'misjudgements', 'transgressions' – or the media – 'affair', 'dalliance', 'secret love life' – affects 'how the sexual exploitation of adult women is articulated and responded to'.[364] Academic research literature on clergy sexual exploitation is little better: it 'almost entirely focuses on the trials and tribulations of the clergy professionals, as opposed to those of their victims'.[365] The 'traditional' stereotype of affairs caused by female 'wantonness' is replaced in academic literature by a 'more contemporary preference for male "sickness"'.[366] Thus clergy who prey on adult women are characterised as 'lovesick' or 'wanderers' who 'fall into' relationships to boost their flagging self-esteem: terms which suggest unintentional, essentially blameless behaviour devoid of agency or responsibility.[367] Only feminist researchers start from principles of accountability linking male clerical power and misogyny with sexual violation of adult women.

In reality, most 'affairs' between clergy and adult women are abusive and exploitative: as Sipe observes, relationships with women will sometimes benefit the sexually immature priest, but

no matter ... how useful they prove to be in the maturation of priests, women get used. By their sinfulness women can save priests. But priests can remain within the system and retain their power – now purified – while women retain their identity in the system as evil unless they are virgins, martyrs or mothers.[368]

These stereotypes are rarely questioned within the clergy itself. In 1996, the public portrayal of the Roddy Wright case was challenged by a Jesuit priest and counsellor:

The real issue is one of sexual abuse or, more precisely, professional malpractice by means of sexual abuse. There is a sense, at least in the popular press, that there is something understandable, romantic, and perhaps even natural in the bishop's situation. It is easy to see how a caring and sensitive man, vulnerable because of loneliness and a woman seeking his help because she has been wounded by a broken marriage or failed engagement, might become mutually attracted and fall in love. Isn't acting on that love and attraction only 'doing what comes naturally'? The answer in this case and others like it must be 'no'. Quite apart from the obvious impediment of clerical celibacy, the genesis of both relationships was professional; both women sought assistance in a time of crisis from a minister they presumed to have been trained and certified by the Church to offer the sort of assistance they required. As a professional, the priest as pastoral counsellor is obligated to act for the good of the parishioner, his client. This entails an awareness of, and sensitivity to, the inequitable power relationship between priest and the person being counselled. Even a healthy, mature parishioner is at a power disadvantage, due to the priest's perceived authority and status. A person in crisis and in need of counselling is at a greater disadvantage and so particularly open to manipulation, exploitation or abuse ... Any priest or professional who exploits this relationship in order to fulfil personal needs, uses this power imbalance in a dangerous, destructive and immoral way. And to allow a pastoral counselling relationship to be sexualised is a prime example of this exploitation ... Because of the power inequity, there is reason to question the validity of the client's consent if and when the relationship becomes overtly sexual. Because of the priest's status or authority, it can be difficult – and at times, nearly impossible – for the client to experience the freedom to refuse or consent authentically – even if an attempt to sexualise the relationship or initiate a romantic involvement comes from this side.[369]

A dissident Irish priest, Father Pat Buckley, also acknowledged the sexual exploitation of Irish women by Catholic clergy in his book *A Thorn in Their Side*.[370] But these aside, the fact that in practice the power imbalance vitiates the woman's consent is routinely ignored. The 'adult abuse' category is assumed to be restricted to adults who by reason of learning difficulties or similar reasons indisputably lack capacity to consent to sex. The sexual exploitation of adult women by clergy – much like the recent sexual exploitation of teenage girls in street grooming cases – is seen as 'different'.

Reflecting society, the criminal law fails to protect vulnerable adult women who have been sexually exploited by priests. The Sexual Offences Act 2003 now criminalises sexual exploitation of vulnerable adults by 'care professionals' in a position of trust towards them, and does so even in cases where the vulnerable adult is legally capable of consenting to sex. The Act recognises the reality that consent alone should not be the determining factor given the power differential between care professional and patient. But the Act does not extend to clergy, even where clergy purport to provide therapeutic treatment. As abuse survivor groups such as MACSAS have argued, clergy should have been included given their role in providing pastoral care to vulnerable people. Indeed, in the discussions which preceded the Act, the wide range of situations which could give rise to vulnerable adult abuse was clearly recognised. In the Department of Health report *No Secrets*, published in 2000, a vulnerable adult was defined as 'a person who is, or may be, in need of community care services by reason of mental or other disability, age or illness; and who is or may be unable to take care of him or herself, or unable to protect him or herself against significant harm or exploitation'. This may sound like a definition aimed at those in institutional care, but the report was at pains to emphasise that 'community care services' should not be narrowly construed; it meant 'all care services provided in any setting or context'. Moreover, the list of possible perpetrators included 'members of any recognised professional group' (which could include priests) as well as volunteers at places of worship.[371] Abuse, the report explained, 'can take place in any context'.[372] *No Secrets* was primarily concerned with developing guidelines for use in healthcare contexts, not with developing the criminal law, but a 2002 Home Office report *Protecting the Public*, drawing on this greater awareness, set out proposals to update the law on sexual offences to protect vulnerable adults. Importantly, *Protecting the Public* recognised that protection needed to be extended in some cases to those adults who in law could consent to sexual activity but whose consent in reality might be compromised by their personal vulnerability given the power imbalance in the caring relationship.

Hence, the report proposed a new offence, 'breach of a relationship of care', which was designed to 'criminalise those providing certain kinds of care who engage in consensual sexual activity with those receiving it'. The report explained that this was necessary to protect those 'who have the capacity to consent but who are particularly vulnerable to exploitative behaviour and thus may agree to sexual activity solely because they are influenced by their familiarity with or dependency on the carer'.[373] The proposed new offence would 'place on a statutory footing matters currently covered by codes of conduct with regard to sexual activity within relationships of care and will create a criminal offence where the current penalty is purely disciplinary'.[374]

The proposed offence was enacted as section 38 of the Sexual Offences Act 2003. But the offence was limited to 'care workers', defined as those working in care homes, children's homes, the National Health Service or other medical settings. So psychologists or psychiatrists providing therapy are covered by the offence; the law recognises that where a patient seeks therapeutic treatment from a healthcare professional, there is almost inevitably an imbalance of power in the professional's favour, and this carries with it the potential for abuse, irrespective of 'consent'. A psychiatrist who initiates a sexual relationship with a patient would not merely be struck off the medical register but could now be prosecuted under s38. Clergy abuse survivor groups argued, rightly, that the same logic should apply to priests, but their arguments were rejected. A priest providing therapeutic services in a pastoral setting and who then goes on to sexually exploit, abuse and harm his vulnerable parishioner suffers no criminal sanction. This means that clergy can purport to provide therapeutic services for adults without those adults having the legal protection which would apply in virtually any other therapeutic setting.

Because most of the adult victims of sexual exploitation by priests are adult women who technically have the capacity to consent to sex, this means that almost no such cases have reached the criminal courts. The same problem applies to civil claims. As we saw in Chapter 5, in 2001 a Father Terence Fitzpatrick, formerly parish priest of St Osburg's Church in Coventry, was ordered to pay £70,000 damages after being held liable by a civil court for sexually assaulting a parishioner, Pamela Brown. Mrs Brown, who had previously been a victim of sexual abuse, had sought support from Father Fitzpatrick in the late 1980s. Over a period of two and a half years, Fitzpatrick had accompanied her to counselling sessions and then assaulted her. Father Fitzpatrick had told Mrs Brown that 'sex games' would be therapeutic, and that they were being conducted 'in the name of our Lord'. Mrs Brown suffered from post-traumatic stress disorder. The allegations had initially been investigated by West Midlands Police in 1993. Father Fitzpatrick claimed that she had consented to the 'relationship', and no criminal charges were brought. Mrs Brown, however, brought a civil claim against Fitzpatrick and in 2001, after many years of trying to defend the claim, Fitzpatrick finally admitted liability. But this case was very rare; in most cases involving clergy sexual exploitation of adult women, the consent issue appears to be fuzzier and thus the perpetrator escapes any legal sanction.

Professional disciplinary sanctions have also been ineffective against offending priests. Canon law provides limited guidance: Canon 277.2 says that 'clerics are to behave with due prudence in relation to persons whose company can be a danger to their obligation of preserving continence or can lead to a scandal of the faithful'. Canon 1395 stipulates that

> a cleric who lives in concubinage, and a cleric who continues in some other sin against the sixth commandment of the Decalogue which causes scandal, is to be punished with suspension. To this, other penalties can be progressively added if after a warning he persists in the offence, until eventually he can be dismissed from the clerical state.

As the clergy abuse survivors' group, MACSAS, has pointed out, the medieval language of the Code of Canon Law, which is simply designed to uphold celibacy, 'clearly does not recognise the abuse of power and betrayal of trust involved where clergy sexualise pastoral/spiritual counselling relationships'.[375] Even in the rare cases where findings of abuse are made, there seems to be a marked reluctance on the part of (male) Church authorities to impose punishment; this no doubt reflects the stereotyping of these relationships in Catholic culture as predatory woman preying on vulnerable celibate priest, when in fact the reverse is true. In 1996 Father Frank Goodall, a Redemptorist priest, was found guilty in a canonical tribunal of raping a nun, but no penalties were imposed and he continued in ministry until his death.[376] Father Fitzpatrick was also allowed to continue within the priesthood and indeed as at 2010 was still in active ministry.[377] Post-Nolan, a priest who had behaved in that way towards a minor would have been unlikely to remain in post, and the case illustrates how adults – particularly adult women who appear to have legal capacity – continue to attract less protection.

The scandal of sexual exploitation of adult women by priests continues to be denied by the English Catholic Church. Despite representations from clergy abuse survivor groups, vulnerable adult abuse was excluded from the Nolan Commission's remit and the Nolan Report mentioned it only as an afterthought, observing blandly that in due course the Church would need to consider 'policies and arrangements in this area'. COPCA was the 'Catholic Office for the Protection of Children and Vulnerable Adults', so the issue was part of its formal responsibilities, but its focus during its five-year lifespan was almost entirely on children.[378] Cumberlege commented that this would need to change 'if the Catholic Church is not to fall behind and find itself in the same position in relation to vulnerable adults as it did … in relation to child protection'. But despite this, and despite recommending that the Bishops' Conference 'should now adopt comprehensive safeguarding policies and procedures' for vulnerable adults, Cumberlege had little to say about the subject, to which it devoted just four pages of a 100-page report.

In fact, and reflecting traditional Catholic prejudices on the issue, Cumberlege's main contribution to the debate was to reject any attempt to define vulnerable adult 'to cover those who are temporarily vulnerable because of circumstances such as bereavement or family breakdown'.[379] In other words, adult women who might approach a priest in a time of distress or personal crisis and then be sexually exploited were to be *excluded* from the discussion. Their inclusion, claimed Cumberlege, would be 'unhelpful' because it would 'blur boundaries and almost certainly lead to inconsistency of approach' and because such people would fall outside the government's definition of vulnerable adults.[380] The problem, Cumberlege concluded, could be addressed by a 'Code of Conduct' for clergy – a code it declined to draw up as being outside its remit. In fact, a draft code of conduct for clergy, produced by a working party organised through COPCA, was rejected by the Bishops' Conference in 2006.[381] Thus, more than a decade after Nolan, the issue of vulnerable adult abuse remains almost entirely ignored in the Catholic Church, which still fails to acknowledge the breach of trust and abuse of power involved in many of these cases.

CHAPTER 12

A PLACE AT THE TABLE

From the start of the abuse crisis in England in the early 1990s, survivor groups have played a leading role in forcing the issue onto the media agenda and campaigning for change. The leading support group for survivors of clergy abuse in the UK is MACSAS (Ministry and Clergy Sexual Abuse Survivors), an organisation born out of CSSA (Christian Survivors of Sexual Abuse), which was founded in the 1980s. Whilst MACSAS has always had a broad interdenominational membership, two themes in particular have underpinned its work. One has been the feminist analysis of child abuse: MACSAS has seen child abuse as another dimension of patriarchy and has sought to challenge a male-dominated power structure. The second principle is that for survivors who want it, the Church itself should become a haven and a place of healing; for many survivors who have been abused in churches, faith is central to their lives, and therefore central to their recovery. This dual challenge – contesting deep-seated clerical prejudices and fighting for 'a place at the table' – has often been bitter and fraught.

CSSA was founded by Margaret Kennedy, an abuse survivor who had emigrated to England and trained as a social worker. Kennedy had undergone psychotherapy for her childhood experiences, but for years felt isolated trying to deal with her

traumas, 'a scared and troubled young adult' who never thought
to question the Church of her upbringing. In her first few
years in England Kennedy was a 'traditional female Catholic
do-gooder', working for the Vincent de Paul Society, meeting
the Pope on pilgrimage and joining a Benedictine community, the
Sisters of Jesus Crucified, as an oblate. 'It was a safe and cosy
Christianity,' Kennedy recalled later. 'There was little challenge and mighty certainty.' It failed to quell her inner turmoil;
Kennedy's childhood experiences of abuse eventually provoked
a profound rethinking about the relationship between abuse and
faith. 'Through all my cosy Christian do-gooding I never found
the peace I longed for ... psychotherapy helped but I longed for
a spiritual understanding of all I'd been through.' At this time of
spiritual confusion, Kennedy was beginning to work, as a social
worker, on the abuse of deaf children. From those experiences,
Kennedy developed a feminist conception of both Christianity
and child abuse:

> Child abuse shaped how I would view the world and it was a
> feminist world view, and remains so ... In trying to become
> more aware of the academic understanding of child abuse I
> was drawn to feminist literature ... what these women were
> writing made profound sense in my own experience within the
> patriarchal church.

But far from leading Kennedy away from religion, this refram-
ing deepened her faith. 'Secular feminism led me on to Christian
feminism ... a whole new way of being "Christian".'[382]

A turning point was when Kennedy attempted to seek help
from Catholic priests regarding her experiences of sexual abuse.

Angry about the abuse and asking herself 'How can I deal with this as a Christian?' she approached a Jesuit priest for guidance. His response – asking her if she was a virgin and telling her to 'go to confession and confess your sins of impurity' – astonished and appalled her; it was voyeuristic and shocking, utterly devoid of humanity. Kennedy then approached a Carmelite priest, who dismissively told her to see a psychiatrist, a bizarre response when she was trying to deal with issues of faith and spirituality. Kennedy concluded that there was much wrong with the institutional Church, and a male patriarchy lay at the heart of it.

Kennedy made contact with other women grappling with similar experiences, and they became CSSA, meeting in a derelict ward in Old Hackney Hospital. From the outset

> CSSA was underpinned by feminist thought but not overtly so. In my mind how it developed would be feminist, but it would also be Christian. Truly Christian, as opposed to what I perceived as 'false' Christianity … trying to secure a new pastoral response, clear in the knowledge that the responses I had received were not those of God.

They started producing literature, intended for people who had been brought up in a Christian context and had been abused in a faith setting. Initially the focus was abuse in the family. The Church took centre stage only later, as the clerical abuse scandal gathered momentum. Clerical abuse survivors contacted CSSA but were uncomfortable with the word 'Christian' in the title, and MACSAS was born.

All the members of CSSA were believers, 'grappling with confusion and fear'. At the heart of this was the Christian injunction to forgive, a weapon all too easily deployed by churches determined to bury the issue. 'If I don't forgive', wondered Kennedy and her fellow survivors, 'will God send me to hell? How does one overcome indoctrination?' But CSSA's meetings weren't prayer groups, they were not meant to be over-holy: 'I wanted us to be allowed to curse God. We needed the space to talk about the confusion of God and abuse.' The group became an authentic community, practising real Christianity, real mutual support and faith. It snowballed; Kennedy was proactive in seeking out new members, but hardly needed to be.

As the group became better known it attempted to engage with the Catholic hierarchy. The initial focus was child abuse in general, rather than clergy abuse specifically. Priests were encountering child abuse within their communities, but lacked the tools to deal with it; Kennedy wanted to educate them so they could carry out their pastoral role effectively. A few bishops were sympathetic: Kennedy speaks with particular fondness about her then bishop, Victor Guazzelli. Guazzelli was a 'saintly man, east London born, knowing hardship. He readily did what I wanted him to do, putting his head above the denial parapet and working with us, sometimes in a limited way, but always open.'

In May 1990 Guazzelli invited Kennedy to present at a senate meeting of all London priests – the first such meeting dedicated to 'childhood sexual abuse and its implications for pastoral care and training of clergy'. Cardinal Hume also attended. The mere fact of the meeting was indicative of a raised awareness of the clerical abuse issue, which was dominating the headlines in the USA. At this stage, however, the focus was on abuse within Roman Catholic families rather than the priesthood. Kennedy remembers 'being very scared. It was like walking into the lion's den. I was the only woman at the meeting. From the community of survivors, there was only me and a priest who was a survivor.'

Kennedy tried to explain to the priests about the dynamics of child abuse:

> Sexual abuse is predominantly about power not sex ... the primary motivation is the need for power and control over a weaker partner (a child) ... The first reaction to abuse is to deny it ... we need to confront this denial and lack of action.

But part of the action needed, she explained, was support for victims and survivors who 'need our continuing prayer, practical support, pastoral services and advice ... I ask you to facilitate a beginning process in pastoral action for the survivors of childhood sexual abuse.'

Nothing Kennedy said at that 1990 meeting would seem controversial now, but the priests she spoke to were conservative, uneasy talking about sex and especially uncomfortable being challenged by a woman. Their reactions ranged from bewilderment to outright hostility. Several insisted that any dialogue had to start with her accepting the possibility of false allegations. 'I said yes, they happen, they are very rare, and often it involves people who have confused events. Why do you ask?' One priest complained that he had been falsely accused; Bishop Guazzelli had to reassure him that nobody in the meeting believed that he was an abuser. Kennedy's impression was that priests were very nervous but 'they were not nervous in a guilty way, but nervous about having to deal with it. Having to talk about it.' Some of the priests talked of parishioners approaching them about abuse in a family setting; as society became more open about abuse, parish priests were getting a lot of this, and it made them uncomfortable.

Kennedy argued that the Church should do three things: openly and publicly state its support of abuse survivors; conduct research to determine how survivors were coping; and appoint pastoral officers with specialist abuse counselling training. The key message was around pastoral care: priests clearly didn't have the skills to provide this so she resolved to pursue more conferences and training. Bishop Guazzelli helped, both in organising and in proselytising. At Stepping Out – Recognising the Need, a joint 1991 conference organised by the Westminster diocese and CSSA, Bishop Guazzelli spoke powerfully in favour of pastoral care, arguing that the Church must not turn its back on people who have been sexually abused; 'their shame, guilt and anger is made worse when they turn to the Church for help only to find rejection'.[383] Bishop Guazzelli spoke of his sense of shame when he heard how some priests had treated survivors: 'Priests have a special role of service to provide and they're not trained for it.'[384]

In 2014, these ideas might seem uncontroversial, but in fact Kennedy's challenge was very discomforting to the clergy, and has remained so: her ambitions for public support for survivors, proper research and specialist pastoral officers remain largely unfulfilled. Priests, says Kennedy, are much more comfortable working with perpetrators than with victims, 'redeeming the man who has abused, which is a one-dimensional problem, whereas victims have multi-dimensional problems – this at any rate is their assumption, although it is not necessarily true'. This is even more the case where the perpetrators are other priests and where the victims are challenging the way male power is abused within the Church. Kennedy challenged the suitability of the confessional as a place for survivors to disclose abuse, pointing out that survivors may be uncomfortable in close proximity to a male priest and intrinsic to the confessional is confession of *sin*. Many survivors would blame themselves for the abuse and would feel that they needed to go to confession to confess their guilt and the part they played in the abuse. 'It should be made quite clear to survivors that this is not something to be brought to the Confessional because there is no blame attached to the survivor.'[385] In saying this, Kennedy was challenging clericalism in a profound way, telling priests that they were out of their depth and that the confessional could deepen a survivor's anguish. This was not well received. Kennedy argued that confessionals should have glass doors to protect children: this was seen as a slander on priests' integrity, but ten years later was essentially accepted by Nolan.

In Kennedy's vision, central to pastoral care was that survivors must have recognition, a place within the Church – a sense that the Church loves and supports survivors rather than shunning them because they ask difficult questions. Kennedy has always acknowledged that this is not the desire of every survivor, but argues forcefully that it should be there for those who want it. At first, the signs were positive. In 1994 CSSA wanted to have its annual interdenominational service in Westminster Cathedral, an event entitled 'Why do we weep?' Bishop Guazzelli was a key influence in procuring this 'powerful event which many survivors still remember with joy'.[386] The ecumenical service was the first in such a high-profile location.

In preparation for the service Kennedy and her colleagues met with Cardinal Hume. Kennedy recalls Hume as 'very caring man' but she was never sure how deep it went – she knew survivors who were rebuffed and at least one who was badly hurt by Hume but in the meeting he was 'nice and open'. A little lamp sat on his desk, a koala hugging the stem. The cardinal's secretary had been concerned when it was explained that participants would be praying for lesbian, gay and transgender victims of clergy abuse. The Archbishop of Westminster was relaxed about this, but nervous about a liturgy written and performed by survivors – 'I don't want this to be a pantomime'. But he didn't ask Kennedy and her colleagues to make any changes, or clear the service in advance. Nor did he attempt to engineer the service into a PR exercise.

It was 'a powerful, very poignant service'. Westminster Cathedral was festooned with banners and wall hangings. All the speakers were ordinary survivors, very nervous. On the day of the service Kennedy told Hume's assistant that the archbishop was not going to be sitting in the sanctuary. He was to be in the congregation with other religious leaders: 'We the survivors will be in the sanctuary.' Hume took this humbly. Kennedy remembers her contribution in the service. 'I was very nervous. My legs were like jelly,' but Hume was welcoming, telling the congregation: 'Thank God for the gift of Margaret Kennedy.' Around 500 people attended and Hume gave a £2,000 donation to CSSA. A wall hanging was dedicated – seventy-two squares – with the title *A Visible Sign of Our Presence*.

The service seemed like a great advance but in some ways, says Kennedy, it was the high point of the hierarchy's acceptance of survivor campaigners. Ultimately, she felt, it turned out to be tokenistic. Hume wanted to be seen to be sympathetic but never really understood how many survivors wanted to be truly welcomed and included by the Church; not to be invisible.

The point was encapsulated by the 1998 controversy over the *Stations of the Cross* in Westminster Cathedral. This famous woodcarving, by the English sculptor Eric Gill, was traditionally regarded as one of the artistic treasures of English Catholicism. Gill himself, who died in 1940, was seen as a profoundly religious figure, remembered not only as a fine artist but as one of the founders of Distributism.[387] However in 1989 Fiona MacCarthy's biography of Gill, drawing for the first time on his private diaries, revealed not so much a life of religious striving as one of prolific sexual perversion and depravity: Gill had repeatedly sexually abused his own daughters, committed incest with his sister and engaged in sexual acts with his dog. The appalling flavour of Gill's private life can be gleaned from a diary entry describing a visit to his youngest daughter's bedroom: 'stayed half an hour – put p. in her a/hole'.[388]

In the ensuing furore some of Gill's supporters in the Catholic press made light of his behaviour in ways which seem inconceivable today – a measure, perhaps, of the impact of twenty years of clerical abuse scandals. The Catholic architect Patrick Nuttgens, reviewing MacCarthy's book in *The Tablet*, claimed that Gill's 'sexual expression was never violent, it was an expression of love … I doubt if he really hurt anyone … He just had an obsession with his own penis and its potentialities.'[389] A Dominican priest dismissed Gill's private activities as 'peccadilloes'.[390] Tom Burns, the leading Catholic journalist and former *Tablet* editor, claimed that the media focus on Gill's sexual behaviour had 'blown it up out of all proportion', risking a 'distorted view of a great and good man' who was 'the humblest and most lovable of men'.[391] Others were appalled by such comments, which revealed a chilling ignorance of the reality of child abuse.

The argument died down but was reignited in 1998 when Cardinal Hume appeared on a television programme, 'Lent in the Park', speaking in reverential terms of Gill and his *Stations*. Kennedy challenged Hume in a controversy immediately seized on by the national press, which was now reporting the Catholic abuse scandal on a daily basis. 'To survivors', said Kennedy, Hume's reverence for the sculpture gave 'a message of gross insensitivity. It spoke to me of the Cardinal's inability to understand that honouring a paedophile's work ignored the suffering of his victims.'[392] The Catholic Church, said Kennedy,

> has a long history of ignoring child sexual abuse, hiding priests, saying when they are caught 'He was a good priest' or 'He was a prayerful man,' denying completely the evil of paedophilia, and the devastation of its victims. Seeing Cardinal Hume under Eric Gill's carving of a station said to me: 'We will not mention Gill's depravity, only his skills, we will use these tainted and contaminated sculptures to call the faithful to prayer, we will not consider the pain of survivors of sexual abuse' ... in other words we will do as we always do ... keep secret our sins. Keep secret the sin of incest.[393]

The *Stations of the Cross*, explained Kennedy, were 'not just another artwork. It is where we pray. You are supposed to be transported into Jesus Christ. You suffer with him. It is one of the fundamentals of Catholicism.'[394] Clifford Longley, writing in *The Tablet*, grasped her point: ordinarily, he wrote,

> the compact between the artist and the viewer does not depend on high standards of personal morality, on either side. But

religious art is a little different. It is here that moral integrity
and artistic integrity converge ... It is a communication from
the viewer to the believer which, as Newman said, speaks heart
to heart.[395]

But in the main the Catholic press was hostile to Kennedy, going
into outrage mode and screaming about censorship, particularly
when she suggested that the *Stations* might be removed. The
notion, argued a letter writer in the *Catholic Herald*, is the 'product of a mind narrow, boorish and pharisaical'.[396] Kennedy tried
to explain that

my concern is not essentially about Gill's art, which I agree is
of substantial merit when he does not digress into pornography.
My concern is with the juxtaposition of Gill's art (and therefore
the man), Westminster Cathedral and prayer. Also with the total
invisibility of Gill's victims and all Catholic (or Christian) victims
by patriarchal churches. It is a pastoral and spiritual concern not
an aesthetic one. Cardinal Hume extols the virtues of a paedophile's art without any reference to either his victims or present
day survivors of child abuse. The Cardinal's insensitivity was felt.
That remains my main point.[397]

• • •

Genuine pastoral care within the Church for survivors who want
it has remained one of MACSAS's central aims. It has also been
the area in which the English Church has failed most abjectly
over the past two decades: survivors continue to have the sense
that the Church wishes they would just disappear. Kennedy

acknowledges that some Catholic bishops have been genuine –
like Bishop Budd, who in 1994 invited CSSA to contribute to
its new Pastoral and Procedural Guidelines.[398] But overall, the
Church's reluctance to engage with survivors seemed to worsen
as the clerical abuse scandal unfolded. It was as if the Church
could cope with child abuse in the abstract, but grew defensive
and even hostile to survivors once the Church itself was exposed
as the abuser, and once survivors started to demand a voice. For
Kennedy the last twenty years have been, in the main, intensely
frustrating. As we saw earlier, Nolan's recommendations around
care for survivors were vague. Donald Findlater, a leading specialist in the treatment of sex offenders, and who assisted the Nolan
Commission, would like to have seen Nolan devote proper
attention to the rights and pastoral care of survivors. Victims of
clerical abuse need a seat around the table with those determining what should happen to the person who abused them:

> Survivors are part of the Church and they have a right to say how
> these things are dealt with. It is a profound offence to them to see
> someone who has committed a crime against a human being take
> any position in the Church which gives them the opportunity to
> misuse their authority again.[399]

Post-Nolan, COPCA established a group on pastoral care for
survivors but very little came of it. There was limited funding for it,
but in any event the approach was fundamentally misconceived.
Kennedy sat on the committee for two years and documents were
drawn up. But what then emerged was a 'charter' for victims and
a 'covenant' for perpetrators. The linguistic distinction was very
telling: 'A covenant', Kennedy points out, 'is more profound. It

implies a higher and better level of treatment. In the end I wasn't clear why different language was used and the church was unable to explain that to me.' Kennedy resigned from the committee, but both documents were dumped and never materialised. It was 'two wasted years'. In March 2006 new guidelines stated that dioceses could use volunteers or members of the clergy to counsel victims – professional qualifications were not considered necessary. Sally Chisholm, a qualified counsellor employed by the Diocese of Westminster who was made redundant following the publication of the guidelines, continued to work unpaid with some adult victims but was clear that the diocese was letting down survivors: 'In many senses, they have been further abused by a Church that held out its hand then withdrew it without notice.'[400]

Both for Kennedy, and for her successor at MACSAS, Alana Lawrence, the critical issue is whether the Church is willing to engage with the survivor or just wants to pass them on to someone else. 'In a nutshell we were looking for honesty and truth. We wanted a leaflet setting out what the church would offer. We didn't want signposting.'[401] MACSAS really wanted the Church to get involved with survivors, but it wasn't really interested. There were other issues too: was the Church using trained people or volunteers? Volunteers, as Cumberlege made clear, were insufficient. Lack of funding was a serious problem, as Eileen Shearer said openly after her resignation. To MACSAS, it is evidence of a lack of genuine commitment. As Lawrence says: 'the Church can set up CAFOD to go round the world and feed the poor. But funding for child protection is pathetic. It is so hypocritical.'[402]

But most of all, there remains in Kennedy's mind the sense

that the Church finds survivors uncomfortable and doesn't want
to deal with them. This goes right to the top:

> For Pope Benedict's visit in 2010 we created a book of survivor
> stories and tried to give it to the Pope. We asked the cardinal, the
> papal nuncio and the Church's child protection team to help us
> give the book to Pope Benedict. They refused. In the crowds at
> Westminster Abbey, we hoped to give it to the Pope as he passed.
> We were barracked, jostled and barred from doing this by Opus
> Dei supporters. Ultimately the meeting between the survivors
> and the Pope was stage-managed – it was held in secret and not
> with people the mainstream survivor groups had come across.[403]

The solution to pastoral care, as MACSAS sees it, would be
for the Church to provide proper funding to employ a core group
of professionals to work with survivors. 'We want a helpline
funded by the church. Counselling funded by the church. An
independent confidential helpline of trained counsellors. As it is
there is nothing within the English church. No spiritual support,
no retreats arranged for survivors, no prayer.' The Church has
become better at safeguarding but is very poor at pastoral support.
It doesn't want to engage. Why not? Kennedy believes that 'there
is underlying all of this, a hatred of victims, a fundamental anger
against victims where we have never really been forgiven for
breaking the taboo of secrecy'.[404] Alana Lawrence says that a
Church true to its beliefs would want to be the antidote to the
suffering caused by abuse:

> If you believe the Church has a mission, it is to be the place where
> broken people can come and find a way of healing – a place of

reconciling and wholeness. That is what it should be – the haven for people we have broken and wounded and harmed. That is what Diarmuid Martin [Archbishop of Dublin] said it should be, and they hated him for it. The Church needs a radical mission statement; for every person harmed in this church we will make this a place where we will walk beside you. Yes, it is about a pastoral programme, but it is as much an attitude of mind as anything else. If you were true to your beliefs you would want all victims to come forward – you'd be calling people out. But the bishops don't want to think about real victims. Names of people hurt.[405]

The Vatican claimed to attach high priority to the needs of survivors and set a deadline of May 2012 for a progress report from each national Church on meeting survivor needs. But in 2011 MACSAS and the Lantern Project, the Merseyside-based survivor support organisation, ended 'exploratory talks' convened with the Church a few months earlier. The Church, they felt, was 'using the discussions as a smokescreen for inaction'.[406] The talks – with the National Catholic Safeguarding Commission (NCSC) and the Catholic Safeguarding Advisory Service (CSAS) – were intended to lead to the creation of a 'comprehensive support package' for victims of sexual abuse by clergy. Graham Wilmer, who heads the Lantern Project and was himself abused by a Catholic priest, said: 'We were prepared to talk to [the institution] that had harmed us, even though it was uncomfortable, because the end of it should be worthwhile ... But we can't trust them. What has effectively happened is nothing.'[407]

Archbishop Vincent Nichols, the head of the Catholic Church in England and Wales, declined to meet Wilmer or the forum before the two groups walked out. Wilmer explained that an aggravating factor for his organisation was that the Church had continued to oppose victims seeking compensation over the past year:

> There certainly is the intention to deliver what looks like an attempt to produce a better response to victims of abuse, but when you test it, you just end up with a bunch of lawyers ... the Catholic Church are not prepared to deal with the victims of its abuse in any way other than to fight them through the courts.[408]

The Catholic Church, said MACSAS in a statement,

> is still not ready to accept responsibility for the actions of its clergy and members of religious congregations who raped and abused thousands of children in this country over the past fifty years. Victims have been reporting this abuse to Church authorities for decades and have yet to receive any compassionate or appropriate response. This failure to hear, to respond and to accept responsibility is a scandal. No bishop attended the 'exploratory talks' and the Archbishop of Westminster refused to have any discussions with any survivor organisations even when it became obvious that the people appointed by the Church to engage in these talks lacked the skills and authority necessary to engage in any meaningful discussion with those representing victims ... MACSAS has stated throughout that we are open to any processes aimed at providing justice and redress for victims and reconciliation between the Church and those so terribly harmed, where appropriate. The Catholic Church in England and Wales does not yet understand the need for these processes and yet over 300 cases are in the civil courts and dozens of cases are currently in the criminal courts.

Graham Wilmer for the Lantern Project also pointed out that 'bishops have continued to argue in the courts that the Church has no responsibility for the actions of its clergy' and that this is 'incompatible with public apologies made by the Conference of Bishops'.[409]

A month later the bishops, meeting in Leeds, acknowledged that 'survivors of abuse who come to the Church for pastoral help rightly expect to be welcomed and listened to, and to be understood and supported' but admitted that 'this has not been adequately developed as an integral part of our safeguarding work'. The bishops referred to 'continuing discussions taking place with a number of survivor organisations' but failed to mention that both MACSAS and the Lantern Project had withdrawn from the talks. More than a decade after Nolan, the Church's failure to meet the needs of survivors is its greatest betrayal.

CHAPTER 13

LEGAL BATTLES

A t least sixty-one Catholic priests who have sexually abused children or vulnerable adults, or who have committed child sex-related internet crimes, have been convicted in the criminal courts of England and Wales since 1990. Many more have escaped justice. Victims too frightened to disclose; families pressured by the Church to stay silent; perpetrators fleeing overseas; prosecutions never brought because of insufficient evidence: for all these reasons, most clerical sex offenders will never be brought to book.[410] But the criminal law is only one element of the legal process and across the world many survivors of abuse have looked to the civil courts for redress, seeking reparation for harm suffered. This redress can only come from the institution, and in England and Wales compensation claims have become a battleground for the Church's corporate liability for sex abuse.

For many survivors, compensation is not an end in itself but a means, albeit imperfect, of forcing the Church to accept responsibility. I have been told many times by clients that compensation, whilst often necessary to rebuild broken lives, is secondary to a proper apology and frank admission of culpability. The inability or unwillingness of the Catholic Church openly to admit past sins and express true remorse forces survivors down legal avenues many would rather avoid. That said, in some jurisdictions, the financial impact of damages claims has been significant in forcing the Church to change. On one estimate, over 3,000 sex abuse lawsuits have been brought against the Catholic Church in the USA[411] and the total damages paid in the USA between 1950 and 2007 exceeded £2 billion.[412] Between 2007 and 2011, eight US dioceses sought some form of bankruptcy protection due to abuse cases.[413] Some jury awards in the USA are reduced on appeal and the eventual settlement is lower than the newspaper headline. Nevertheless, in the USA the financial imperative for the Catholic Church to stamp out child abuse within its ranks has become irresistible: it simply cannot afford to carry on paying out claims of this magnitude and remain financially solvent.

In England, civil claims for child abuse – against the Catholic Church or anyone else – are a relatively recent phenomenon. It was only in the late 1990s that such claims became commonplace. Initially, child sex abuse claims were brought against individual perpetrators. However, legal and practical obstacles came into play. In the early 1990s, Lesley Stubbings attempted to sue her foster father and brother for sexual abuse committed against her many years before. Her claim was struck out by the House of Lords in 1995 on time-limit grounds. The judges held that, as the law then stood, any claim against an individual abuser was subject to a strict six-year time limit running from the date on which the claimant turned eighteen (the limitation 'clock' does not tick against a child.) After the six years the claim was automatically extinguished, even if the delay was an entirely understandable consequence of the shame and fear that invariably accompany sex abuse.

Miss Stubbings appealed to the European Court of Human

Rights, but to no avail. The Stubbings decision, which was not overturned until 2008, thus placed an almost insuperable hurdle in the way of claims against individual abusers, although some claims of this kind continued to be made: in 2000 a Coventry priest, Father Terence Fitzpatrick, was ordered to pay £70,000 damages to a vulnerable adult parishioner.[414] Claimants could only surmount the six-year time limit if they lacked legal capacity throughout the whole of the period between the assaults and the start of the claim. But even if this condition could be met, an individual perpetrator might not have money to pay the claim and therefore any legal action could be futile. Of course, this outcome is almost inevitable with those Catholic priests who upon ordination take a vow of poverty.[415]

In the mid- to late 1990s, therefore, claimants and their lawyers started to sue not only individuals, but organisations which had failed to protect children in their care. This trend was spurred by a growing awareness of the extent of abuse of children in institutional settings such as residential care homes. The Waterhouse Report in 2000, *Lost in Care*, exposed a damning catalogue of abuse and neglect in children's homes in north Wales. The early claims which came before the courts involved secular organisations like local authorities. In 1996, Leicestershire County Council accepted liability in a group action brought by claimants who suffered abuse at children's homes in Leicestershire in which the serial abuser Frank Beck was employed. A template was established for subsequent group litigation against other organisations. The first stirrings of litigation against the Catholic Church followed shortly afterwards: the first compensation cases against the Church seem to have been brought in relation to Father Samuel Penney.[416]

Over the last fifteen years, thousands of compensation claims have been brought against local authorities, churches, schools and youth organisations. But contrary to popular myth England has not become like America. Under English law, such claims have been bedevilled by a number of legal and practical difficulties, which the Catholic Church, more than most defendants, has not been slow to exploit.

VICARIOUS LIABILITY

Child abuse litigation in England and Wales over the past two decades has been dominated by arguments about the extent of corporate or organisational liability for individual misconduct. In tort law, the concept that an organisation is liable for the actions of a person whom they employ is known as 'vicarious liability'. In order for vicarious liability to arise, the actions in question have to have been within the 'course of employment': self-evidently, as an employer I am not liable for the wrongful actions of my employee if those actions fall outside the employment context. Before 2001, no organisation could be held vicariously liable for the actions of an employee who committed sexual assaults. Such behaviour was not deemed to be 'within the course of employment'. A school, it was reasoned, does not employ a teacher to sexually abuse pupils. A teacher who did that was on a 'frolic of his own'. He might be personally liable to pay damages, but his employer was not.

However, his employer might be liable if it knew or ought to have known that the teacher was committing abuse or was at risk of doing so: then liability would arise in 'negligence', the failure of the employer to take proper care. So, before 2001, a claimant seeking to hold the Church liable for damages had to prove that the Church knew or ought to have known of the abuse: one had to fix the diocesan hierarchy with knowledge of the abuser's propensity.

This was generally a tall order evidentially, even if the claimant had suspicions of institutional knowledge and cover-up. Suspicions are one thing, actual proof another. Proving what one priest knew of the behaviour of another, or what a distressed and concerned parent may have said to a Church official some years earlier, is often difficult. In the cases reviewed in this book only dogged detective work by police, lawyers and investigative journalists unearthed the truth of institutional knowledge and cover-up.

Even where it could be shown that the institution knew something, the Church would often resist liability, for example by claiming that what was known fell short of true knowledge of actual or threatened abuse: if there were concerns, it would be claimed, they related to nothing more serious than 'over-familiarity' between priest and child, which might be entirely innocent.[417] Another disputed area was information or allegations imparted in the confessional. A victim might 'confess' the abuse or the abuser might do so to another priest.[418] The legal question is whether information imparted in this way could be said to fix the Church with knowledge of the abuser's behaviour. The Church, of course, would invariably advance the sanctity of the confessional as excusing its failure to act on the information received.

Although the issue has been debated in legal cases, the status of information received in the confessional has never been the subject of a court decision and it seems that the Church has been reluctant to fight the point to trial. In the law and culture of the Catholic Church, the sanctity of the confessional is absolute.

According to the 1983 Code of Canon Law, 'the sacramental seal is inviolable. Accordingly, it is absolutely wrong for a confessor in any way to betray the penitent, for any reason whatsoever, whether by word or in any other fashion.'[419] So absolute is this sanctity that even the penitent cannot release the priest from it. It is not a form of confidentiality that can be waived; it is inviolable and stands for all time. Canon law also imposes restrictions on what information can be sought from the penitent: 'In asking questions the priest is to act with prudence and discretion, taking into account the condition and age of the penitent, and he is to refrain from enquiring the name of a partner in sin.'[420] So the priest faced with an allegation of child abuse imparted in the confessional may not even ask the name of the abuser, this has to be volunteered.[421]

Both the Pastoral and Procedural Guidelines (1994) and the Nolan Report assumed that the sanctity of the confessional would remain absolute.[422] However, the relationship of priest and penitent is not, in my view, a relationship to which privilege attaches in English law, although it does in some other jurisdictions. Where a priest becomes aware that someone has a propensity to sexually abuse children, his duties under canon law would not have the effect of displacing his obligations under English law to take reasonable care for a parishioner's safety. The obligations imposed by secular law are not ones which the representatives of the Church are free to disregard simply because they conflict with the Church's own scheme for its internal regulation. Therefore, I believe that a failure to act on information obtained during confession would be considered negligent by an English court. But perhaps sensibly, the Church never pushed to point to a judicial decision.

The issue is not now likely to be decided in England and Wales, because over the past decade a set of judicial decisions have gradually whittled away the need to prove negligence, and most claims against the Church can now be framed in terms of vicarious liability. In a landmark decision in *Lister* v. *Hesley Hall* (2001), the House of Lords held that an employer could be vicariously liable for sexual abuse committed by an employee where the employee's misconduct was 'so closely connected with his employment that it would be fair and just to hold the employer vicariously liable'.[423]

From the claimant standpoint, this was a significant advance in the law, although due to problems concerning the Limitation Act (see below), the full benefit of this decision was not felt until the House of Lords decision in *Hoare* in 2008. The *Hoare* case involved an imprisoned rapist who won £7 million on the lottery during a weekend release. One of his victims who had been raped decades earlier tried to sue him but was stymied by the strict six-year limitation period; she appealed her case to the House of Lords, who changed the law. The *Hoare* decision, which enabled the courts to waive the normal limitation period in direct assault cases provided a fair trial was still possible, paved the way for large numbers of historic abuse claims to be successfully argued on the basis of vicarious liability.

Post-*Lister* and especially post-*Hoare*, with vicarious liability firmly established in principle and the limitation defence having been narrowed down, the Catholic Church then tried to contest the *scope* of vicarious liability. In essence, the Church sought to argue that it could not be vicariously liable for a priest. The argument was initially put on the basis that certain of a priest's activities were not sufficiently 'closely connected' with the Church. When that failed, the Church argued that vicarious liability should not apply because a priest is not an employee.

That issue first came before the English courts in the *Maga* case.[424] This was a claim against the Archdiocese of Birmingham. Father Christopher Clonan had befriended and abused Maga, a child living in the archdiocese who was a non-Catholic.[425] Clonan and his victim initially met through their shared interest in sports cars. Clonan then employed Maga to do odd jobs at the presbytery and subsequently some of the abuse took place on Church premises. At trial, the fact that Father Clonan's association with the claimant started with his use of the claimant to wash his car and do his cleaning, in other words 'non-priestly activities', was fatal to the claim; the judge concluded that the Church was not vicariously liable as 'the association [i.e. between Clonan and Maga] was not part of evangelisation'.

However, overturning the trial judge, the Court of Appeal found that there was the requisite 'close connection' between the Church and the abuse for vicarious liability to arise. Lord Justice Neuberger listed multiple reasons for this close connection. These included such things as the fact that Father Clonan was normally dressed in clerical garb and was so dressed when he first met the claimant, and was referred to as 'Father'; the fact that his functions as a priest included the duty to evangelise amongst non-Catholics; the fact that Father Clonan had special responsibility for youth work in the Church; and the fact that some of the grooming and abuse took place on Church premises. In a memorable passage Lord Justice Longmore explained the court's reasoning:

For centuries the Church has encouraged lay persons to look up to (and indeed revere) their priests. The Church clothes them

in clerical garb and bestows upon them their title Father, a title
which Father Clonan was happy to use. It is difficult to think of
a role nearer to that of parent than that of priest. In this circum-
stance the absence of any formal legal responsibility is almost
beside the point.

Other common-law countries, particularly Canada and Australia,
have also been grappling with Catholic Church scandals and their
courts have also had to determine the extent of Church liability
for clerical misconduct. Commonwealth decisions are persuasive
in our courts and in finding for the claimant in *Maga* the Court
of Appeal drew on the earlier Canadian case of *Jacobi*.[426] In this
decision the Canadian Supreme Court applied to Church liability a concept of 'enterprise risk'. In order to establish vicarious
liability, the claimant must show that the 'employment significantly contributed to the occurrence of the harm'; in other words
the risk of abuse was inherent in the defendant's enterprise.
Newspaper headlines had been suggesting for some years that
few enterprises carried a greater risk of abuse than the Catholic
priesthood. *Jacobi* laid the ground for *Maga*.

In *Maga* the Archdiocese of Birmingham had conceded that in
principle it could be vicariously liable for the actions of its priest.[427]
However, in the next test case, *JGE*,[428] the Church tried to argue
that it could not be vicariously liable for the actions of a priest
in any circumstances because a priest is not an employee of the
Church, or even akin to one. If this argument had succeeded, then
effectively the Catholic Church would cease to have any liability
whatsoever for abuse committed by priests, save where negligence
could be proved – a return to the old pre-*Lister* battleground.

The anonymised claimant JGE was a woman who alleged she

was sexually abused by Father Wilfred Baldwin, who worked in the Diocese of Portsmouth during the 1970s. She said that she was raped by Father Baldwin (now deceased) when she was a six-year-old resident in a local children's home. She sought compensation from the diocese on the basis that because the priest was engaged to work in the Portsmouth diocese, it was vicariously liable for his behaviour.

For the court, the issue turned on the relationship between Father Baldwin and the diocese. The diocese argued that a priest is not an employee. As the judge in *JGE* noted, there were certainly features of Father Baldwin's position with the diocese which distinguished it from normal employment. There was no written contract of employment. Father Baldwin was not paid by the diocese, but relied on his parish to generate the income to support him. The diocese could not dismiss him; this could only be done by the Vatican. The Inland Revenue treated Father Baldwin as an office holder not an employee.

However, and as the Church conceded, there are many English case law authorities which confirm that a formal contract of employment is not a prerequisite for vicarious liability. As the Court of Appeal explained in another case, the issue is control: who has control over the actions of the person who is committing the wrongful act.

And the answer is that a bishop has control over his priests.

There are many canons in the Code of Canon Law which confirm that the relationship between a priest and his bishop is one of obedience:

Christ's faithful, conscious of their own responsibility, are bound to show Christian obedience to what the sacred pastors, who represent Christ, declare as teachers of the faith and prescribe as rulers of the Church.[429]

Clerics have a special obligation to show reverence and obedience to the Supreme Pontiff and to their own ordinary.[430]

Appointment to the office of a parish priest belongs to the diocesan bishop, who is free to confer it on whomsoever he wishes.[431]

A parish priest ceases to hold office by removal or transfer affected by the diocesan bishop in accordance with the law; by his personal resignation, for a just reason, which for validity requires that it be accepted by the diocesan bishop.[432]

In the exercise of the office of preaching, everyone is moreover to observe the norms laid down by the bishop of the diocese.[433]

Likewise, Pope Paul VI's 'Decree on the Ministry and Life of Priests'[434] said of the relationship between priest and bishop that 'priests, never losing sight of the fullness of the priesthood which the bishops enjoy, must respect them in the authority of Christ, the supreme shepherd. They must therefore stand by their bishops in sincere charity and obedience…'

Moreover, whilst the issue in *JGE* had not previously been decided by the English courts, once again an identical point had been considered by the Canadian courts – and had been decided against the Church. In *Doe* v. *Bennett* (2004), the Canadian Supreme Court held that a Catholic bishop was vicariously liable for the actions of a paedophile priest. Whether or not the bishop and the priest had an 'employment contract' in the strict legal sense was beside the point. The bishop exercised control over the priest and therefore they had a relationship 'akin to that of employment'. Therefore, said the Canadian Supreme Court, it was fair and just to impose vicarious liability on the bishop.

Applying these precedents, the trial judge held that the diocese was vicariously liable for the actions of Father Baldwin: 'By appointing Father Baldwin as a priest, and thus clothing him with all the powers involved, the defendants created a risk of harm to others, viz. the risk that he could abuse or misuse his powers for his own purposes…'[435]

The Court of Appeal upheld the trial judge's decision, confirming that in certain circumstances organisations can be vicariously liable for persons they do not formally employ, i.e. where the relationship is akin to employment and where the organisation exercises control, a Catholic priest being a good example. The Court of Appeal decision in *JGE* proved to be the end of the road for the Catholic Church on the issue of vicarious liability: it sought to appeal the case to the Supreme Court, but permission was refused. The Supreme Court regarded the issue as having been settled for good.

The Bishop of Portsmouth attacked the ruling, claiming that it is wrong that

> a bishop should be automatically liable for the actions of a priest simply by virtue of the fact that he or one of his predecessors appointed the priest. The diocese is aware of no other organisation which can be held liable for the actions of its office holders in this way.[436]

The decision also provoked hysteria in the Catholic blogosphere, with many traditionalist Catholics seemingly outraged at the judgment: how could the courts possibly believe that a priest is an 'employee' of the Church? But this reaction betrayed a fundamental misunderstanding of the doctrine of vicarious liability, which is not restricted to employment situations. *JGE* was about the scope of vicarious liability in circumstances where the perpetrator of abuse is 'akin to an employee', which every priest is. If anything, by seeking to evade claims on the basis of the legal peculiarities of the position of priest, the Catholic Church was seeking immunity in respect of the actions of the people who work for it granted to no other organisation. This seems an unattractive argument, especially for an organisation which has had an endemic problem of child abuse and which publicly professes to be dealing with it. Perhaps belatedly recognising the reputational damage caused to the Church by its legal sophistry in *JGE*, the chair of the National Catholic Safeguarding Commission publicly criticised the diocese's stance in the case. Speaking at the launch of the NCSC's 2011–12 annual report, Danny Sullivan said it was 'important to avoid the perception that the needs of victims of clerical abuse were not the Church's priority'.[437]

The decade-long war over vicarious liability, therefore, has now been emphatically won by claimants. Negligence with all its evidential difficulties need not be proved; it is enough to show that the priest was acting under the umbrella of the Church. That is obviously beneficial for individual claimants, who can get their compensation more quickly. However, if liability attaches irrespective of fault, it is no longer necessary for lawyers to probe into how the Church handled abuse cases, and whether it was guilty of negligence or worse. The requirement to prove negligence exposed the church's historic failings; under a vicarious-liability regime, more favourable though it is for claimant compensation, none of this will come to light. Ironically, the very result that the Church has resisted may actually protect it from greater scrutiny in the future.

LIMITATION

But vicarious liability is only one of the hurdles which a claimant has to surmount. Arguments about time limits have been even more fraught. This is because a very high proportion of child abuse cases involve 'limitation' issues; in other words the case is brought well after the expiry of the normal time limit, so the court has to decide whether to allow a late claim. Many abuse cases are very old: some involve allegations dating back to the 1950s. In a case relating to a local authority care home, Lord Justice Sedley explained why:

> Inevitably there is a problem of limitation in these proceedings. I say 'inevitably' because it is in the nature of abuse of children by adults that it creates shame, fear and confusion, and these in turn produce silence. Silence is one of the most pernicious fruits of abuse. It means that allegations commonly surface, if they do, only many years after the abuse has ceased.[438]

Typically cases may surface ten, twenty or even thirty years after the assault complained of. Limitation law for many years suffered from the fundamental flaw that it was never designed with child abuse in mind. A child abuse claim is a personal injury claim; therefore, the time limits which apply are essentially the same as those which apply to a road traffic accident, a pavement trip or an industrial illness. The Limitation Act 1980 gives the claimant no more than three years to come forward: a hopelessly unrealistic requirement.

It took the courts many years to appreciate the unique problems faced by child abuse victims in summoning up the psychological resources to disclose, and to reframe the law accordingly. Before the courts got around to doing that, the Catholic Church was not slow to take advantage of the limitation defence in order to try to deny victims a hearing of their substantive allegations.

Fortunately, the law has now changed. Since the *Hoare* decision in 2008, an abuse claim is generally permitted even many years after the event *provided it is possible to have a fair trial.* This is right. Justice should not be time limited; to make it so would reward the abuser who is best at terrifying and silencing his victim. Following the revelations of celebrity child abuse dating back to the 1970s, some have argued that dredging up ancient allegations inevitably leads to unfairness to a defendant: the perpetrator may have died; memories will have faded; documents will have gone missing. On that logic, some argue that abuse claims should be automatically extinguished after a fixed period, as they were when Miss Stubbings tried to claim.[439] But justice demands that an allegation be tried if it can be tried fairly. That will vary from case to case. In some old cases a fair trial will no longer be possible; in others it will. Post-*Hoare*, the courts now assess each case on its merits, weighing the available evidence, considering what might have been lost and how much real prejudice will have been suffered by claimant and defendant respectively by the passage of time.

Of course, defendants invariably contend that any time delay renders a fair trial impossible. In Church cases, claimant lawyers have learned to subject such contentions to careful scrutiny. In one case, which turned on the decisions of a senior Catholic cleric, it was asserted that the cleric, at that time aged seventy-six and retired, was in an extremely poor state of health and was consequently 'unable to assist' the court. But just as that assertion was being made in court proceedings, the senior cleric was making several public appearances: delivering a celebratory Mass, receiving an honorary degree and speaking at the reopening of a church. Subsequently, when questioned by *The Observer*, the retired cleric denied that his state of health had ever prevented him from responding to questions about the litigation: 'The suggestion that his health had become an issue has come as a complete surprise.'[440] The case was subsequently settled.

TACTICAL GAMES

Limitation is not the only area where the Catholic Church has resorted to technical ruses and smokescreens in an effort to evade paying compensation. Some of these tactics relate to the internal structure of the Church, which is surprisingly complex. The Catholic Church is not a single legal entity. Rather, it is divided into legally distinct dioceses and orders. A priest will be attached either to a particular diocese, for example the Diocese of Leeds, or to a particular order, for example the Benedictines. The 'employer' of the priest for the purposes of the compensation claim is likely to be either a diocese or an order, and this should be identifiable from the *Catholic Directory*. Having established which diocese or order the priest is working for it is necessary to identify the correct technical legal title for that defendant. In the case of a diocese there are two possibilities: the bishop (being the senior priest of the diocese), or the trustees of the diocese, bearing in mind that the diocese will be a charity. This can then raise a host of additional problems, the chief of which has been whether the bishop himself can be sued.

For historical reasons, some uncertainty appears to exist in English law as to whether a Catholic bishop is a legal entity. In canon law, Catholic bishops are certainly legal entities, but the position in civil law at first glance seems less clear. *Halsbury's Laws*, the traditional legal reference work for lawyers in the pre-digital age, asserts that a Roman Catholic bishop or other dignitary of the Roman Catholic Church is 'not a corporation sole'; in other words, is not a legal entity.[441] Of course an individual bishop can be sued, simply as a person like any other, but this would be in his personal capacity, not as an office holder, and so would not facilitate a claim against the institution.

At one stage it appeared that the Catholic Church would try to evade liability by trying to strike out a claim against a bishop on the basis that he was not a legal entity; but the Church has never pushed the point to a judicial decision. This is partly because the authorities cited by *Halsbury's* in support of the proposition were decided when the position of Catholics in England was very different from today, i.e. before the Catholic Emancipation Act of 1829.

One very old case relied upon by *Halsbury's*, for example, is the decision of the Court of Appeal in Ireland in 1809 in *Attorney-General* v. *Power*, which concerned a bequest made to a Roman Catholic bishop.[442] The bequest was held to be void, as 'no such character' as a Catholic bishop was 'known to the laws of Ireland'; the very notion was 'against public policy'. Similar, if slightly less insulting, reasoning was employed in an 1893 decision from Ireland.

That 1893 decision, however, made no reference to the position in England, where the status of Catholics had considerably altered in the intervening period. Catholicism was, of course, unlawful in England following the Reformation in the 1530s. The Roman Catholic hierarchy was re-established in England in 1850. Accordingly, in 1809 (the date of the main authority relied upon by *Halsbury's*) Catholics in England were forbidden from holding any public office and the very office of a Catholic bishop was contrary to public policy. But the position is entirely different today. That seems to have deterred the Church from testing the point. But not only that: it would obviously be politically unattractive for the Catholic Church to argue in open court that a Catholic bishop has no legal existence, relying, in the process, on ancient cases which were the by-product of anti-Catholic discrimination.

These technical arguments may excite lawyers, but behind every legal technicality lies a real person – a victim of abuse whose life will have been profoundly scarred by those childhood experiences. The Catholic Church has developed a reputation for being unusually aggressive and obstructive in legal cases – taking every point and often fighting losing arguments to the bitter end, as in cases like *Grey, A.* v. *Archbishop of Birmingham*, *Maga* and *JGE*. The rationale of this strategy from the Church's standpoint is far from clear. Of course it may not even be primarily the Church's strategy: it may be its insurer's. But it is done in the name of the Church. Every case which is fought to a contested trial generates more publicity and more claims, as other victims are emboldened to speak out. Claimant lawyers are now well organised and know every ruse, so these tactics have rarely succeeded. But they have aggravated the experience of the legal process for survivors and, understandably, caused immense mistrust of the Church. The Church's legal strategy has done significant and long-term damage to its image and particularly to its reputation amongst victims – damage to which it seems strangely oblivious, but for which it pays a heavy price in public standing. Every survivor campaigner knows someone who has had to fight tooth and nail to secure just compensation; this fosters a profound sense of anger. It has damaged the reputations of some individual bishops – the current Archbishop of Westminster, Vincent Nichols, is mistrusted by survivors because of legal cases fought by the Archdiocese of Birmingham, where he was formerly archbishop, and yet various diocesan child protection officials to whom I have spoken on the whole viewed Nichols as a champion of child protection. Legal cases mean this is not reflected in his public reputation. The Church is, of course, legally entitled to take every point; it is entitled to argue its case and lose, as it has done. But the Church leadership should reflect on the damage it does to its standing amongst survivors. You cannot seriously purport to be a moral beacon in society yet respond to the devastation wrought by child abuse 'with the gimlet eye of a canon lawyer'.[443]

DAMAGES

Even when all these hurdles are overcome the levels of damages awarded in the English courts can sometimes seem insulting to victims. In English law, damages awards are made by case-hardened judges, not juries. Awards are purely compensatory; they seek, as far as money can, to put the claimant back in the position he or she would have been in but for the wrong which has been committed. There are a number of separate elements to the award. The first is the award for the physical and psychological pain and suffering caused by abuse – what lawyers term 'general damages'. These are often modest. They are calibrated strictly by reference to past cases so the judge does not have a free hand to give vent to his or her personal sense of revulsion at the perpetrator's behaviour as an American jury could.

Punitive damages, which enable American juries to punish the offender or the institution itself, are not available in England. In addition to 'general damages', the claimant can seek to recoup his or her financial losses, for example loss of earnings. In principle, it has always been possible for substantial awards for loss of earnings to be made in child abuse claims. In practice, however, this is unusual. A victim of child abuse has no established earnings pattern pre-dating the abuse which can serve as a benchmark for what he or she would have earned if the abuse had not occurred. Also, many victims of child abuse come from vulnerable or disadvantaged backgrounds. Therefore, it will be suggested that their earnings potential may have been modest in any event, irrespective of the abuse. These are often very difficult hurdles for a claimant to overcome. Awards can also be made for the cost of private therapeutic treatment; the claimant does not have to rely on the NHS. But again these sums tend to be modest.

As a result the largest reported award against the Catholic Church in England has been £635,000. This is unlikely to be the largest settlement figure actually paid by a Catholic diocese or institution in England. I happen to know that there have been larger settlements, paid under conditions of strict confidentiality. Nevertheless, the award of £635,000 was at the very top end of the scale of awards for abuse in the English courts. The case involved a claim against the Archdiocese of Birmingham arising from assaults by Father Christopher Clonan. In this case, the abuse was very extreme and lasted for eleven years. The claimant, who had an otherwise untroubled background and siblings who had gone on to successful professional careers, was able to secure a substantial award for loss of earnings; he successfully cleared the causation hurdles which have defeated many other claimants. The vast majority of cases are fought and settled for less.

IMPACT OF CLAIMS

Whilst not impacting on the Church to anything like the extent which has occurred in the USA, damages claims have been an important factor behind reform of child protection in the Church. Financially, whilst most individual claims have been settled for relatively modest amounts, there have been many of them, and they add up. They have led to important evidence being unearthed. As we saw, until 2008 claimants and their lawyers had to prove, not only that the abuse occurred, but that the Church hierarchy negligently failed to vet or supervise the activities of the priest suspected of abusing children. This requirement to prove negligence has cast a spotlight on the Catholic Church's historic failings. In many cases claimants have alleged that the abuse they suffered was preventable because the Church knew that a particular priest was a paedophile but covered this up to avoid embarrassment. Forensic digging by lawyers has propelled some of these murky facts into the public domain. And the publicity surrounding damages claims has been important too, especially when the headlines speak of 'cover-up'. The damages claims launched against Cardinal Cormac Murphy-O'Connor in 2000 alleged that Murphy-O'Connor had personally turned a blind eye to Father Michael Hill's paedophile activities whilst he (Murphy-O'Connor) was Bishop of Arundel and Brighton and responsible for the supervision of Hill, who he knew had been suspected of an unhealthy interest in children. These claims were settled in 2000, subject to strict confidentiality. When the settlements were subsequently leaked to the press, a media firestorm ensued, with allegations that Murphy-O'Connor had attempted to 'cover up' his own failings and 'silence' the victims. The Nolan reforms were the result. The Hill affair is only the most prominent example of how damages claims have turned the media spotlight onto the Catholic Church's past failings, forcing the Church to reform itself. That publicity is self-reinforcing: it encourages more potential claimants to come forward, thus repeating the cycle. The publicity attending any damages award emboldens more victims to break their silence and challenge the culture of denial. This has also been true in the USA, Canada and Australia. Thus, common law systems of personal injury litigation have played a role both in exposing child abuse in the Catholic Church, and in forcing the Church to reform itself.

• • •

Even where claims in England and Wales have been successful, many victims have expressed frustration that the damages claim fails to focus accountability at the top of the Church, i.e. on the papacy itself. In his polemic *The Case of the Pope*, Geoffrey Robertson QC argues that the Vatican has deployed canon law as secret legal system that shields clerical abusers from criminal trial around the world, and therefore stands at the apex of a world-wide conspiracy. Whether one accepts that thesis, the Catholic Church is undoubtedly a uniquely centralised operation. Canon 331 of the Code of Canon Law gives the Pope 'supreme and full power over the universal Church'. In US litigation against the Holy See the plaintiffs point out that the Holy See is a unique entity, with an organisational structure and chain of command that mandates that the Holy See and its head of the state, the Pope, have a significantly high level of involvement in the routine and day-to-day activities of its agents or instrumentalities, particularly with respect to the handling of clergy who have engaged in certain specified conduct, including child sex abuse.[444]

The Holy See controls the hiring of individual priests, directs and mandates their morals and standards, and possesses supreme and universal power over the Catholic Church worldwide. There is no doubt that Popes bear considerable moral responsibility for the child abuse scandal. So could the papacy itself be sued? Robertson certainly thinks so, suggesting that in English law

there would be no immediate bar to a civil action against the Holy See in relation to child sex abuse committed by a priest employed by the Catholic Church in [England], so long as a causal connection could plausibly be alleged with negligent orders or directives or decisions issued from the Vatican.[445]

There have been claims against the Holy See in the USA; Minnesota attorney Jeff Anderson has instigated a 'child sex and cover-up lawsuit against the Vatican'.[446] One American case, *Doe v. Holy See*, reached the US Supreme Court on the question of whether the negligent conduct took place in the United States; the Supreme Court ruled that part of it did.[447] In 2010, Jeff Anderson opened an office in London, highlighting his desire to bring litigation against the Vatican.[448]

However, claims against the papacy, at least in the English

courts, are likely to encounter many obstacles. As we saw, the Roman Catholic Church is not a single body, but rather a communion of different dioceses. Claims have been brought against either the bishop or the trustees of the diocese. A claimant looking to sue the leadership of the Church in Rome would be faced with two other legal entities: the 'Holy See' (the preeminent worldwide jurisdiction of the Catholic Church) and the Vatican (a mini city-state in Rome).

This raises problems of state immunity. The State Immunity Act (1978) sets out the immunities enjoyed by states and the exceptions to them. Something is a 'state' for the purposes of SIA 1978 if the Foreign Secretary so certifies.[449]

The Church's position is that the Holy See is a state in international law. Robertson challenges this assertion, arguing that the claim relies 'squarely' upon the 1929 Lateran Treaty, which created the Vatican City State, giving the Holy See a physical territory over which it could exercise sovereignty. 'The Lateran Treaty', Robertson contends, 'cannot serve as a credible basis for the Holy See to claim statehood. The grant of 108 acres – the size of a large golf course – was not pursuant to any international treaty.'[450] However, others maintain that Robertson is confusing and conflating the two separate legal entities. Sir Ivor Roberts, a former British Ambassador to the Vatican, argues that the Holy See, which goes back to early Christian times and to an era where the concept of the nation state was unknown, has long existed as the pre-eminent episcopal jurisdiction of the Catholic Church 'and as such, diplomatically and in other spheres, the Holy See was and is acting for the whole Catholic church'.[451] Both before and after the Lateran Treaty, Roberts argues, the Holy See has been recognised, 'both in state practice and in legal scholarship, as a subject of public international law, with rights and duties analogous to those of States'.[452] The Holy See is recognised by the United Nations as an observer state in the UN system and is a full member of a large number of UN specialised agencies. It maintains diplomatic relations with 178 states; foreign embassies are accredited to the Holy See, not to the Vatican City; and it is the Holy See that establishes treaties and concordats with other sovereign entities. In US child abuse litigation which has been brought against the Holy See it has been accepted that the Holy See is a sovereign state.

An argument that the Holy See does not enjoy statehood for these purposes is unlikely to be successful. The State Immunity Act (1978) then affords immunity to states in respect of personal injury claims caused by acts or omissions outside the UK. It provides for some exceptions: 'A state is not immune as respects proceedings in respect of a death or personal injury ... caused by an act or omission in the UK.'[453]

So, on the face of it the Holy See would enjoy the benefit of state immunity unless it could be demonstrated that the acts or omissions giving rise to the personal injury claim occurred in England. Sometimes cases surface where Vatican officials have been directly implicated in negligent decision making about paedophile priests. In these cases actual Vatican decisions will have been taken 'outside the UK', in an office in Rome, although this definition has not yet been tested in court. In *Doe* v. *Holy See* the US Supreme Court rejected the Holy See's technical defence that its conduct did not occur in the USA, on the basis that it was sufficient that the injury and some of the conduct alleged to be negligent took place there.[454] But where the acts or omissions giving rise to the claim occurred outside the UK the Holy See would seem to enjoy state immunity.

That may prove an insuperable obstacle, although the scope of state immunity has been challenged in recent years in civil damages claims arising from allegations of torture. Sulaiman al-Adsani, a dual national of Britain and Kuwait, who was severely tortured after offending the Emir of Kuwait, attempted to bring a civil damages claim in England against the government of Kuwait. His claim was struck out by the UK courts on state immunity grounds: acts of torture committed in Kuwait, because they were not committed in the UK, did not fall within the exceptions to the immunity conferred by the 1978 Act. That decision was upheld by the European Court of Human Rights.[455] More recently, some British expatriates tortured in Saudi Arabia have attempted to bring damages claims in the UK courts against the individuals allegedly involved in their torture, including the Saudi Interior Minister. Those cases were struck out by the House of Lords in 2006, and at the time of writing the House of Lords decision has just been upheld by the European Court of Human Rights, although the court indicated that the matter should be kept under review, and there may be an appeal to the Grand Chamber. The claimants in this case argue that the prohibition of torture has become a peremptory norm of international law, overriding national law and political and diplomatic considerations, including state immunity.

In the event that the appeal – or some subsequent case – were to succeed, creating an exception to state immunity in cases of torture, could clerical sex abuse ever be brought within that category? Torture is defined legally as

any act by which severe pain or suffering, whether physical or mental, is intentionally inflicted on a person for such purposes as

obtaining from him, or a third person, information or a confession, punishing him for an act he or a third person has committed
or is suspected of having committed, or intimidating, coercing
him or a third person, or for any reason based on discrimination
of any kind, when such pain or suffering is inflicted by or at the
instigation of or with the consent or acquiescence of a public
official or other person acting in an official capacity.[456]

Amnesty International has asserted that the physical and sexual
abuse of children by Catholic priests and nuns in Ireland described
in the Ferns, Ryan, Murphy and Cloyne reports 'included acts that
amounted to torture and inhuman and degrading treatment'.[457]
However, whether or not one accepts this view, is not suggested
that the alleged acts of torture were themselves committed by
officials of the Holy See. The charge against the Holy See is not
that its officials have been personally involved in child abuse,
torture etc., but that they have created and maintained a worldwide legal system and culture in which such acts could flourish,
and that from time to time they have been actively involved in
perpetrating cover-ups. Morally this may make the Holy See as
culpable as those who commit these acts, but legally it places the
Holy See at one remove from a damages claim. That said, the law
in this area is ever developing and the possibility of changes to
state immunity cannot be ruled out. In the US litigation against
the Holy See, the claimants (known as plaintiffs in the USA)
argue that the US courts have jurisdiction 'because the Holy See
engaged in commercial activity in Illinois and throughout the
United States'. It remains to be seen whether the same argument
could be applied in a UK context.

But this leaves a multitude of hurdles in suing the Vatican.

Robertson (cited above) suggests that 'there would be no immediate bar' to such a claim 'so long as a causal connection could
plausibly be alleged with negligent orders or directives or decisions
issued from the Vatican'. But issues of state immunity aside, this
assertion falls foul of recent English case law regarding vicarious
liability in abuse cases. *JGE* clearly gives rise to two difficulties
in suing the Holy See: claims based on vicarious liability render
obsolete any claim based on 'negligent orders or directives'; and
vicarious liability will likely rest with the organisation vested
with day-to-day control of the priest, i.e. the English diocese or
order rather than the Holy See.

JGE means that it will not normally be necessary for a
claimant to contemplate bringing an action in negligence and
therefore the type of claim suggested by Robertson which aims
to evidence 'a causal connection' between the abuse and 'negligent orders or directives or decisions issued from the Vatican'
would almost certainly not arise. Vicarious liability will likely
rest with the diocese or order to which the abuser priest is
attached. That organisation will, in theory, be operating under
the ultimate direction of the Holy See. But in some ways the
papacy has the best of both worlds: supreme and full power
over the universal Church yet at the same time a devolved
diocesan structure, which enables it to deflect legal liabilities
onto local entities.

• • •

In any case, survivors want both justice and healing: criminal
prosecution and civil litigation may offer neither. Many criminal prosecutions of sex offences are unsuccessful. Litigation can

often be successful in material terms and compensation can help rebuild a damaged life. But litigation is generally far from therapeutic. Because of its length, adversarial nature and uncertain outcomes litigation may retraumatise victims and even if successful may fail to provide a deeper sense of justice and fair reparation. As one claimant attorney observed after a settlement of litigation against the Catholic Church in Boston, USA: 'It's not uncommon for victims to feel pain after a settlement because the validation ... does not fill the spiritual and emotional void.'[458]

By contrast, advocates of *restorative justice* seek to offer a more holistic approach, aiming to 'make things right while focusing on healing for the victim-survivor and offender and accountability by Church representatives'.[459] The concept of restorative justice dates back to the 1970s when a Victim–Offender Reconciliation Programme (VORP) began in Canada. Fostered by the Mennonite community, the idea spread to the USA and in the 1980s started to attract the attention of lawyers and academics. Proponents of restorative justice contrasted it with the 'retributive' paradigm of traditional legal processes, which focused on the past and on blame fixing; restorative justice would encourage responsibility for past behaviour but 'its focus would be on the future, on problem solving, on the obligations created by the offence' and on healing.[460]

The concepts underlying restorative justice are best understood by contrasting it with more traditional legal processes. In the criminal process an offender is put on trial, then if found guilty will be sentenced; if the sentence is adequate, justice is then assumed to have been done, irrespective of whether the victim actually feels it has. The victim is a passive participant; technically he or she is simply a witness in a process controlled by the state. The focus is on the offender, not on the victim, although a victim impact statement may be read out in court.

In the civil litigation process, as we saw, the focus is on the corporate liability of the organisation, which may hinge on technicalities; the feasibility of a fair trial after time delay, a similarly technical issue; and the damage or loss caused by the assault, which then has to be translated into a monetary figure. But generally any liability will be met by an insurer, so the process will not involve the perpetrator or the organisation behind it taking personal financial or moral responsibility. The broader needs of the victim, the offender and the community are largely ignored.

In the restorative justice model, the victim is placed centre stage, but in the broader context of the needs of the victim, offender, institution and wider community, which will also need protection from the offender. Victim and offender meet; talk about their experience of the wrong which was committed; discuss and seek to agree on how the wrong should be righted, which may include compensation; and discuss the future, which might (for example) involve (in a clerical abuse case) agreeing binding restrictions on the priest's future ministry. The two people most directly involved in the crime take centre stage in the restoration of the harm done, alongside others such as a victim advocate, family members and Church leaders, and the process is holistic, covering all issues: apology, compensation, measures to prevent future offences. A restorative justice process could be adapted if criminal or civil processes are already underway; the processes are not necessarily mutually exclusive. So a restorative justice meeting could embrace settlement of a civil claim, but encompass other aspects like genuine apology and future prevention.

Advocates of restorative justice see it as empowering the victim, thus helping to rectify the power imbalance between victim and perpetrator at the heart of the offence. In effective restorative justice, victims can feel a true sense of justice not achievable through traditional legal processes where their needs are subordinated to the state and legal technicalities. But there are limitations. Restorative justice can only come into play when the offence is admitted; it cannot play a role in determining the truth of an allegation. It obviously has less application if the offender has died, although a process could still take place involving victim and Church. It is strictly voluntary on all sides. It depends on both the offender and the organisation sincerely wanting to right the wrong. Crucially for abuse in religious settings, it cannot be seen as a means of imposing a demand for forgiveness upon the victim. And most of all, as Graham Wilmer has pointed out, it cannot be used if the survivor is at risk of being retraumatised by the process; it can only come when recovery is sufficiently advanced.

To date, restorative justice has not been employed in Catholic abuse cases in England; there have been some limited attempts to use it in the USA. But as victims want both justice and healing, not simply money, and given the problems inherent in civil litigation, it deserves more attention. Unfortunately it would require rather more imagination and engagement with survivors than the Church has been willing to demonstrate to date. But if the Church genuinely wishes to make good the damage done to victims and communities, it should be considered.

CHAPTER 14

CONCLUSION

The most honest assessment of the impact of the abuse crisis from within the Church came from Bishop Kieran Conry in 2010. The Church, he asserted, is 'holed beneath the waterline'. Rejecting accusations of media bias, he said the problems of child abuse dominating headlines in the UK and across the world were problems of the Church's own making. 'The Roman Catholic Church sets itself up to be the great moral authority. When it does fail its own rigid standards, it deserves to be attacked and criticised.'

Bishop Conry believed the problems had not been exaggerated:

I think what we will find is the number of cases will grow. We can't pretend it is something we can ignore or dismiss. The Church is one of the great moral champions in terms of its own rigid moral codes. When it fails it deserves to get hit.

Asked whether the Church could recover, he said: 'It probably can; again, it depends on how it deals with it.' In Britain, he maintained, the issue was now dealt with 'fairly effectively' and strict guidelines were now in place. But in other parts of the world, such as Ireland, it had done 'lasting' damage.[461]

Twenty years on from the Penney scandal and the torrent

of revelations which followed, how 'safe' is Catholic safeguarding now? Against the backdrop of continuing concerns about child protection, and the Church's known history of hushing up abuse allegations, the current focus of campaigning by survivor groups is *mandatory reporting*: formal legislation that would require certain categories of people to report suspected cases of child abuse to police or social services. Currently, in England and Wales (and Scotland) there is no formal requirement in law to report child protection concerns to the statutory authorities. There are professional reporting obligations, for example for teachers or carers, which are emphasised through local and national guidance, and various inter-agency protocols. But the failure to report abuse does not constitute a criminal offence. As Jonathan West pointed out about St Benedict's Ealing:

> The amazing fact is that in failing to report abuse at the school to the police or social services, St Benedict's didn't break any laws. It is possible for a head teacher to know for certain that a member of staff has raped a pupil on school premises, and the head teacher has no statutory obligation to report anything to anybody. Any obligation towards the child and its parents exists only as contract law, a school's child protection policy being an implied part of the contract between school and parents.[462]

Campaigners have therefore argued for 'Daniel's Law', named after Daniel Pelka, a little boy starved and beaten to death by his mother; his bruising and emaciation was ignored by his school. Daniel's Law would make it mandatory for child protection concerns to be reported by professionals working with children, introducing clarity especially in circumstances of conflicting duty, where a teacher or pastor might be torn between child welfare and protection of the institution. As a legal change, it would be relatively simple; there are ample precedents from the USA and Australia, and in Northern Ireland, section 5(1) of the Criminal Law Act 1967 already provides for a criminal offence of failing to disclose an *arrestable* offence to the police, which, de facto, includes most offences against children. Something similar could be brought onto the statute book in the rest of the UK.

Mandatory reporting laws would apply to many different organisations, but the championing of these laws, in the UK and internationally, is more than anything else a reaction to widespread child abuse identified the Catholic Church and the belief that the institution has fostered a culture of secrecy and denial that puts children at continuing risk. In the Republic of Ireland the backlash against the Church inspired a constitutional amendment making it mandatory to report any complaint from a child about abuse, thus enshrining children's rights in a state constitution which, traditionally and in conformity with its Catholic origins, placed much more emphasis on privacy and the authority of the family.[463] And indeed it is not difficult to see how mandatory reporting could have made a dramatic difference to child protection in virtually all of the cases discussed in this book; the risk of criminal liability on the part of a bishop or parish priest for failing to report suspicions or allegations would have protected thousands of children from abuse by clerical sex offenders over past decades. Mandatory reporting laws are particularly relevant where people feel a conflict of loyalties between the protection of children and their fealty to an all-powerful institution, and there is no institution where that conflict has proved so toxic as the Catholic Church.

But whilst the case for Daniel's Law is compelling, it would be wrong to view the issue of safeguarding in the Catholic Church in 2014 primarily through the lens of mandatory reporting. I believe that the most significant advance in safeguarding in the Catholic Church over the post-Nolan period has been that *new* allegations are now, in the main, reported to the statutory authorities. I say 'new' allegations, because I doubt that the Church has entirely come clean about older, historic cases. But so far as new allegations are concerned, the principle of external reporting is probably now embedded in most parts of the English Church. As we saw in Chapter 10, even St Benedict's, which for so long resisted the calls of campaigners for mandatory reporting, in 2013 introduced a new safeguarding policy which removed any remaining 'wriggle room' about the reporting obligations on school staff. Of course, it remains to be seen if the policy will be adhered to, but the wording is crystal clear. And the Benedictine institutions, having remained outside the Nolan process, were playing catch-up: following Nolan, most Catholic dioceses and orders had started to embrace the principle several years earlier. This is not to say that the Church's systems are failsafe. As Lord Carlile put it, there remains an ever-present 'backsliding tendency' and 'constant vigilance' is essential. A UK-wide mandatory reporting law should be an essential part of that vigilance. However, thanks to the Nolan reforms and the relentless media glare which accompanied them, we have probably reached a point where external reporting of new allegations, and the accompanying oversight, is an accepted norm in the English Church. This is no thanks to the Vatican, which as we saw earlier has continued to maintain at best a studied ambiguity on the question of reporting to civil authorities – and indeed has failed to give legal recognition to Nolan. But the change in England is real, and even if it has not been universally welcomed, clergy and laity now know that a failure to report will not only be a breach of agreed safeguarding rules, but a red flag to the media.

So if 'defensive safeguarding' in the English Church is better than it was, what of other aspects of child protection? In this book I have attempted to highlight the continuing problems. Dioceses will vary in their standards of child protection, depending most of all on the commitment and ethos of the individual bishop. But I believe there has not yet been a systematic and comprehensive trawl of past ('historic') allegations and suspicions; whilst new allegations now generally get reported to the police, I fear we can be far less confident about the older ones buried in diocesan files and institutional memory. Bishop Conry is right to predict that old cases will continue to come to light. Within the priesthood traditional attitudes still hold sway: just as I finish this book a client tells me that she has been told by her local Catholic priest that to 'rake over the past is a mortal sin'. Survivors argue that they cannot have confidence in Church institutions until the stables have been properly cleansed, and if the Church ducks that challenge, then it is not too fanciful to suggest that the growing pressure for a public inquiry into abuse in the churches, along the lines of inquiries in Australia and Ireland, may lead to state intervention.[464] And as we have seen, there are other problems too: for one, a continuing aura of secrecy and lack of independence in the Church's safeguarding institutions, reinforced by events like Clifton in 2012 involving the resignation of highly experienced and committed child protection officials, and by ambiguity and lack of transparency over issues like laicisation. There has been an unwillingness to properly address safeguarding issues in regard to vulnerable adults, and, worst of all, a continuing failure to engage with survivors, as regards both pastoral support and compensation. 'Defensive safeguarding' has undoubtedly improved, but these major issues remain.

This should not be a surprise. As Eileen Shearer observed, cultural change takes many years. Abuse allegations may now be better handled, but the factors which gave rise to the abuse crisis – clericalism, authoritarianism, sexual immaturity in the priesthood – have not gone away. Indeed, as I have argued, clericalism has not only been a cause of the crisis; the resistance to Nolan, and to a secular model of child protection, has been driven above all by a clericalist presumption that priests are entitled to be treated as a special case, exempt from the procedural norms and standards of proof that govern child protection in other professions. Canon law has provided a handy pretext for justifying clerical exceptionalism, but the law of the Church simply reflects its culture: the belief that priests, as 'Christ's real image and representative', are a caste apart is deeply rooted in Catholic theology. Simply tweaking the Church rulebook – say to permit a bishop to temporarily withdraw a priest from active ministry[465] – will not change age-old beliefs and attitudes, and certainly not overnight. Similarly, whilst the Church has introduced tighter selection procedures for aspiring priests, the issues of sexual formation and maturation of clergy throw up a much more profound challenge for the Church, one it seems currently to be ducking. As Donald Findlater observed: 'There is within the Catholic Church a denial of sexual identity and a refusal to admit problems which are then left to fester.'

So whilst progress since Nolan should be acknowledged, the

deeper change necessary to avoid future scandal and harm to children has yet to take place. During the papacies of John Paul II and Benedict XVI, with conservatives wielding an iron grip on the Vatican, it was difficult to imagine that it ever could. Since the accession of Pope Francis, the possibility of a 'Catholic spring' seems less remote. We do not yet know whether Pope Francis's admonishment to Catholics not to be 'obsessed' by traditional doctrine heralds a deeper revolution, or whether the change may only be skin deep. But at least it inspires hope. If – but only if – the Catholic Church can leave behind the clericalism, authoritarianism and sexual denial which have dominated the institution for so many years, it may yet become a place of safety for children.

NOTES

1   A figure the authors subsequently described as a 'conservative costs projection'. Yallop, *Beyond Belief*, p. 28.
2   Robertson, *The Case of the Pope*, p. 34.
3   See Chapter 8.
4   'Historic' in the sense that the abuse occurred many years ago. But they are not 'historic' to victims, who continue to live with the consequences many years afterwards.
5   To use the words of the Cumberlege Report in 2007; see Chapter 9.
6   See interview with Baroness Cumberlege, *The Tablet*, 21 July 2007.
7   Benedict, *The Light of the World*, p. 26.
8   Fox, *The Pope's War*, p. 126.
9   Ibid., p. 129.
10   Mooney, *All the Bishop's Men*, p. 167.
11   Ivereigh, 'Guilty until proved innocent', *The Tablet*, 14 July 2007.
12   Robertson, op. cit., p. 50. At pp. 42–62, Robertson provides a multitude of detailed reasons why canon law is inappropriate for sex abuse cases.
13   See Chapter 9.
14   Murphy Report, p. 8.
15   Ibid., pp. 7–8.
16   Benedict, op. cit., p. 50.
17   Quoted in *Time* magazine, 27 January 2003.
18   Liebreich, *Fallen Order: A History*.
19   Benedict, op. cit., p. 24.
20   Ibid., p. 68.
21   John Jay Report, 'The Nature and Scope of Sexual Abuse of Minors by Catholic Priests and Deacons in the United States 1950–2002', John Jay College of Criminal Justice, February 2004, p. 69.
22   See Chapter 11.
23   See Chapter 11.
24   See e.g. Jenkins, *Paedophiles and Priests*, p. 78.
25   Cozzens, *The Changing Face of the Priesthood*.
26   Wolf, *Gay Priests*; Sipe, *A Secret World: Sexuality and the Search for Celibacy*.
27   'The Causes and Context of Sexual Abuse of Minors by Catholic Priests in the United States, 1950–2010'.
28   Conversation with author.
29   Quoted in *New York Daily News*, 13 April 2010.

30   Quoted by Catholic News Agency, 16 April 2010.
31   *New York Daily News*, op. cit.
32   Quoted ibid.
33   Tatchell, conversation with author.
34   Quoted on CatholicCulture.org, 15 April 2010.
35   *National Catholic Reporter*, 23 February 2009.
36   Cozzens, op. cit.
37   Goodstein, 'Church Report Cites Social Tumult in Priest Scandals', *New York Times*, 17 May 2011.
38   Cited in Keenan, *Child Sexual Abuse in the Catholic Church*, p. 13.
39   Quoted in Boston Globe, *Betrayal: The Crisis in the Catholic Church*.
40   Also, as Cozzens asked: why, if homosexual orientation is 'intrinsically disordered', does God appear to be calling so many homosexuals to the priesthood?
41   Conversation with author.
42   Quoted in Jenkins, op. cit.
43   See Chapter 12.
44   Jenkins, op. cit., p. 79
45   Murphy Report, p. 8.
46   Conversation with author.
47   Australian Bishop Porteous, quoted in Keenan, op. cit., p. 236.
48   *The Guardian*, 5 April 2010.
49   Quote from Ryan, quoted in Keenan, op. cit., p. 236.
50   *Pastoral Review*, Vol. 2, Issue 5, September/October 2006, p. 44.
51   Conversation with author.
52   *The Guardian*, 11 March 2010.
53   Professor David Pilgrim, PhD thesis, 'Sexual Abuse in Catholic Settings' (University of Central Lancashire, unpublished).
54   Sipe, *Celibacy in Crisis: A Secret World Revisited*.
55   'Celibacy "drives some priests to be sex abusers"', *The Times*, 4 December 2002.
56   Pilgrim, op. cit.
57   Serene Jones, president of the Union Theological Seminary, speaking to CNN's *Amanpour*, 18 March 2010.
58   Penny Jamieson, *Living at the Edge*, pp. 122–3.
59   Canon, p. 489.
60   See Chapter 13 for further discussion.
61   *Quanta Cura*, Encyclical Letter of Pope Pius IX, 8 December 1864, para. 5.
62   Richard Scorer, 21 January 2011. http://www.pannone.com/media-centre/blog/abuse-blog/secret-vatican-letter-exposes-catholic-church-abuse-cover.
63   Robertson, op. cit.
64   'Decalogue': the Ten Commandments.
65   The word 'Sacred' was dropped from the title of the CDF when the revised Code of Canon Law was promulgated in 1983.
66   *Sex Crimes and the Vatican*, BBC, 2006.
67   John Allen, *National Catholic Reporter*, 11 October 2006.
68   Quoted in Keenan, op. cit., pp. 212–13.
69   Ibid., p. 211; also Doyle, 'The 1922 Instruction and the 1962 Instruction *Crimen Sollicitationis*', promulgated by the Vatican, unpublished note, 3 October 2008.
70   *Crimen* (Appendix B).
71   Murphy Report, Chapter 4, para. 82.

72   Stated in *De delictis gravioribus*, 2001.

73   Robertson, op. cit., p. 53.

74   Doyle, op. cit.

75   Ibid.

76   Ibid.

77   Father Paul Bruxby, a canon lawyer, justified this omission to me by pointing out that 'the Vatican has to legislate for the whole world'. A requirement to report to civil authorities might work in the West but might not be appropriate in less developed countries where civil authorities could not be guaranteed to protect victims and investigate sex crimes properly. However, I cannot see why that rationale would apply to Ireland, England or indeed most Western countries.

78   I.e. sanctity of the confessional.

79   It was Scicluna who extended the canonical limitation period and extended the scope of canonical crimes to include possession of child pornography in the 2010 reforms.

80   Murphy Report, p. 5.

81   Comments at press conference following publication of Murphy Report.

82   Murphy Report, p. 6.

83   Murphy Report, p. 4.

84   Words of Graham Wilmer, see below. In 2003 Graham founded the Lantern Project, which provides support and counselling to abuse survivors: http://www. lanternproject.org.uk.

85   Comment by Bishop Kieran Conry, see Chapter 14.

86   Confidentiality agreement, shown to author by Graham Wilmer.

87   *Barnet Times*, 8 February 2007.

88   Conversation between author and 'John'.

89   John Gerard McClean (1914–78), Bishop of Middlesbrough 1967–78.

90   Ingram was found guilty of sexual offences involving six boys between 1970 and 1978, committed on camping trips and weekend trips to a farmhouse near Melton Mowbray.

91   'Sex-case officers praised', *Leicester Mercury*. Date not visible on author's copy.

92   Ingram, 'The Participating Victim: A Study of 92 Cases of Sexual Contact between Adult and Child', *British Journal of Sexual Medicine*, Vol. 6, No. 44, January 1979, p. 22f (Part 1), and Vol. 6, No. 45, February 1979, p. 24f (Part 2).

93   Ingram, 'FILTHY: Reaction to Paedophilic Acts', *Libertarian Education (Leicester)*, No. 21, Spring 1977, pp. 4–5.

94   O'Carroll, *Paedophilia: The Radical Case* (available on internet).

95   Middleton (ed.), *The Betrayal of Youth: Radical Perspectives on Childhood Sexuality, Intergenerational Sex, and the Social Oppression of Children and Young People*, p. 102.

96   Ibid., p. 103.

97   Although he later claimed that the encounters were fictitious and were intended simply as a 'provocation'.

98   Coren, *Why Catholics Are Right*, p. 24.

99   Thompson, 'How Hattie's friends defended paedophilia', *Daily Telegraph*, 19 October 2012.

100   Hewitt served as general secretary of NCCL from 1974 to 1983.

101   Thompson, op. cit.

102   Ibid.

103   Ibid.

104   'Apologists for Paedophiles', *Daily Mail*, 14 December 2013.
105   Benedict, op. cit.
106   Mary Kenny, *Catholic Herald*, 26 March 2010.
107   See Chapter 7.
108   Quoted in 'Catholic Church in new sex abuse row', *The Observer*, 17 December 2006.
109   Ibid.
110   Ibid.
111   Roman Catholic Diocese of Leeds press statement following Crowley conviction.
112   Conversation between author and victim's mother.
113   Particulars of claim for victim represented by author.
114   Quoted in Yallop, op. cit., p. 37.
115   Archbishop of Westminster statement following Crowley conviction.
116   See Chapter 6.
117   Conversation with author.
118   Couve de Murville obituary, *The Guardian*, 7 November 2007.
119   Hence 'archdiocese'.
120   *Everyman: Breach of Faith*, BBC documentary, 1993.
121   Flanagan, *Father and Me*, p. 51.
122   Ibid.
123   Ibid.
124   Interview with BBC *Everyman*.
125   Letter to *The Tablet*, 5 June 1993.
126   Alan Draper, 'The Impact on a Parish of Child Sexual Abuse by a Priest: An Action Plan for Healing', Maryvale Institute.
127   Interview with BBC *Everyman*.
128   Flanagan, op. cit., p. 129.
129   Interview with BBC *Everyman*.
130   Draper, op. cit.
131   Conversation with author.
132   *The Tablet*, 22 May 1993.
133   Letter from Brendan Flanagan, *The Tablet*, 29 May 1993.
134   Nichols, interviewed during closing sequence of BBC's *Kenyon Confronts: Secrets and Confessions*, 8 October 2003.
135   *Sunday Mercury*, 26 January 2003.
136   Carrie's account is from conversations with author and his book, *Tolkien Is Klone'it*.
137   See Chapter 4.
138   Editorial, *Sunday Mercury*.
139   *The Age* (Melbourne), 16 June 2004.
140   *Maga (by his Litigation Friend the Official Solicitor)* v. *Trustees of the Birmingham Archdiocese of the Roman Catholic Church* (2009), EWHC, p. 780, para. 71.
141   See Chapter 13.
142   *Maga*, op. cit., para. 72.
143   Ibid., para. 69.
144   See Chapter 10.
145   *Maga*, op. cit., para. 73.
146   *Sunday Mercury*, 3 August 2003.
147   Quoted in *Birmingham Mail*, 6 May 2012.
148   See Chapter 13.
149   Quoted in *The Guardian*, 30 April 1998.

150   *The Independent*, 1 May 1998.

151   Father Hudson's Society statement, quoted in *Sunday Mercury*, 10 March 2008.

152   *Sunday Mercury*, 19 August 2012.

153   Quoted in *Birmingham Evening Mail*, 18 September 2001.

154   Report in *Sunday Times*.

155   Quoted in *Coventry Evening Telegraph*, 3 July 2001.

156   'Pastoral and Procedural Guidelines', pp. 11–12.

157   Speaking to the BBC *Panorama* programme 'Power to Abuse', 2000.

158   'Pastoral and Procedural Guidelines', p. 8.

159   Ibid., p. 31.

160   Ibid., p. 16.

161   Ibid., p. 17.

162   Ibid., p. 14.

163   Anthony Howard, *Basil Hume: The Monk Cardinal*, p. 257.

164   John Cornwell, 'Get real about the press', *The Tablet*, 18 May 2002.

165   See, for example, Westminster diocesan directory website: 'An outstanding and much-loved priest, as remarkable for his holiness as for his outreach to the marginalised.'

166   *The Spectator*, 24 February 1996.

167   *The Independent*, 25 February 1996.

168   At that time Assistant General Secretary, Bishops' Conference of England and Wales.

169   *The Independent*, ibid.

170   'Pastoral and Procedural Guidelines', p. 16.

171   *The Independent*, ibid.

172   Ward himself was also arrested in 1999 after a woman claimed that he had raped her when she was a seven-year-old girl in the 1960s. The offence was alleged to have occurred when Ward was a parish priest in Peckham. Ward was released without charge.

173   Conversation with author.

174   Conversation with author.

175   Conversation with author.

176   This and other quotes from Mr B: conversation with author.

177   Now Cardinal Murphy-O'Connor.

178   Conversation with author.

179   Nicholas Coote, at that time a senior diocesan official and subsequently, in the 1990s, one of the Catholic Church's most senior officials for child protection – see Chapter 6. He confirmed to *The Tablet* in July 2000 that he met with Belinda and her husband, and advised them to go to the bishop.

180   Press statement, 19 June 2000.

181   Quoted in *The Tablet*, 29 July 2000.

182   Ibid.

183   Ibid.

184   Murphy-O'Connor interview with Jeremy Paxman, *Newsnight*, BBC, 6 December 2002.

185   Press statement, 19 June 2000.

186   Conversation with author.

187   O'Keeffe to Bishop Murphy-O'Connor, 11 February 1983. Documentation in the *Tablet* archive.

188   For more discussion on this institution, see Chapter 9.

189   *The Tablet*, 29 July 2000.

190   Murphy to Bishop Murphy-O'Connor, 28 June 1983. The first line quoted reads: 'I must say I am weary about another assignment for him.' However, 'weary' was presumably intended to mean 'wary'.

191   Quoted in *The Tablet*, ibid.

192   Interview in *Catholic Herald*, 27 August 2012.

193   Ibid.

194   Conversation with author.

195   Clark to Bishop Murphy-O'Connor, 19 July 1983.

196   Ibid.

197   Letter from victims to Hume, passed to author.

198   See Chapter 10.

199   Howard, op. cit., p. 256.

200   Ibid., p. 110.

201   Letter to victim represented by author.

202   When elevated to Westminster in 1976, Hume did not initially take the presidency of the Conference of Catholic Bishops of England and Wales, ceding that role to George Dwyer, the Archbishop of Birmingham, who was his senior in length of service (although Hume's position at this time was unusual for a new Archbishop of Westminster in that he had not previously been a bishop). See Howard, op. cit., p. 110.

203   See Chapter 10.

204   See Chapter 6.

205   A reference to changes in 2001 in the canonical statute of limitations.

206   See Chapter 9.

207   See Chapter 11.

208   See Chapter 12.

209   See Chapter 6.

210   Interview in *Catholic Herald*, 27 August 2012.

211   Interview in *Daily Telegraph*, 20 January 2003.

212   Murphy-O'Connor interview with Jeremy Paxman, *Newsnight*, BBC, 6 December 2002.

213   Quoted in report of press conference in *The Tablet*, 4 January 2003.

214   Interviewed just a few weeks later by the *Daily Telegraph*, Murphy-O'Connor seemed to suggest precisely that: 'Q: With canon law it is not easy to enforce discipline against priests. What will the procedures be? A: The Nolan recommendations make provision for this. They are doubly careful now. If there is a written contract with a priest you rely on him to keep it. If he doesn't keep it he is called to account.' *Daily Telegraph*, 20 January 2003.

215   Canon lawyer quoted in *The Tablet*, 4 April 2003.

216   Ibid.

217   *The Guardian*, 6 March 2003.

218   See Chapter 12.

219   'Cardinal's £50,000 bribe to silence beast priest', *News of the World*, 12 January 2003.

220   *The Tablet*, 25 January 2003.

221   Philip Jenkins, *The New Anti-Catholicism: The Last Acceptable Prejudice*.

222   *The Guardian*, 28 July 2003.

223   Conversation with author.

224   Quoted in *Daily Telegraph*, 20 July 2003.

225   'Their law' refers to the Church regulations and guidelines currently in force concerning priests accused of sexual abuse.

226   'Assassination of a Cardinal', *The Tablet*, 23 November 2002.

227   Conversation with author.

228   Quoted in *The Times*, 9 December 2002.

229   Ibid.

230   Announcement from Catholic News Agency, January 2002.

231   *The Tablet*, 25 May 2002.

232   'Abuse allegations reach new high', *The Tablet*, 2 July 2005. The article summarised the figures in COPCA's 2005 report, which referred to allegations lodged in 2004.

233   'Does Nolan go too far?' *The Tablet*, 25 February 2002.

234   Ibid.

235   Ibid.

236   *Directory on the Canonical Status of the Clergy: Rights, Obligations and Procedures*, Catholic Bishops' Conference of England and Wales, 2009. Canon 1722 of the 1983 Code of Canon Law provides that a cleric may be prohibited from the exercise of ministry only once a penal trial has been initiated.

237   *The Tablet*, ibid.

238   'Responding to Allegations of Clerical Child Abuse: Recommendations for Harmonising the Nolan Report and the Code of Canon Law', Working Party of the Canon Law Society of Great Britain and Ireland, 2004, p. 3. See Chapter 3 with regard to *Sacramentorum Sanctitatis Tutela*.

239   Ibid.

240   Ibid., p. 14.

241   Ibid., p. 15.

242   Private conversation with author.

243   'Guilty until proved innocent,' *The Tablet*, 14 July 2007.

244   Ibid.

245   'Moral certainty' is a standard of proof somewhere between the criminal standard of beyond reasonable doubt, and the civil standard of the balance of probabilities, but probably closer to the former.

246   Speech to National Conference of Priests meeting, reported in *The Tablet*, 2006.

247   Archbishop Nichols acknowledged that accused priests are unlikely ever to be reinstated: of the forty clergy in England and Wales who had been accused by 2005, only two had been restored to ministry (four were dismissed).

248   *The Tablet*, 25 May 2002.

249   *The Tablet*, ibid.

250   *The Guardian*, 1 September 2004.

251   'A parish betrayed', *The Tablet*, 25 September 2004.

252   Quoted in *The Tablet*, 11 September 2004.

253   Quoted in *The Tablet*, 20 November 2004.

254   Quoted in *The Tablet*, 11 September 2004.

255   Quoted in *The Tablet*, 20 November 2004.

256   Quoted in *The Tablet*, 11 September 2004.

257   Ibid.

258   Quoted in *The Observer*, 6 August 2006; report of Gallanagh's 1960 conviction is in the *Belfast Telegraph*, 24 June 1960.

259 MACSAS submission to Cumberlege review.
260 Ibid.
261 Cumberlege Report, para. 2.14.
262 Cumberlege Report, para. 2.8.
263 Cumberlege Recommendation 41.
264 *The Tablet*, 21 July 2007.
265 'The child still comes first', *The Tablet*, 4 August 2007.
266 Quoted in *The Tablet*, 16 June 2007.
267 *The Guardian*, 15 July 2007.
268 Shearer, 'The child still comes first', *The Tablet*, 4 August 2007.
269 Quoted in *The Tablet*, 6 October 2007.
270 See Chapter 3.
271 See below.
272 'Child Protection Five Years On', *Pastoral Review*, September–October 2006.
273 Ibid.
274 Cumberlege Recommendation, p. 72.
275 See note 239 above.
276 Anne Lawrence, quoted in *The Times*, 14 January 2012.
277 *Catholic Herald*, 10 February 2012.
278 Dr Phillip Gilligan on his blog, 'Concerned about abuse in the Catholic Church'.
279 Ibid.
280 Conversation with author.
281 Quoted in historical summary of Paracletes by US lawyer Jeff Anderson.
282 Gilligan, 'Clerical Abuse and Laicisation: Rhetoric and Reality in the Catholic Church in England and Wales', *Child Abuse Review*, 2012.
283 Ibid.
284 [2010] 1 WLR 1441.
285 Cumberlege Report, p. 18.
286 Item 2, Section 2.3.5.9, Catholic Safeguarding Advisory Service manual (2010).
287 See Chapter 10.
288 Congregation for the Doctrine of the Faith.
289 Quoted in Liebreich, op. cit., p. 266.
290 Owen, 'The scandal of child abuse in the Church', http://www.piperpost.net/archives-204.htm.
291 *Sins of the Fathers*, BBC Scotland, 29 July 2013.
292 Saint Laurence Papers V, *Ampleforth: The Story of St Laurence's Abbey and College*.
293 *The Guardian*, 18 November 2005.
294 *Workington Times and Star*, 25 November 2005.
295 *The Independent*, 28 November 1995.
296 *Daily Mail*, 17 April 1996.
297 Ampleforth statement quoted in article in *Cherwell*, 5 October 2005. Green was later appointed to a fellowship at St Benet's Hall, an Oxford college associated with the Benedictine Congregation, and in 2005 was accused of harassing a student at the college; the allegation was dealt with internally by the college, and Green apologised (ibid.).
298 'Pervert priest admits to 14 charges', *This Is York*, 29 July 2005.
299 BBC News, 23 September 2005.
300 A sentence reduced to three years on appeal.
301 'Letter from the Abbot', 27 September 2005.

302   Quoted in *Workington Times and Star*, 25 November 2005.
303   Details confirmed by Judge Beaumont, hearing Carroll's appeal against sentencing in 1999.
304   Saint Laurence Papers V, op. cit., p. 77.
305   Ibid., p. 85.
306   Ibid., p. 84.
307   *Workington Times and Star*, 20 March 2005.
308   *Workington Times and Star*, 30 December 2005.
309   Conversation with author.
310   Carlile Report, p. 1.
311   Ibid., p. 4.
312   Ibid., p. 4.
313   Ibid., p. 3.
314   Conversation with author.
315   Jonathan West blog, 'Confessions of a Skeptic', 11 October 2011.
316   He continued to run the local Scout troop until 1975.
317   Carlile Report, p. 17.
318   Conversation with author.
319   Carlile Report, p. 35.
320   Ibid., p. 17.
321   [2006] EWHC 166 (QB) at para. 28. However, in a later interview with the BBC Radio 4 programme *Sunday*, Shipperlee said that Pearce had first 'formally' come to his notice only in 2004.
322   [2006] EWHC 166 (QB).
323   Ibid., para. 83.
324   Ibid., para. 116.
325   Letter from Shipperlee read out at Pearce's trial.
326   Quoted on West blog, October 2008.
327   Ibid.
328   Ibid., summary.
329   West blog, October 2008.
330   Ibid.
331   Charity Commission report, p. 6.
332   Ibid., p. 8.
333   At this trial, Maestri was acquitted.
334   *The Guardian*, 9 September 2011.
335   Ibid.
336   However, it appears that most if not all of the restrictions on him were lifted by the abbot soon afterwards, without consulting the diocesan safeguarding team, who were unaware of any change in his status.
337   J. West.
338   Details provided by West.
339   Carlile Report, p. 10.
340   Ibid., p. 13.
341   Conversation with author.
342   Ibid., p. 10. However, these words were not original to Carlile. They were originally in a report on the school prepared by the ISI.
343   Ibid., p. 29.
344   Ibid., p. 22.

345   West blog, 6 October 2013.

346   Quoted in *The Guardian*, 14 January 2012.

347   *Sins of the Fathers*, BBC.

348   See Chapter 14.

349   *Downside School: Inspection Report*, OFSTED, 9 December 2010.

350   'Independent Schools Inspectorate: Downside: Follow-up Inspection', 23 June
       2011. Until recently, Downside was in a slightly odd position of being inspected
       both by OFSTED and the ISI. As a boarding school, its boarding welfare
       provision was inspected by OFSTED, and as an independent school, the rest is
       inspected by the ISI. Hence the mixture of reports from both sources.

351   *The Times*, February 1995.

352   BBC News, 28 October 2011.

353   Conversation with author.

354   Curti, *The Tablet* blog, 11 November 2011.

355   West blog, 6 October 2012.

356   Carlile Report, p. 25.

357   Kennedy, 'The Well from Which We Drink Is Poisoned: Clergy Sexual
       Exploitation of Adult Women', PhD thesis, London Metropolitan University
       (2009).

358   Not her real name.

359   Conversation with author.

360   Kennedy, op. cit., p. 26.

361   Quoted ibid., p. 10.

362   Ibid., p. 14.

363   Ibid., p. 10; Roddy Wright, *Feet of Clay*.

364   Kennedy, ibid., p. 39.

365   Flynn, *The Sexual Abuse of Women by Members of the Clergy*, p. 7.

366   Kennedy, op. cit., p. 37.

367   Kennedy, op. cit., p. 34 gives examples from academic literature.

368   Quoted ibid., p. 10.

369   'Playing with sore hearts', *The Tablet*, 12 October 1996.

370   Pat Buckley, *A Thorn in Their Side*.

371   *No Secrets*, para. 2.12.

372   Ibid., para. 2.14.

373   *Protecting the Public*, p. 28.

374   Ibid.

375   *The Stones Cry Out*, MACSAS (2010).

376   Kennedy, op. cit., p. 12.

377   See Chapter 5.

378   Cumberlege Report, p. 85.

379   Ibid., p. 87.

380   Ibid.

381   *The Stones Cry Out*, MACSAS (2010).

382   Conversations with author.

383   Report in *The Universe*, 23 June 1991.

384   Ibid.

385   Report of talk at senate meeting, 21 May 1990, Margaret Kennedy, 'Catholic
       Women Together', East London Pastoral Area

386   Kennedy, letter to *The Tablet*, 11 January 2003.

387 An economic doctrine based on Catholic social teaching.

388 Fiona MacCarthy, *Eric Gill*, p. 156.

389 *The Tablet*, 28 January 1989.

390 *The Tablet*, 11 February 1989.

391 Ibid.

392 Quoted in *The Times*, 16 April 1998.

393 Letter from Kennedy to Roger Bolton, *Right to Reply*, BBC, 22 February 1998.

394 Conversation with author.

395 *The Tablet*, 25 April 1998.

396 *Catholic Herald*, 24 April 1998.

397 *Network* (MACSAS publication), No. 55, June 1998.

398 See Chapter 6.

399 Quoted in 'Problem Priests', *The Tablet*, 4 January 2003.

400 Quoted in *The Tablet*, 7 July 2007.

401 Kennedy, conversation with author.

402 Lawrence, conversation with author.

403 Kennedy, conversation with author.

404 Ibid.

405 Lawrence, conversation with author.

406 *The Guardian*, 14 October 2011.

407 See Chapter 4.

408 *The Guardian*, ibid.

409 A reference to the JGE case – see Chapter 13.

410 In the John Jay study of 4,392 priests accused of abusing children between 1950 and 2002, only 226 were charged with crimes and of these 138 were convicted. See Chapter 2.

411 *Philadelphia Inquirer*, 25 June 2012.

412 MSNBC, 14 July 2007. 413 The eight dioceses are: Davenport, Fairbanks, Milwaukee, Portland, San Diego, Spokane, Tucson and Wilmington.

414 See Chapter 5.

415 Members of some religious orders (some of whom are ordained priests) take a vow of poverty. However, contrary to popular myth, most priests, especially diocesan priests, do not. Most priests (not all) are relatively poor because they have small incomes from the diocese. However, some priests will have private means and/or relatively well-paid jobs.

416 See Chapter 5.

417 See Chapter 5, the Penney case for example.

418 Ibid., see the Robinson case for example.

419 Canon 983.1.

420 Canon 979.

421 This reinforces Margaret Kennedy's argument about the total unsuitability of the confessional as a place for disclosing abuse, see Chapter 12.

422 Nolan suggested changes to the visibility of the confessional so that abuse could not take place within it.

423 [2001] UKHL 22.

424 [2010] 1 WLR 1441.

425 See Chapter 5.

426 (1999) 174 DLR (4th) 71.

427 This concession was stated to be made solely for the purposes of that case.

428   [2012] EWCA Civ. 98.
429   Canon 212.1, Code of Canon Law (1983).
430   Ibid., Canon 273.
431   Ibid., Canon 523.
432   Ibid., Canon 538.
433   Ibid., Canon 772.1.
434   *Presbyterium Ordinis*, Pope Paul VI, 7 December 1965.
435   [2012] EWCA Civ. 98.
436   Quoted in *The Guardian*, 15 November 2011.
437   Quoted on Philip Gilligan blog, 'Concerned about Abuse in the Catholic
      Church', 1 August 2012.
438   *Ablett and others* v. *Devon CC and others* (2000), (unreported), (CA).
439   See Neil Addison blog, 'Religion and the Law', 17 July 2012.
440   *The Observer*, 17 December 2006.
441   Vol. 10(2), para. 1112.
442   (1809) 1 Ball & B 145.
443   To use the words of Irish Prime Minister Enda Kenny.
444   *John Doe 100* v. *Holy See (State of the Vatican City)*, United States District Court,
      Northern District of Illinois.
445   Robertson, op. cit., p. 155.
446   *John Doe 100* v. *Holy See*, op. cit.
447   Robertson, op. cit., p. 156.
448   *The Guardian*, 20 January 2011.
449   There are differing views about whether that certification could be challenged in
      the courts.
450   Robertson, op. cit., p. 70.
451   Sir Ivor Roberts, 'Is the Holy See above the Law?', *The Times*, 13 April 2010.
452   Ibid.
453   State Immunity Act (1978), section 5.
454   Robertson, op. cit., p. 155.
455   *Al-Adsani* v. *United Kingdom* (2001) 34 EHRR 273.
456   UN Convention against Torture.
457   *In Plain Sight: Responding to the Ferns, Ryan, Murphy and Cloyne Reports*,
      Amnesty International (Ireland), September 2011.
458   Mitchell Garabedian, quoted in *Washington Post*, 2004.
459   Noll and Harvey, 'Restorative Mediation: The Application of Restorative Justice
      Practice and Philosophy to Clergy Sexual Abuse Cases', *Journal of Child Sexual
      Abuse*, Vol. 17, Issue 3, November 2008.
460   Ibid.
461   *The Times*, 16 March 2010.
462   West blog, 17 October 2013. St Benedict's is a fee-paying school so there would
      be a contract between school and parents. No such contractual relationship
      would exist in a state school context, potentially putting a state school child at a
      disadvantage.
463   See *The Guardian*, 9 November 2012.
464   See 'Stop Church Child Abuse!' campaign: http://stopchurchchildabuse.co.uk/
465   *Directory on the Canonical Status of the Clergy: Rights, Obligations and Procedures*,
      p. 81: provisions added to facilitate administrative leave.

INDEX

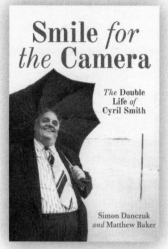